D0078362

Landscapes of Despair

Boxes filled with the homeless – Los Angeles Street in LA's Skid Row
Los Angeles Times photo.

Landscapes of Despair

From deinstitutionalization to homelessness

MICHAEL J. DEAR AND
JENNIFER R. WOLCH

Princeton University Press
Princeton, New Jersey

OESTERLE LIBRARY, NCC
NAPERVILLE, IL. 60566

Copyright © Michael J. Dear and Jennifer R. Wolch 1987

First published in 1987 by Princeton University Press,
41 William Street, Princeton, New Jersey 08540

All rights reserved. Except for the quotation of short passages for the
purposes of criticism and review, no part of this publication may be reproduced
stored in a retrieval system, or transmitted, in any form or by any means,
electronic, mechanical, photocopying, recording or otherwise, without the prior
permission of the publisher.

Library of Congress Cataloging-in-Publication Data
Dear, M.J. (Michael J.)
Landscapes of Despair
Bibliography: P.
Includes Index.
1. Urban Poor. 2. Public Welfare. 3. Institutional Care.
4. Community Organization. 5. Homelessness.
I. Wolch, Jennifer R. II. Title.
HV4028.D43 1984 362.5 87-3435
ISBN 0-691-07754-1

Typeset in 11/12 Baskerville
by DMB (Typesetting), Oxford
Printed in Great Britain

362.5
D34l

Contents

JESTERLE LIBRARY
NORTH CENTRAL COL
NAPERVILLE IL

Contents

OESTING LIBRARY
NORTH CENTRAL COLLEGE
NAPERVILLE, ILLINOIS

Contents

List of tables

List of maps and figures

List of maps and figures

Preface

The focus of this book is the discharge of dependent populations from large-scale institutions and their subsequent fate in the community. This practice of discharge, termed deinstitutionalization, has been the most important change in the delivery of human services in modern times – both in North America and in other Western capitalist countries. The book is also about the parallel development of 'service-dependent population ghettos' in many of our inner cities – spatial concentrations of welfare populations and the facilities designed to assist them. The emergence of this new type of urban ghetto was an unforeseen solution to the problem of developing community-based care for a variety of service-dependent populations, including the mentally disabled, physically handicapped, ex-offenders and addicts. The ghetto was and is an ambiguous solution. For example, it provided a source of client support; the ghetto acted as a coping mechanism for deinstitutionalized groups. At the same time, however, the ghetto was the object of community antagonism; it is already being destroyed or dismantled in many American and Canadian cities.

This book provides the first comprehensive analysis of the service-dependent ghetto in North America. We ask: how did the ghetto arise? What is the nature of its structure and evolution? What are its benefits and costs? And how should we plan for its future? To answer these questions we have adopted two broad research objectives: first, to explain the formation and evolution of the service-dependent ghetto; and secondly, to develop an appropriate policy perspective on the multifaceted problems related to it.

We believe that this is the crucial moment to address these issues. It is a time of major economic and political uncertainty, when continued cutbacks threaten to undermine the 'safety net' of our national social programs. We are already witnessing the dismantling of an essentially untried community-based social support network, when we have no replacement in position. This poses an enormous threat to service-dependent populations. They face the destruction of their rudimentary coping mechanisms in the city. This implies either a retreat to institutional care, or a life-threatening fall between the cracks of the collapsing welfare system. The imminent demise of this system is already foreshadowed by the massive explosion in the numbers of homeless people and in the misassignment of many service-dependent groups (for example, of the mentally ill into the prison system).

In this book, we confront the challenge posed by community-based care of service-dependent groups. We hope to be able to understand the service-dependent population ghetto, and in doing so to inform the debate on the development of a more humane human-service delivery system in North America and the other Western capitalist nations that have, to a greater or lesser extent, embarked on a policy of deinstitutionalization and community-based service provision.

M. J. Dear
J. R. Wolch

Ocean Front Walk
Venice, California
1987

Acknowledgements

It is a pleasure to acknowledge the assistance provided by many friends and colleagues in the preparation of this book. Gordon Clark, Derek Gregory, Chris Philo and Martin Taylor read and commented upon the entire manuscript: their constructive criticism was invaluable. Others helped by reading various chapters and include Bill Baer, Louis Gentilcore, Peter Gordon and Marjorie Robertson.

We have worked with many colleagues and students who have contributed directly to the materials in this book. They include Ruth Fincher, Stuart Gabriel, Glenda Laws, Adam Moos, Cynthia Nelson, Annette Rubalcaba and Martin Taylor. Gwyn Barley, Cecil Beamish, David Day, Nick Oatley, David Bestvater, Robin Kearns and Clodagh Stoker-Long also helped along the way.

At various stages of research and in the preparation of the book, Dear was assisted by grants from the Canadian Social Sciences and Humanities Research Council and by generous leave provisions from McMaster University. Michael Webber was instrumental in arranging leave during a critical period of final revision. The Department of Geography at the University of California, Los Angeles, and the School of Urban and Regional Planning at the University of Southern California, provided congenial settings for completing the manuscript. Funding support from the National Science Foundation, Program in Geography and Regional Science, allowed Wolch to undertake portions of the research. Bill Baer generously provided respite from teaching duties at a key phase of the work. The Institute for Urban and Regional Development at the University of California, Berkeley, offered a supportive environment during this period.

Lastly, Manuel Castells, Julian Wolpert, Mike Teitz, and Martin Taylor provided ongoing and vital intellectual encouragement for which we are indebted.

to Julian Wolpert

Part I
Introduction

1

Service-dependent populations in the city

In the 1960s and 1970s, the deinstitutionalization movement was translated from philosophy into a tangible social program. It represented a well-intentioned effort to remove the mentally disabled, physically handicapped, mentally retarded, prisoners and other dependent groups from asylums and similar places of incarceration, in order to place them in community settings. For most groups, this policy represented a fundamental change in practices that had been in place since the early nineteenth century.[1]

It is a major part of our purpose to explain why things went wrong with deinstitutionalization. *It is not our intention to argue against deinstitutionalization, or for reinstitutionalization*; we believe that the discharge of the dependent from large-scale institutions has been a necessary and humane stage in the evolution of our service system. But today as we survey some of the human and social costs of the movement, we feel an urgent need to tell the full story so that some overdue policy initiatives may be developed and implemented rapidly.

This is, therefore, a book with a very particular purpose and viewpoint. It is written by two social scientists closely involved with the organization and planning of human-service systems. We are not directly involved in providing services, so we have some degree of detachment from the problem of front-line caring. This perspective, has, we believe, allowed us to provide some fresh insight into the problems of deinstitutionalization and of providing for society's dependent persons.

What we would like to achieve here is to remove the sense of shock and unpleasant discovery which seems to accompany each new phase in the deinstitutionalization history. In retrospect, we should not have been surprised that the deinstitutionalized should have become 'ghettoized' in our inner cities.[2] Similarly, it should not now be surprising that the atrophying service system should be accompanied by a massive surge in homelessness amongst service-dependent populations. Nor is it unexpected that many groups are being misassigned to inappropriate social settings and reinstitutionalized (for instance, in prisons) because they lack other shelter options.[3] The historical wheel has turned full circle. Current newspaper accounts of prison officials' attempts to separate the mentally disabled from the regular inmate population in many jails echo similar efforts of wardens in the seventeenth century – efforts that eventually culminated in the birth of the asylum during the late seventeenth and early eighteenth centuries.

One of the most fascinating aspects of the contemporary crisis in human services is its focus in the city. As institutions have been closed, discharged populations have gravitated toward specific zones in our urban areas. These have typically been core areas of the inner city, where the service-dependent have found helping agencies and housing opportunities. As dependent persons migrated to those urban locations (often from considerable distances outside the city), they attracted more services which themselves acted as a magnet for yet more needy persons. A self-reinforcing cycle of ghettoization was thus begun.

This specific urban manifestation of the deinstitutionalization process is, we believe, the key to understanding the history and possible future of our current social welfare dilemmas. We have previously referred to this phenomenon as the growth of the 'public city'. Other commentators have drawn attention to the deep-rooted social changes currently affecting modern cities. Manuel Castells, for example, has referred to the essentially anarchistic process of contemporary urbanization in what he calls the 'wild city' (Castells, 1976). Stanley Cohen (somewhat more sinisterly) views the development of community-based care as an exercise in the dispersal of social control – in what he calls the 'punitive city' (Cohen, 1979).

Our narrative is therefore an explanation of a social process (deinstitutionalization) and its particular urban manifestation (the ghetto). In attempting to unfold the logic of this historical process and to avoid any unpleasant future surprises, we have drawn extensively on experiences in the US and Canada, and especially the State of California and the Province of Ontario. In no sense do we provide a complete picture of either experience. However, the cumulative comparative analyses based on these examples build a compelling explanation of the current crisis of deinstitutionalization in the North American city.

A NOTE ON METHODS OF ANALYSIS

In preparing this narrative, we have drawn extensively on conventional historical, social-theoretic, geographical and policy-analytic methods. First, we sythesize the major events marking the history of deinstitutionalization in North America – particularly in the State of California and the Province of Ontario. Our research relies on both primary and secondary historical sources to arrive at an understanding of the evolution of service-dependency and social welfare practices. In recounting this history, we have considered both the *longue durée* and *durée*, to portray both the structural continuity of historical experience in urban social welfare and the important role of changing social practices that shape the more immediate context of service provision.

Secondly, the research approach is shaped strongly by a conceptual framework based on contemporary social theory (Giddens, 1984; Gregory and Urry, 1985; Thrift, 1983; Dear and Scott, 1981). In particular, we have drawn on theories of the duality of structure and agency in social life and the role of political economic factors in social change, in order to interpret the historical experience of social welfare provision. This implies a multilevel analysis that accounts for the interaction of macrolevel political economic structures and constraints; the role of institutions such as the state in translating those structures into policies and programs; and the activities of knowledgeable and capable human agents involved in the social welfare system.

Third, our narrative is clearly geographical and place-specific. Rather than providing an aspatial analysis that discounts the time–space contingency of social welfare practice, we emphasize the geographic dimensions of service provision. Hence we have chosen to focus on particular locales that constitute the settings in which structural forces, institutional practices and everyday routines of agents interact to produce a concrete manifestation of deinstitutionalization outcomes. We have not attempted to provide complete accounts of the experiences in the locales that we consider; instead, we have woven together cross-cultural and intertemporal analyses in a way which allows us to move between study areas, to preserve a consistent narrative and a chronological integrity and yet to provide generalized conclusions relevant to other geographical areas.

Lastly, and perhaps most distinctively, we have wedded a critical perspective on social welfare in the city with pragmatic tools of public policy analysis. This may seem unconventional and is certainly problematic; however, as planners we feel compelled to move from interpretation to praxis. Designing an adequate human-services delivery system for cities is in part a technical planning problem involving the assignment of service-dependent clients to community-based service settings. Such an exercise calls for normative rules, decision criteria, operating principles and institutional means for conflict resolution and program implementation. Thus our recommendations for praxis, while remaining fully informed by a critical interpretation of deinstitutionalization, also use the technical language of planning to provide practical guidance to policy-makers attempting to ameliorate the everyday crises of community-based human services.

ORGANIZATION OF THE BOOK

The ten chapters examine three broad themes. The first theme (chapters 1–3) explores the nature of the ghettoization problem, its historical background and our theoretical approach. The second theme (chapters 4–7) examines the rise and fall of the service-dependent ghetto and the growth of misassignment and homelessness. Finally (in chapters 8–10), we synthesize the implications of our analysis and explore the public policy dilemmas surrounding community-based care for the dependent.

To aid understanding of our extended (and at times complex) account, we present in the remainder of chapter 1 an abbreviated account of the arguments presented in the book. Chapter 2 addresses the central question about the ghetto: what set of social forces could have produced this particular urban form? The answers are sought in the processes of urbanization and of the restructuring of the Welfare State. These structural (or contextual) features have intersected decisively with the actions of import human agents to give rise – inevitably, predictably – to the ghetto of the service-dependent. The ghetto has, however, a very long history. In chapter 3, a general survey of the social history of 'dependency' during the nineteenth and twentieth centuries explains the evolution of the ghetto landscape.

Against the theoretical and historical backdrop provided in the first two chapters, Part II of the book begins a careful unravelling of the place-specific nature of the ghetto. The long narrative begins (in chapter 4) by explaining how general philosophies of treatment and care in Ontario became manifest as a specifically *urban* phenomenon in one locale (downtown Toronto). In chapter 5, a detailed analysis of the anatomy of the service-dependent ghetto in one city (Hamilton) shows how the deinstitutionalization movement affected many diverse populations which all gravitated to the downtown 'host' community. Here they congregated with the helping facilities designed to serve them.

In order to advance the narrative beyond the initial creation and consolidation of the ghetto, we shift the *locus* of our analysis in later chapters to California. In chapter 6, the systematic destruction of the service-dependent ghetto in San Jose is described as a consequence of public and private actions. Then in chapter 7, the present episode of the deinstitutionalization saga is unfolded. Here, we document the crises of misassignment and homelessness and the looming threat of reinstitutionalization.

In Part III we examine the normative implications of our analysis. Chapter 8 argues that deinstitutionalization remains a worthy policy objective for assisting dependent populations and that the current service interventions are pathological and iatrogenic. Two levels of intervention are subsequently identified: first, the need to adjust the mechanisms of community-based service planning; secondly, the need for a renewed political commitment to the development of a community-based alternative. Hence, in chapter 9, we explore the rights and obligations of communities and the need for planners to take into consideration community self-interest as well as client rights in devising service solutions. Finally, in chapter 10, we argue for a rebirth of the commitment to deinstitutionalization in order to relieve the homelessness crisis and to provide for successful social welfare in the city.

2

The social construction of the
service-dependent ghetto

The patterns of everyday life sometimes appear to be deceptively simple. The impetus for this book, for example, derives from the now-familiar observation of the ghettoization of ex-psychiatric patients in the inner city. Yet a knowledgeable observer might quickly surmise that ghettoization is a complex phenomenon – the result of a wide range of forces, including aspects of supply and demand for housing. For instance, on the supply side, in the inner city there are large properties available for conversion to group homes; an established supply of transient rental accommodations like single-room occupancy hotels; and established support networks (both of service facilities such as missions and of personal ties to other community residents). Demand for housing and jobs by ex-psychiatric patients has led to an informal spatial filtering of patients to the core area; a significant amount of interregional migration (from rural areas to core areas of cities with major psychiatric hospitals); and the formal referral of ex-patients to core-area housing alternatives. These 'market' forces encouraging ghettoization have been reinforced by two other factors: an apparently extensive community opposition, which has effectively excluded ex-patients from most suburban residential neighborhoods; and the development of planning strategies that attempt to avoid community conflict over locational decisions by seeking out uncontested sites for neighborhood mental health facilities.

Curious observers may, however, be tempted to look beyond this appealing overview. They will quickly learn that the mentally ill have been joined in the ghetto by a host of other deinstitutionalized populations, including the dependent elderly, the mentally retarded, the physically disabled, ex-prisoners and substance abusers. The past decade has witnessed the unprecedented growth of a 'public city' – the spatial concentration of service-dependent populations and the agencies and facilities designated to serve them.[1] As an urban phenomenon, the public city represents a significant change in the form of cities. As a social welfare phenomenon, it acts as a reservoir of potential clients and as a primary reception area for the deinstitutionalized. As more people arrive in the ghetto, so more services are needed to care for them; the new services themselves act as a catalyst in attracting further clients and so a self-reinforcing cycle is intensified.

What set of social forces could have produced this particular urban form? How did deinstitutionalization give rise unexpectedly to the ghetto? And what will now happen to the ghetto as social welfare policies are restructured? To begin to answer these questions, we first establish in this chapter some general theoretical arguments about the relationship between *social forces* (deinstitutionalization) and *spatial form* (the urban ghetto). The precise nature of our concept of the relationship between society and space is explored in the next section. This is followed by consideration of the two longer-term, macroscale trends that have provided a necessary context for ghettoization: the process of suburbanization and the policies of an evolving Welfare State. Exactly how these contextual factors give rise to a particular spatial form is explored by looking at the short-term, microscale practices of the relevant 'actors' or agents in the deinstitutionalization process. Here, the daily activities of professional, client and community will be seen to create the service-dependent ghetto as a common element in city form.

SOCIETY, SPACE AND THE GENESIS OF THE GHETTO

There has been much debate about the precise relationship between societal processes and spatial form. We take the view that the geographical configuration of the landscape (including cities and regions) is a concrete reflection of underlying social processes. However, this translation from the social to the spatial is neither a simple nor a well-ordered sequence; neither is space simply the passive stage on which social events are played out. As Giddens (1984, p. 368) has observed: 'Space is not an empty dimension along which social groupings become structured, but has to be considered in terms of its involvement in the constitution of systems of interaction.'

The wider logic of the social construction of the service-dependent ghetto lies in the dual notions of *society and space* and *structure and agency.*[2] The service-dependent ghetto has been created by skilled and knowledgeable actors (or agents) operating within a social context (or structure), which both limits and enables their actions. It is impossible to predict the exact geographical outcome of the interaction between *structure* and *agency*. The reason for this is that while individual activities are framed within a particular structural context, they can also transform the context itself. Any narrative about landscapes, regions, or locales is necessarily an account of the reciprocal relationship between relatively long-term structural forces and the shorter-term routine practices of individual human agents. Economic, political and social history is therefore *time-specific*, in the sense that these relationships evolve at different temporal rates; it is also *place-specific*, in that these relationships unfold in recognizable 'locales' according to some precise logic of spatial diffusion. So geographical patterns, such as the ghetto, are evolving manifestations of a complex social process. As society evolves, so does its spatial expression; but by the same token, the geographical form will have repercussions on the social forces themselves.

This reflexive impact of space on society can be achieved through many different avenues. In the simplest terms, many social relations are necessarily *constituted* through space (for example the relations of production in resource-based activities and environments); other relations are *constrained* by space (such as the inertia imposed by obsolete built environments on change); and finally, some social relations will be *mediated* through space (including the development of ideology and beliefs within geographically confined regions or locales). In the case of the service-dependent population ghetto, the influence of society on space is clear in the trend toward inner-city rehabilitation and gentrification which is absorbing housing opportunities in the ghetto for the deinstitutionalized. The influence of space on society is demonstrated through the ghetto's effect in heightening community awareness of the plight of the service-dependent, especially the homeless. This awareness has, in turn, caused adjustments in the allocation of resources and the practices of service delivery.

The landscape of the ghetto is thus a complex text allowing multiple interpretations. Our task in this chapter is to deconstruct this terrain in search of its origins.[3] The point of departure is to view the *ghetto as a landscape of power*. This approach is prompted by Foucault (1980, p. 148), who wrote: 'A whole history remains to be written of *spaces* – which would at the same time be the history of *powers*.' The terrain of the service-dependent ghetto is most heavily inscribed by the power of the Welfare State, but it also intersects decisively with the process of capitalist urbanization. This is not to imply that a simple logic of state and capital have consciously worked in concert to produce the ghetto. Instead, the development of the ghetto can be seen through the lens of Foucault's notion of 'micropowers', those minute details of everyday relationships, which together provide the basis for more centralized or global powers. A focus on micropowers directs attention to the actions of specific agents in every sphere of conflict and to the essential unpredictability of social life. However, Foucault has essentially ignored the links between these micropowers and the wider logic and structures of centralized power. He thus omits consideration of how power relations are combined and crystallized in the state apparatus, or how state institutions act strategically in everyday routines (Driver, 1985, p. 438). This structural or institutional level of analysis is crucial to understanding the landscape of power.

The *organizational locus* of power that is most prominent in our analysis is the apparatus of the Welfare State.[4] This power is exercised through many sites, or instances. In *Discipline and Punish*, Foucault (1977) asserts that the modern state aims for a disciplined mind rather than a subjugated body. Social norms should be individually internalized, thereby ensuring the homogeneity of the whole. In the practice of social control, the division of space and time is essential to the discipline and surveillance of individuals (Foucault, 1977, pp. 141–62; Giddens, 1984, pp. 145–58). The designs of prison, asylum, schoolroom and even home are all testimony to this principle.[5] Spaces and timetables are all choreographed to manage activities and individuals. As the level of the individual is approached, the power of the state apparatus is necessarily articulated and attenuated through time–space constructs (Clark and Dear, 1984, chapter 7). The total ensemble of social control (including the Welfare State) is termed the 'carceral archipelago' by Foucault (1979) – a society permeated by a network of surveillance institutions and disciplinary procedures.

The *geographical locus* of the carceral archipelago is, for our study at least, the inner city. The rise of the ghetto is associated with the totally separate logic of capitalist urbanization (Dear and Scott, 1981). The landscape of the ghetto has resulted from interactions between social process and urban process; it has taken on an iconographic dimension that serves as a constant remainder of the crisis in human services.

Thus in order to understand the service-dependent ghetto as a land-scape of power, we need to discover the ways in which surveillance and disciplinary procedures of the Welfare State are articulated by and penetrate the routines of the principal agents of human-service delivery in the inner city. To this end, we examine the urban process; the Welfare State; and the dynamics of everyday life as the agents in both systems interact over time and space (see figure 2.1).

URBANIZATION, SUBURBANIZATION AND THE INCIPIENT SERVICE-DEPENDENT GHETTO

The appearance of the 'industrial city' in the late nineteenth century followed closely behind the rise of modern capitalism as the dominant form of economic relations.[6] Clusters of firms gathered at sites of raw materials or at transportation nodes, where costs of production could be minimized. The evolving industrial landscape had two fundamental geographic elements: the core area – a complex, integrated hierarchy of industrial centers of different functions and sizes; and a periphery – a hinterland subordinate to the core, functioning mainly as a supplier of resources to the core and consuming the core's products.

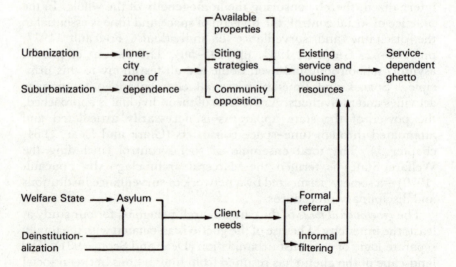

FIGURE 2.1 Social process and spatial form: factors influencing the creation of the service-dependent ghetto

Within each urban center, a further degree of spatial differentiation materialized. Commercial areas developed, devoted to market exchange, financing industrial growth and urban expansion. Workers moved into dense residential districts around the rapidly growing commercial and industrial districts, serving to attract yet more firms to the area. These processes of industrial agglomeration and labor-force concentration created the characteristic internal geography of the early industrial city, which consisted of

1 production space, where goods were produced and exchanged;
2 residential (or reproduction) space, where workers lived and raised their families; and
3 circulation space, devoted to roads, railroads and other forms of transport, designed to distribute goods, capital and workers.

At the center was the dense commercial core; surrounded by an ever-widening ring of industry and segregated residential neighborhoods.

One such neighborhood, located close to the commercial–industrial core, was the city's soft underbelly, lying in the path of core-area expansion. Here, speculation was accompanied by land-use conversion and disinvestment as property-owners waited for the land values to rise. This neighborhood was populated by the city's low-income, socially misfit groups and charitable agencies. Known as the 'zone of transition', this district was the first geographical expression of the incipient service-dependent ghetto, or 'zone of dependence'.

The massive concentration of population and economic activity associated with industrialization caused intolerable congestion, overcrowding and other social ills in the city, eventually prompting a decentralization of activities. Very early in the nineteenth century, upper-income residents began to move to peripheral areas in search of better properties and healthier surroundings (Walker, 1981). But the growth of residential suburbs exploded at the turn of the century when advances in transportation (especially trolley cars and railways) and mortgage lending practices enabled the suburbanization of the professional and managerial classes. Improved transportation technology and communications (including the telephone) also facilitated the decentralization of economic activity. The stage was thus set for the long march of people and jobs to the suburbs – a movement that has continued to dominate patterns of urban growth throughout the twentieth century.

Twentieth-century suburban growth has been characterized by successive waves of decentralization, as industrial expansion, advances in communications and transport technologies, investment in urban infrastructure and population movements have reinforced each other in an outward surge. In the most recent waves, these activities have been joined by retailing and other service activities. By 1950, the long-term trends toward residential suburbanization and economic decentralization had diverted the flow of population and investment capital away from the inner city; suburban 'booms' accompanied inner-city 'busts' and 'redlining' by financial institutions. For many cities, inner-area disinvestment hit just as the city's physical fabric was becoming obsolete. The depopulation of the inner city also created a fiscal disparity between central city and suburb. As well-to-do households suburbanized, taking their tax dollars to new jurisdictions and leaving the low-income earners, unemployed and dependent behind to be served by a dwindling tax base, an acute fiscal squeeze added to the growing political, social and economic woes of the city.

In many cities, especially in the North-eastern US, physical and functional obsolescence was accelerated during the 1960s and 1970s by the process of deindustrialization (Bluestone and Harrison, 1982). As the older industrial base of these cities declined, fundamental shifts in the patterns of interregional and international migration occurred. The 'snowbelt' inner cities now no longer received an influx of migrants who had formerly taken up the space left behind by their suburbanizing predecessors. New migrants headed for the 'sunbelt' suburbs (Sawyers and Tabb, 1984). In the inner-city vacuum created by suburbanization and deindustrialization, urban decay and abandonment became common and extensive. The zone of transition, traditionally an area of property speculation, housing conversion and cheap accommodation and services, had become more than ever the home for society's marginal people. This inner-city zone of dependence became, in fact, the eminently suitable target of the deinstitutionalization juggernaut (figure 2.1).

DEINSTITUTIONALIZATION AND THE WELFARE STATE

In large part, the modern state developed in order to protect and maintain the system of social relations in so far as this was not achieved 'automatically' by market forces. Its functions eventually extended to encompass three primary roles: to secure social consensus by guaranteeing acceptance of the prevailing social contract by all groups in society; to secure economic conditions by regulating investment and consumption; and to secure social integration by providing for the welfare of all groups, especially the lower classes. These objectives were realized through the development of an extensive set of state apparatuses. These institutions included the entire panoply of parties, elections, government and constitution; statutes and court systems; law-enforcement agencies; public-service bureaus; fiscal and monetary control boards; information centers; administrative and regulatory units; and health, education and welfare agencies (Clark and Dear, 1984, chapters 3, 4).

This last group included hospitals, all levels of education and a range of social welfare programs such as (eventually) unemployment benefits and social insurance. The welfare-oriented activities emphasized the material support offered by the state to most social groups. While providing support, however, they also involved some degree of regulation or control over the serviced populations. This not only promoted the social integration of the serviced group, but it also had a profound ideological effect. It situated social pathology at the level of the individual, group or community and resulted in the penetration of modern state regulation deep into the fabric of social relations.

The relative prominence of governmental health, education and welfare services, their extension to an ever-growing share of the population and the expansion in the size and numbers of public and quasi-public welfare institutions (agencies, bureaus, etc.), has enabled analysts to characterize many governments (including the US and Canada) as 'Welfare States'. Much of this growth was catalyzed by the need to alleviate political crises, including depression and social unrest. Under a process usually referred to as 'corporatism', the state increasingly attempted to reduce conflict by institutionalizing collective aspirations into the political process. This in turn resulted in an increased centralization of governmental functions; increased state intervention in the economy; and an expanded representation of labor, business and other social groups in institutionalized conflict. One outcome of the corporatist dynamic is that class or group interests increasingly became constituted within specific governmental institutions, which reflected the power relations between groups. Conflict between institutions thus became a primary manifestation of the way in which group interests were aggregated, represented and mediated. The outcome of such conflicts depends upon the balance of power between these institutions (Clark and Dear, 1984, chapter 4).

The history of American and Canadian social welfare policy reflects a slow but progressive absorption of state responsibility for programs devoted to the satisfaction of human needs and to the improvement of human welfare (Gilbert, 1981; Guest, 1980). These programs had hitherto been the responsibility of voluntary and charitable organizations. Very early in its history of intervention in welfare matters, the public sector developed an *institution-based* mode of response (figure 2.1). This included lunatic asylums, hospitals, almshouses, orphanages and houses of industry (see for example, Rothman, 1971). With the exception of the asylum, these institutions were usually located close to the heart of the urban population, where the need was greatest. However, the rural-based asylums were quickly engulfed by the spread of adjacent urban areas.

The institutions were destined to endure until well into the twentieth century. They acted as urban-based 'reservoirs' of disabled persons. During the 1960s, however, the release of the pent-up pressure in institutions was engineered via the 'deinstitutionalization' movement. Deinstitutionalization referred to the move away from large-scale institution-based care to small-scale community-based facilities. The movement assumed many particular manifestations, and incorporated widely diverse populations including the mentally disabled, the retarded, the dependent elderly, ex-offenders and substance abusers (Lerman, 1982; Dear and Taylor, 1982, chapter 3).

Overcrowded and essentially custodial institutions had increasingly come under attack for failing to provide adequate care and treatment and for the deplorable physical conditions that inmates were forced to endure. At the same time, a libertarian philosophy began to infiltrate the practice of social welfare. This philosophy was composed of two convictions: first, that prolonged institutionalization did more harm than good; and second, that it was an abuse of the civil rights of those who were subjected to it. As a result, in the 1950s several experiments were undertaken to demonstrate the utility of a noninstitution-based care. The most spectacular success was reported in the field of mental-health care, where programs designed to maintain patients in their homes showed the inappropriateness of a policy of universal hospitalization. The emergence of these new treatment philosophies coincided with the appearance of new chemotherapies for behavior disorders. This meant that the more acute symptoms of mental disorders could be controlled. Finally, a political and fiscal impetus in favor of deinstitutionalization arose. In the US for example, federal funds were made available to establish 'community mental health centers', with an explicit mandate to deliver grass-roots care at the local level. In addition, cash grant programs were extended to the disabled during this period, allowing individuals to be supported outside an institutional context. The federal programs were welcomed by many counties and states, which recognized that such funds would enable them to transfer a significant portion of the burden of care away from the state and county institutions, for which they had financial responsibility, to the community, which federal funds would support. In short, an unstoppable coalition of libertarian concern, treatment philosophy, chemotherapeutic advances, and politics and money came together almost by coincidence (Klerman, 1977). The 'deinstitutionalization' movement had been born (figure 2.1).

This birth represented, in effect, the creation of a new configuration of old and new governmental institutions, voluntary organizations and professionals – a new apparatus of the Welfare State. Conflict was inevitable. The existing welfare establishment was obsolete, propelled only by inertia; the birth of a new, innovative system to deal with changing social conditions challenged its legitimacy; and it had become captive to various class and special-interest groups, rendering it incapable of responding to new needs. As the structure and territory of the welfare institutions are being renegotiated, we can anticipate that the lives of the individuals affected will be unusually turbulent and precarious.

SUBURBANIZATION, DEINSTITUTIONALIZATION AND EVERYDAY LIFE

The longer-term tendencies toward suburbanization and deinstitutionalization define the necessary background for explaining the ghettoization of the service-dependent. However, the actual creation of the ghetto must also incorporate (as explanatory variables) the routine practices of human agents involved in suburbanization and deinstitutionalization. The everyday practices of three types of agents are especially significant in explaining the essentially unanticipated rise of the ghetto: these are the professional care-givers; the clients; and the community. Two other groups play minor but nevertheless vital roles: the land-use planner and the service operator. The routine practices of these five agents involved in social welfare have caused a specific geography to emerge in the city.

Professions

Professions are powerful. They have a 'gatekeeper' function in the distribution of society's resources. They have specialist knowledge which is exercised through a state-sanctioned code of practice usually linked to a service ethic. Professions act to monopolize their position and status, emphasizing the dangers that may arise if their professional skills are ignored or misused.

In the instance of the sick and needy, professional care has always proceeded from fundamental principles of isolation and separation of individuals in space (Dear and Taylor, 1982, chapter 3). In the penal systems, for example, the most intense architectural manifestation of these principles was Bentham's 'Panopticon', which arranged individuals in isolated cells on tiered circles about a central observation area. More generally, the spatial separation of individuals for care requires four actions:

1 *enclosure*, or the definition of a protected place of treatment;
2 *partitioning*, or the creation of an internal spatial organization in which each unit has its specific place;
3 identification of *functional sites*, in which internal achitectural space is coded for different uses, reflecting, for instance, the need for therapy, administration and work areas; and
4 *ranking*, or the definition of the place occupied by clients in a classification hierarchy.

These actions enable professionals to describe a functional–analytic space and to allocate patients for treatment within that space (Foucault, 1977, pp. 141–9).

The power of professions derives from the labeling process that identifies a client as socially distinct, with some form of 'illness' or 'deviance' that may be 'treated' or 'cured'. This involves the 'normalization' or resocialization of the client, which consists of several tasks: referring individuals to a normative social model that acts as a basis of comparison; labeling and thereby differentiating among individuals in the system with respect to the normative model; measuring and categorizing the specific defects and potential of the individual establishing the level of conformity that has to be achieved by each individual; and lastly, defining by these tasks the operational limits of the social model of the abnormal person. Hence, the professional service offered compares, labels, categorizes, homogenizes and excludes; that is, it normalizes (Foucault, 1977, pp. 182–3). The professionals operating this service not only diagnose the *needs* of individuals, but also specify the appropriate course of treatment and judge when it has been successful (figure 2.1).

The consequence of such power for the burgeoning profession is well described by Foucault (1977) in his account of the birth of the prison in France. He points out that in the space of only 80 years (1757–1837), punishment changed from the 'art of unbearable sensations' (i.e. torture) to an 'economy of suspended rights' (i.e. imprisonment for varying time-periods). As a result, a whole army of wardens, doctors, chaplains, psychiatrists, psychologists and educationalists took over from the executioner. By the beginning of the nineteenth century, public executions preceded by torture had almost entirely disappeared. In their place, a whole panoply of assessing, diagnostic, prognostic and normative judgements concerning the criminal was lodged in the penal framework. Prison had failed to eliminate crime; indeed, after a century and a half of 'failures', the prison still exists, producing the same results, and there is the greatest reluctance to dispense with it. According to Foucault, the supposed failure of the prison is part of its true function; that, in effect, prisons participate in fabricating (or at least merely managing) the delinquency they are supposed to combat. In penal systems, as in other institutions, loyalty to the profession often seems to transcend the needs of the client.

In the modern Welfare State, professional care-givers face an acute contradiction. They have largely supported the move toward deinstitutionalization, but as care has moved into the community, they have been forced to relinquish control over their traditional clientele. Their 'charges' (patients, inmates) are usually *referred* to the care of others, for example community workers (figure 2.1). The new asylum without walls permits some degree of isolation and professional control of the client group within the community. However, this extension of professional control beyond the institution has sparked an acute distrust of discretionary authority. Some have suggested that the authority of the professional care-giver has been exceeded and the rights of the cared-for have consequently been trampled upon. In the search for a 'doctrine of least harm', the problem becomes one of defining a decent, caring social policy that is not simultaneously coercive or dehumanizing (Rothman, 1978).

Clients

Deinstitutionalization poses enormous personal challenges. Forgotten or dormant skills need to be resurrected; new friends, a new home, a new job, have to be established; and the accustomed support-service network may be withdrawn abruptly. It is hardly surprising that many individuals are quickly reinstitutionalized – back to jail, asylum or hospital. The others who manage to remain on the outside often survive on the margin – poor, lonely, isolated.

The ability to cope in the community depends on a number of factors, including type of disability (physical, social, mental); institutional experience; preparedness for discharge; availability of aftercare or follow-up; personal characteristics such as socioeconomic status, extent of personal networks, beliefs and attitudes; community setting, including availability of housing, jobs and transportation; and resident attitudes and preparedness in the host community (Laws and Dear, forthcoming). These characteristics merge to define a unique coping 'matrix' for each discharged individual, making it extremely difficult to predict their fates in the community. It is now incontrovertible that many deinstitutionalized have gravitated to the core areas of North American cities, which seem to provide the best opportunity for them to remain outside the institution. The groups actively seeking out the inner city include disabled people without family and friends and persons with chronic conditions.

Ghettoization is an informal process of spatial filtering, whereby a mobile minority of the more severely disordered individuals gravitate toward areas of transient accommodation in the core areas of North American cities (figure 2.1). This drift to the inner city is motivated by hopes and fears that are similar to many groups planning a new move. The deinstitutionalized share common concerns over housing and neighborhood quality, their ability to find work and to make ends meet. They are not ignorant of the hazards of coping in a new environment and begin to formulate plans, however tentatively. Some of these plans reflect a depressingly accurate realism: many people expect to receive an income that is below the poverty line; others expect to be isolated from family and friends. For most people, optimism is dashed upon discharge: few are prepared for acute problems with housing; a clear desire for employment is overridden by the reality of bleak job prospects; and the anticipation of support services and recreational programs is soon tempered by lack of access to such program resources (Dear et al., 1980). It is in the ghetto that the deinstitutionalized find help in the search for jobs and homes, can locate other support facilities, begin or renew friendships, start self-help groups and operate newsletters. In short, the ghetto is functional for the deinstitutionalized; it is a spatially limited zone where individual support is made possible through proximity. The inner city has become a coping mechanism and is recognized as such by professionals who refer clients to the resources in the zone of dependence.

Community

Prejudice is an extremely common human failing. People have always found it difficult to accept 'outsiders' in whatever shape or form. In an address to the Royal Society of Canada in 1898, T. W. Burgess noted the grounds for community opposition to a new asylum. His remarks would require no modification to describe many contemporary conflicts over facility siting.

The chief grounds on which the plaintiffs based their [opposition to the new asylum] were: that the erection of the building and the maintenance and carrying on of an asylum on the site chosen constituted a public nuisance, and was a source of injury and damage to them, decreasing the value of their property, especially as sites for villas and elegant dwellings; and that they, the plaintiffs, would be exposed to constance annoyance, inconvenience, and danger, with great risk of disease through the contamination of the air and the pollution of the Rivers St. Lawrence and St. Pierre by the sewage from the hospital.

(Burgess, 1898, p. 86)

A remarkable range of health and welfare services are acknowledged as being necessary but are not wanted by residents adjacent to a potential site. This attitude has been variously characterized as the NIMBY syndrome (not-in-my-backyard), or the NOOS syndrome (not-on-our-street), (see Dear and Taylor (1982). Community opposition in its initial phases often seems to be based on irrational expectations and prejudices. Later it is usually modified to include at least some 'objective' propositions. The bases for opposition include decline in property values; increased traffic or parking problems; decline in neighborhood quality; fears for the safety of persons or property; fear of bad example; lack of supervision of facilities; introduction of 'outsiders' into the community; and secrecy surrounding facility siting plans.

Little is known about the qualities that define a good 'host' for community-based facilities. However, three basic factors seem to determine community acceptance or rejection: community characteristics, resident characteristics and facility characteristics (Segal and Aviram, 1978).

Many researchers have attempted to establish those *community characteristics* that identify accepting and rejecting 'hosts' for human service facilities for the deinstitutionalized population. Experience indicates that homogeneous suburban neighborhoods tend to close ranks and exclude such facilities which consequently become concentrated in more varied, transient neighborhoods (typically in the inner city). However, it is impossible to predict with certainty what the likely reaction in any specific neighborhood will be. In the case of mental illness, community attitudes seem to resolve into four attitudinal dimensions:

1 authoritarianism, which implies a view of the mentally disabled as an inferior class requiring coercive handling;
2 benevolence, a paternalistic, kindly view of patients, derived from humanistic and religious principles;
3 social restrictiveness, viewing the mentally ill as a threat to society; and
4 a community mental-health ideology, representing an anti-institution bias in the care of the mentally disabled (Dear and Taylor, 1982).

The patterns of acceptance and rejection depend upon the *net balance* between these dimensions of a community's 'personality'. Canadian research in the field of mental disability has evidenced a reasonably high level of community tolerance and sympathy for the mentally disabled. This has been confirmed by the positive experiences of group home operators in the US (US General Accounting Office, 1983).[7] However, such findings would appear to contradict everyday experience, where media reports seem frequently to refer to another outbreak of local opposition to a home's establishment. Two related factors might explain the apparent inconsistency between a high level of general community acceptance and the outbreak of local 'firestorms' of opposition. First, levels of acceptance may be eroded as the potential location approaches closer to one's own home. And secondly, opposition tends to be confined to a small vocal minority in the immediate vicinity of a potential site. Under such conditions, it is not difficult to reconcile the actions of a highly localized, vocal minority with a general climate of tolerance.

The kinds of people who live in community facilities (the *residents*) have an important impact on the host community's response. Such factors as age, sex and other sociodemographic variables can aid or hinder the process of acceptance (Heal et al., 1978; Weber, 1978). The most prominent concerns however, focus typically on the unpredictability and/or dangerousness of the new residents. These dimensions are compounded by a more traditional, moralistic judgement of resident disabilities. There is, for example, a well-established hierarchy of disability-group acceptance (Harasymiw et al., 1976). At the bottom of the scale are those groups which appear to reject community values and are 'unproductive' (for example drug addicts, ex-offenders); much more acceptable are people with less debilitating disabilities, (certain physical disabilities for instance) who can engage in productive activities. However, these observations must be tempered by the fact that people who are more aware of and familiar with disabilities tend to be more accepting, and that deinstitutionalized residents who were originally from a host neighborhood are more acceptable than 'outsiders'.

Two aspects of the *facility* itself are important in influencing community acceptance: its operating characteristics and its design. Operating characteristics are primarily determined by the type(s) of resident(s) being served, but variations in levels of supervision and in daily routine (for instance) will also determine the profile a facility will present to its host neighborhood (Segal and Aviram, 1978; Weber, 1978). Less well understood are the implications of facility design for community acceptance. It might be expected, for example, that relatively small-scale facilities may be accepted more readily. Yet other factors also play a role, such as home layout, availability of yardspace and parking facilities. Studies have pointed out that relatively minor architectural or design concessions can be made in order to gain community acceptance. Examples include enlarging a facility lobby to allow visitors to congregate inside instead of on the sidewalk; altering entrance arrangements to move activity around the corner to another street; and the erection of screening walls.

It seems likely that the entrance of the service-dependent into a community is perceived as a threat to the environmental resource base of the neighborhood and thus to the people who live within it. Accordingly, the community's power for spatial exclusion is often marshalled to protect its 'turf' from the incursion of such groups. The net result is that powerful (often suburban) jurisdictions have been very successful at excluding service-dependent groups and their facilities. Inner-city neighborhoods (more tolerant? less powerful?) have, in contrast, frequently ended up with more than their 'fair share' of facilities and service-dependent populations (figure 2.1).

Land-use planners and service operators

The issue of zoning (and other legal procedures such as licensing) has become important because many attempts have been made to establish human service facilities in areas where they are non-conforming land uses.[8] Typically, group home living arrangements may breach strict zoning specifications for single-family units. In many instances, applications to allow zoning variances have acted to alert community opposition to a proposed home; in other areas, permissive zoning laws enable relatively conflict-free facility siting. Usually it has been the suburban jurisdictions, with more stringent zoning ordinances, which have succeeded in using planning laws to exclude community facilities.

Service providers have responded to increasing community opposition by developing siting strategies that minimize conflict over facility location decisions (figure 2.1). Most of these strategies have reinforced the trends toward isolation and exclusion prompted by the behavior of the community, clients and professionals. Initially, the planners' strategy was aimed at *containment of opposition*. The locational search was directed toward sites where opposition could be manipulated through one of two siting strategies. The first of these is the 'low-profile' approach, whereby a facility is opened by stealth, without informing the host neighborhood. The hope is that by the time the facility's presence is discovered, the community will realize that any fears it might have conjured up were groundless. A second strategy has been called the 'high-profile' approach, in which an attempt is made to educate and persuade the host community to accept the facility before it is opened. The high-profile approach may target community leaders, or could take the form of a more general public awareness campaign (through mailings, public meetings and so on). Needless to say, neither approach is risk-free; in fact, if such strategies are perceived as subterfuge by the host community, the potential for inciting a most vitriolic opposition is great.

It was because of the unpredictable outcomes of the containment strategies that a second phase of siting approaches developed. These may be termed *risk aversion* strategies. These had, as their objective, the complete avoidance of any siting conflict. And, since such conflict typically arose around the need to apply for a zoning variance, providers next sought out areas where such variances were not needed. Of course, such opposition-free sites proliferated in the mixed land-use/zoning districts typical of our inner cities. As a consequence, during this period, a large proportion of facilities were sited in core areas.

The most interesting recent developments in locational strategy, constituting a third phase of siting policy, is the growth of a *fair-share* zoning movement. Many communities perceived themselves as 'saturated' with different kinds of facilities, while other neighborhoods had none. Thus, community opposition developed in neighborhoods that felt they were being asked to shoulder more than their 'fair share' of the caring burden. In many areas local zoning ordinances were passed to prevent further facilities from opening in over-burdened communities. This was most commonly achieved through the introduction of minimum distance-spacing standards that were intended to prevent further saturation and to ensure some degree of geographical separation between facilities. It was only a matter of time before the cry to 'open up the suburbs' was heard and the fair-share zoning or zoning 'as-of-right' movement was born (Dear and Laws, 1986).

So far, fair-share zoning has had only a minor impact on siting practices. Service providers still prefer to locate close to the hub of client need or where properties large enough for conversion to communal living-quarters are available (figure 2.1). Even if suburban properties were to be made available, they are typically beyond the pocketbooks of most service-dependent people and have less access to important services available in the core area. In addition, many key agents in service delivery are now beginning to realize the positive aspects of ghettoization, for example the ghetto as a coping mechanism. The problem is that the land and property market has in many places already outstripped our analytical expectations. Some ghettos are slowly being dismantled as the process of gentrification and urban renewal begins to absorb cheaper inner-city districts, often under the impetus of new planning legislation. It seems highly ironic that the service-dependent ghetto should have grown 'organically' as an unexpected outcome of deinstitutionalization; and that now, when we are recognizing the need to adopt a deliberate policy attitude toward the ghetto, it is undergoing another market-induced change that could lead to its attrition and demise.

SYNTHESIS

The care and treatment of the service-dependent are currently being provided under conditions of extreme duress. Deinstitutionalization has caused the obsolescence of one set of institutional arrangements and its successor is emerging slowly and painfully. While this professional territory is being renegotiated, the *locus* of care has shifted into a community-based asylum without walls. This geographical concentration has zeroed in on the inner-city zone of dependence, which had been abandoned by its suburbanizing population. The human-service professionals have taken up residence in the service-dependent ghetto. The clients, cast adrift, search in vain for the promised community care network. For many, the right to deinstitutionalization has become a new legitimacy for neglect. Faced with the apparent onslaught of the homeless deinstitutionalized, the community shrinks from its responsibility as host and erects fences to protect its turf. Somewhere on the periphery of this battlefield, service operators and land-use planners attempt to provide for the casualties of deinstitutionalization. The operators continue to open facilities wherever communities will allow them, and wherever there are people in need. Land-use planners facilitate openings of community-based facilities, except where communities are powerful enough to block their efforts. The few existing resources meet up with the deinstitutionalized in the 'service-dependent ghetto' (figure 2.1).

In the everyday practices of these agents, space plays a key role. It is a necessary design in the professional program of isolation and treatment. It is the constitutive element of the inner-city coping networks of service-dependent populations. And it is a fundamental mediating factor in the creation and perpetuation of geographically separate residential and resource environments through the isolation

of the disabled, the private-market process of residential differentiation and the state-sanctioned practice of exclusionary zoning. It is
paradoxical that the processes of the land and property markets now
threaten the future of the ghetto in a manner that seems essentially
beyond the control of the human-services system.

3

The social history of
service-dependency

Over the course of the past century, there have been radical changes
in the social construction of service-dependency and in the manner
in which services are provided. In a departure from nineteenth-
century notions of the elderly, physically infirm and mentally disabled
as being deviant, dangerous and a drain on collective resources, the
service-dependent population has increasingly been viewed as
worthy of support and as an integral part of the urban community.
Similarly, support services targeted at the dependent have been
dramatically transformed, shifting from confinement in large,
repressive institutions segregated from society, towards a model of
service delivery in which clients remain in the community supported
by small-scale and less restrictive service facilities situated close by.

But behind this aura of liberal reform, older ideas about the
service-dependent persist and confound these new trends. Attempts
to reintegrate clients into the community fabric are foiled by
municipal jurisdictions and neighborhood residents who fear client
presence and who avoid the burdens of support by shutting them
out. Segregation and control within institutions has been replaced
by an informal control system in which the mentally ill, physically
handicapped, ex-offenders, elderly and retarded are forced to
huddle in an asylum without walls: the cheap, deteriorated fringe of
the central business district.

In this chapter, we trace the social history of service-dependency
in North America (particularly the US) since the nineteenth
century. We explore the scale of dependency during the 1850–1900
period, between the turn of the century and World War II and in
contemporary times. At each juncture we examine prevailing public
attitudes toward dependent groups, the philosophies of those charged
with their treatment and care, and how the service delivery regimes

became translated into a distinctive element of urban spatial form and organization. Through this historical filter, we see the service-dependent ghetto emerge as a logical outgrowth of social attitudes and values, prevailing professional practices, and the interplay of industrial, commercial and residential activities in the expanding North American metropolis.[1]

THE BIRTH OF THE INSTITUTION

Institutions for the confinement of dependent populations gained widespread popularity in North America during the Jacksonian period (Rothman, 1971). By the late nineteenth century, dependents of every kind were housed in almshouses, workhouses, penitentiaries and hospitals of various sorts. Although cash and in-kind relief was provided to the 'deserving' poor in order to maintain civil order, institutionalization remained the preferred professional prescription for eradicating the undesirable effects of social disorganization. Away from the turbulence and illicit attractions of the industrializing city, well-ordered institutions would provide 'moral treatment', and thereby instill the appropriate behavioral norms among the dependent classes.

By the middle of the century, however, the promise of the asylum, penitentiary and almshouse had faded. Overcrowded and underfunded, the large institutions had become custodial warehouses with a decidedly poor public image. Nevertheless, they continued to be erected in isolated areas and filled with residents; the institutional approach retained its legitimacy among human-service professionals despite its unconvincing record of treatment. Back in the city, teeming with immigrants and beset by recurrent periods of economic booms and busts, the poor and dependent population that escaped the institutions settled along the fringe of the expanding central business district, in cheap rooming houses, tenements and temporary shelters.

Deviant, dangerous and dependent classes in the nineteenth-century city

Society in the late nineteenth century distinguished numerous categories among that portion of its membership unable to exist without assistance. These categories included idiots, lunatics, inebriates, paupers, tramps, vagrants, the aged, sick, feebleminded, disabled, orphans and criminals. While recognizing their detailed distinguishing characteristics, these classes were conceived of as an undifferentiated whole: 'the deviant, dependent and dangerous classes,' united by popular beliefs in a 'morphology of evil,' perpetuated by heredity, which was regarded as a common etiology of all forms of dependency. Despite such views, a moral division among the dependent classes persisted and affected policy responses. The able-bodied were typically castigated as morally corrupt and undeserving of assistance, while lunatics, widows, orphans and the sick were deemed worthy of philanthropic aid. However, according to Rothman (1971), in practice the category of worthy poor 'was so narrow as to be practically irrelevant. The difference between dependency and deviancy narrowed, with the poor standing as potential criminals' (p. 164).

Definitive quantitative estimates of dependency are difficult to obtain for the nineteenth century. The first nationwide American census to estimate the size of the mentally ill and deficient population was taken in 1840; along with later census figures, these estimates were subject to numerous errors and fundamental problems of categorization. There exist even less reliable figures for other segments of the dependent populations: unemployment data were not collected, nor was the size of the poor population ever quantified adequately.

Nevertheless, census figures, anecdotal evidence, popular impression and a well-documented and visible influx of poor, immigrant groups during the late nineteenth century fueled fears about a rapid expansion in the dependent classes. Such fears are apparent in descriptions of the dependent and in the design of social control efforts and they reveal popular theories of causal attribution. Generally, the dependent were seen as responsible for their own plight. For instance, the tramp population in New York City during the 1870s was characterized most ungenerously by prominent analysts of the day:

A lazy, shiftless, incorrigible, cowardly, utterly depraved savage . . . he seems to have wholly lost all the better instincts and attributes of manhood. He will outrage an unprotected female, or rob a defenceless child, or burn an isolated barn, or girdle fruit trees, or wreck a railway train, or set fire to a railway bridge, or murder a cripple, or pilfer an umbrella, with equal indifference . . . Having no moral sense, he knows no gradations in crime. He dreads detection and punishment, and he dreads nothing else . . . Practically, he has come to consider himself at war with society and all social institutions . . . He has only one aim – to be supported in idleness.

(Katz, 1983, pp. 160–1)

Even the mentally defective had, by the late nineteenth century, become 'undesirable, frequently viewed as a great evil of humanity: the social parasite, criminal, prostitute, and pauper' (Scheerenberger, 1983, p. 116). In fact, the President of the Association of Medical Officers of American Institutions for Idiotic and Feebleminded Persons reflected popular images in his characterization of the mentally retarded:

Is it because there are in the United States an army of perhaps half a million tramps, cranks, and peripatetic beggars crawling like human parasites over our body politic, and feasting upon the rich juices of productive labor? Many of these human parasites have committed no crime and are guilty *per se* of no wrong, unless it is a crime and a wrong to be brought, without one's volition, into this world, burdened with the accumulated inherent sins of a vitiated and depraved ancestry; to be bred in filth, to be born in squalor and to be raised in an atmosphere tainted of course with crime. Many of these wretches are what they are because they are what they were made, not what they have made themselves. Handicapped by the vices of their inheritance they are simply not strong enough to keep up to the social, civil and moral ethics of the ages, and as an inevitable consequence, just as water seeks its level, they drop back by degrees to become in turn deficient, delinquent, defective and dependent. (A. Osborne, 1894, as quoted in Scheerenberger, 1983, p. 116)

Fears were exacerbated by the common perception of urban life itself as dangerously disorganized, threatening and overstimulating. As Boyer argues: 'Fears about industrialization, immigration, family disruption, religious change, and deepening class divisions all focused on the growing cities. Social thinkers, reformers, philanthropists and others whose assumptions and activities seemed otherwise different were often linked by a shared preoccupation with the city' (Boyer, 1978, p. viii). Moreover, the growing spatial segregation and social isolation of the dependent in warren-like slums fostered an image of these groups as different and threatening. According to Ward (1976):

The accelerated rate and new scale of urbanization created cities in which the poor, removed from their familiar traditional world and completely isolated from their moral and social superiors, were assumed to live a sordid and deviant life in districts known as slums . . . once isolated from their social superiors it was believed that worthy poor would rapidly be degraded by the contaminating influences of the most depraved and discontented among them . . . Cities came to be seen as dichotomous social orders; when this segregated social geography was described as two nations the slums gained unambiguous recognition of their identity and of their potential to be an insurgent state.

(Ward, 1976, p. 323)

Concentration of population in fast-growing urban–industrial centers may have heightened social awareness and fear of their presence, but in all likelihood dependent groups had actually expanded their numerical share of total population. By the century's end, several hundred thousand persons suffered from poverty, insanity, mental retardation, or other forms of dependence. As Katz (1983), Scull (1981) and others argue, this rise in dependency was linked to the growing dominance of wage labor and an increasing casualization of the work force as highly competitive firms sought least-cost production and labor arrangements. This process implied constant economic uncertainty for many families and individuals. In response, interurban mobility rates soared as people looked for work. Mobility mounted with each plunge in the business cycle. The depression of 1873 led to drastic population shifts, in fact prompting the popular appellation of 'tramp' to refer to the single men moving across the countryside and through cities looking for employment (Katz, 1983). Economic dislocation, minimal wage rates, seasonal fluctuations of production, and the use of flexible 'casual' and sweated-labor systems eliminated job security and led to periodic destitution for many.

The internal physical structure of the nineteenth century city was largely a result of the system of wage labor and the technology of both transport and manufacture. But the spatial form and organization of the city itself affected rates of dependency. The spatial pattern of jobs and housing created specific hurdles that heightened the risk of dependency. The casual-labor market was a socially inefficient way of organizing work, premised on abundance and redundancy of labor. The need to wait on call early each morning at a particular factory or workshop required highly accessible shelter. It also obviated the possibility of employment elsewhere; not only would jobs be allocated early in the day, giving workers only one chance for day-long employment, but furthermore, the transport costs of job searching inhibited the job-worker matching process. The need for two-earner families to locate in order to maximize joint probabilities for work also restricted the range of residential choices and reduced the ability of families to respond to the job loss of one member by moving the household residence. Finally, the restricted supply of cheap housing and neighbourhood credit severely limited mobility for marginal populations. Thus when economic crises hit, urban spatial structure and activity patterns inhibited adjustment processes and exacerbated problems of dependency and poverty (Stedman-Jones, 1971).

Both economic organization and urban spatial structure therefore affected dependency rates dramatically. These forces also helped to shape policy responses to the problem. In order to insure social and economic stability, maintain an ongoing supply of cheap labor and thus promote capital accumulation, some relief to families at home was a vital political–economic necessity. But at the same time, the very ghettoization of the dependent led to beliefs in their dangerousness and its contagion, prompting policies of massive removal of poor, insane, deficient and delinquent persons to institutions.

Nineteenth-century treatment: moral treatment and community protection

Despite a recognition of basic differences among the dependent population, approaches to their support were surprisingly uniform. Almost all the helping professions – medical superintendents, jailers, overseers of the poor – favored institutionalization as a form of treatment. As the nineteenth century unfolded, however, their rationale for this treatment setting shifted radically from a belief in the capacity of such regimes to cure or correct, to a belief in the inevitability of disorders and the necessity for removing the dependent in order to protect the community and to provide cheap custodial care to clients.

The theory of 'moral treatment', which first gained ascendancy during the late eighteenth and early nineteenth centuries, prescribed institutionalization in asylums, prisons, almshouses and poorhouses as a cure for dependency. The notion behind moral treatment was strictly environmentalist: that individuals were susceptible to the degenerating influences of an imperfect society and disorderly community. If afflicted with lunacy, pauperism, or criminal tendencies, clients could be 'cured' via placement in a well-ordered institution designed and run according to strict moral precepts of work and deference to authority. As Rothman (1971) suggests, early in the nineteenth century reformers argued that human nature was malleable, a product of circumstances: schools would eradicate the effects of a poor home environment; the healthy milieu of mental hospitals would cure the insane; and the rehabilitative atmosphere of prisons would transform the criminal.

During the early and middle decades of the nineteenth century, such notions led to a massive wave of asylum building, poorhouse and almshouse construction, prison development and of course compulsory public schools. For example, between 1850 and 1869, 35 new state mental institutions were established and a further 59 (much larger) institutions were opened by 1890. According to the 1880 census, there were almost 92,000 insane persons out of a population of 50 million; this compares with 15,610 out of 21 million in 1850 (Grob, 1983, p. 25). Increasingly, responsibility for these institutions was public, their construction and operation funded by state and local tax dollars. Rapid expansion of the dependent population stimulated a large-scale response in order to insure social control and as reformers pressed for 'scientific treatment' in institutions as a cure for dependency of most any kind.

In the middle of the century, institutions of almost every type had dropped pretenses of providing therapy or cures, becoming almost purely custodial in function.

For predictable reasons, none of these happy outcomes [cures] occurred. The reasons rest in the way in which institutions had been created. They were too large, too crowded, too inherently punitive, and too under-financed to operate in a manner remotely approaching their ideal . . . Nonetheless, the producers and managers of institutions, unwilling to accept the responsibility for failure, blamed the victim. Environmentalism gave way to heredity as the theory of human nature. The problem with the children of the poor, the mentally ill, and the criminals resided in their genes, not in their environment.

(Rothman, 1971)

According to this view, pauperism, idiocy, lunacy and criminality were hereditary, passed on from generation to generation, making cures almost impossible.

The demographic and industrial dynamics of the period in question insured that institutions would fail in their initial mission. Excessive demands placed on the care system created deplorable physical conditions and an increasingly harsh and punitive institutional environment. In most cases, these pressures resulted in the willy-nilly mixing of various classes of dependent inmates, segregation and treatment remaining an ideal that was impossible to reach in practice.

Managers of institutions, eschewing the notion of curable dependency, instead sought legitimacy for their activities by claiming for them an invaluable role as places of last resort for dependent populations exposed to a harsh world. Moreover, institutional life was seen as a necessary if coercive instrument of social control – its very drabness, isolation and potential for abuse serving to inhibit all but the most desolate and decrepit from seeking aid and forming a powerful incentive for adherence to a proper life-style and work ethic. If the asylum could not provide moral treatment, it could nevertheless impose morality simply by its fearful image. In doing so, the burden of dependency had shifted from the environment to rest squarely on the shoulders of the dependent themselves. The widespread perception that the dependent caused their own problems, reinforced by psychiatric theories linking debauchery and insanity, in large part explains the minimal public fiscal support for their assistance and treatment.

Popular views of the poor were legitimized in the 1870s and later by the emergence of Charity Organization Societies (COS), first established in the US in 1878 (Katz, 1983, p. 91). These societies, the forerunners of modern-day social work, claimed to be engaged in 'scientific charity,' which had as its most basic premises the notion that excessive almsgiving in the home only served to exacerbate pauperism and encourage slothful, spendthrift, intemperate, illicit and immoral behavior among the poor.

In practice, Charity Organization workers sought to train the poor along with their almsgiving, via a system of 'friendly visitors' who offered advice as well as censure to poor families seeking relief. But in addition, Charity Organization Societies, imbued with a Social Darwinist ideology, argued that provision of such 'outdoor' support in fact weakened all of society by allowing the least fit to survive and propagate. Their conviction concerning the evils of outdoor relief led them to campaign vociferously against public outdoor provision, to demand its abolition and to advocate the exclusive use of 'indoor' – almshouse – relief.

During the 1870s, this repressive approach to the poor was actually implemented in 10 cities of the Eastern seaboard. The severe economic downturn of the decade had increased dependency rates, creating fiscal stress for local authorities responsible for poor relief. The COS-backed policies of indoor relief were cheaper than outdoor provisions, because localities could in fact shift some of their support obligations onto the state-run institutions. Such experiments were short-lived, however, because of popular demands for the restoration of in-home assistance. Nevertheless, the battle for institutionalization reflected the strong desires for social control over potentially threatening and disruptive elements in society.

Thus institutions remained the dominant form of dealing with dependency. As Rothman (1971) notes in regard to poor relief, after 1850 'the almshouse maintained a firm hold over public policy while its physical plant decayed and even the pretense of rehabilitation disappeared' (p. 287). Despite obvious failings and defects, officials were deeply dependent on them. 'Officials did not attempt to differentiate carefully among the poor, to devise and administer one solution for the aged and another for the vagrant. Convinced that all groups at the bottom were more or less bothersome, culpable, and unfit for extended relief at home, they continued to rely upon the almshouse solution' (p. 290).

This hegemony was not without challenge, however. First, advocates for the deserving segment of the dependent population, such as widows and orphans, argued that removal was both harmful and unnecessary as a means of socialization or prevention of pauperism. Outdoor relief had many advocates who spoke out against the abuses of institutions and their dangers for children. In fact, a considerable portion of both public and private support was allocated to clients in their homes, despite the campaigns of Charity Organization Societies to eliminate outdoor relief (Coll, 1969, p. 62). Generally, between 20 percent and 50 per cent of total aid to the poor was given in the form of outdoor relief, although this portion diminished during the 1870s and 1880s. Beyond theory, outdoor relief was a political necessity, as a result of demands of the urban working class suffering periodically from economic dislocation and crisis (Katz, 1983, p. 230).

Although it was difficult to find supporters of outdoor relief in influential journals or in national or statewide organizations, opposition to its abolition remained strong. For instance, in New York State county superintendents of the poor refused to vote for its total abolition. Even though most of them, at least for the record, deplored outdoor relief, they argued that its abolition would create unjust hardships for the worthy poor and foment social discontent, which they would be unable to stem. Indeed, running throughout the comments of superintendents on outdoor relief was the theme of popular demand.

(Katz, 1983, p. 191)

Secondly, in addition to outdoor relief for the poor, a brief movement focused on 'boarding-out' of the insane surfaced in the 1870s, led by neurologists critical of state asylums. But the threat of waning professional control led medical superintendents to crush this fledgling community care strategy (Bell, 1980, p. 55).

Thirdly, the late 1800s witnessed the establishment of the Settlement House movement, devoted explicitly to assisting the urban

poor and immigrant population in their adjustment to urban industrial life. Precursors of progressive era reforms, settlement workers
sought to live among the poor and provide services aimed at education
and socialization to middle-class norms. But in spite of their belief in
the centrality of the family and communal life for social development,
settlement leaders were fully behind the incarceration or commitment of the deviant, dependent and dangerous classes in large-scale
institutions. Robert A. Woods and his associates at South End House
in Boston decried the fact that *all* such persons were not removed, as
they corrupted the community and made service delivery problematical.

No civilized community undertakes to carry within its corporate life the
criminal and the lunatic. The South End attempts to carry these equally
dangerous types, the confirmed pauper, the confirmed prostitute, and confirmed drunkard. . . Persons of these types, who now go to and from the
harbor institutions (the poorhouse) an incredible number of times, must be
dealt with upon the principle of the habitual criminal act, the length of term
rapidly increasing with each commitment, and reaching ere long a sentence
that will last until the persons either are cured or die. . . So much of the
social wreckage must be dredged out.

(Woods, 1970, pp. 291–2)

State Intervention and the Specialization of Care-giving

During the early part of the nineteenth century, the state slowly
expanded its role in the area of dependency. In the 1820s most state
legislatures reformed colonial 'poor laws,' and under the influence
of advocates of institutional treatment, required each constituent
county to maintain a poorhouse or farm in addition to any outdoor
relief they might elect to provide (Katz, 1983, p. 5). Local government continued to have prime fiscal responsibility for the construction and operation of such institutions, funded out of local taxes.
Similarly, other types of institutions were local responsibilities, i.e.,
jails and insane asylums.

Later in the century, state governments entered into some
institution-building (penitentiaries, reform schools, asylums). They
also sought to coordinate and supervise institutions of many types,
after zealous reformers attacked their quality of care. This effort to
centralize, rationalize and bureaucratize the relief system resulted in
the establishement of State Boards of Charities, first begun by
Massachusetts in the early 1860s (Grob, 1973, p. 258). This trend
quickly spread throughout the country, where state boards were

charged with the task of administrative oversight of public systems for correction, health care, mental health and poor relief, as well as private institutions receiving government support and, in time, the development of standards of practice for many sorts of institutions (Perlman and Gurin, 1972, p. 26). Later, lunacy commissions were implemented in some states specifically for the mental institutions (Bell, 1980, p. 57), but in others state and local as well as private asylums were under Boards of Charity, placing them squarely within the emerging public welfare system. According to Katz,

these boards gathered statistics, visited institutions, and collected other forms of evidence, which they used to make recommendations to state legislatures. With little power, and often resented by the institutions and voluntary agencies they supervised, state boards accomplished little by themselves and often had a rocky history . . . these state boards were the precursors of the state departments of public welfare established in the early decades of the twentieth century.

(Katz, 1983, p. 7)

States also mandated important shifts in the treatment settings available to specific subgroups of the dependent population. Reacting to almshouses in which poor widows, orphans, syphilitics, criminals, lunatics and the infectiously ill were housed side by side, some states during the 1870s ordered the removal of children from poorhouses and almshouses, despite the fact that often removal to more specialized institutions or to foster homes meant the separation of children from parents (Katz, 1983). Removal orders, however, such as that of Massachusetts in 1879, excluded mentally impaired children, who remained either in special institutions (a minority) or almshouses (Scheerenberger, 1983, p. 112). Similarly, the insane were ordered to be removed from almshouses by many states during the middle decades of the century, to be housed in state insane asylums, severely taxing their capacity and vitiating attempts at providing more than custodial care. Despite these mandated removals, however, many children and lunatics remained in almshouses. Moreover, almshouses provided the major source of general hospital care available to the urban poor during this period (Coll, 1969, p. 24). The private sector retained its prominence for the care of the affluent sick or insane; corporate hospitals were theoretically designed to redistribute fee revenues from rich paying clientele in order to subsidize indigents, but in fact institutional economics and affluent patient aversion to such social mixing obviated this strategy. Care of the poor was left to the public sector and to charity clinics, thereby establishing a dual system of care (Grob, 1973, pp. 76–7).

Throughout the century, state and local government played the primary public roles in support of the dependent. The sole federal endeavor came with the Reconstruction-era Freedman's Bureau. The Bureau provided a variety of services to Southern blacks and some whites and constituted the major source of public welfare in the South during 1865–9.

Despite a lack of federal involvement, the state's role in the realm of dependency was far more significant than is often acknowledged (Katz, 1983). As Katz argues, 'It is important to stress that after the initial period of settlement, and outside of the South, public relief always has been more widespread than private' (p. 6), and that 'there has never been a golden age of voluntarism in America. Some level of government always has been active, usually providing most of the money' (p. 240). By 1900, private societies in New York City aided 30,560 persons or families, while public outdoor relief alone served over 200,000 (ibid., p. 190). Thus even in locales with a strong private philanthropic base, 'relief had a mixed economy' and 'throughout most of America it [relief] was a public/private venture' (Katz, 1986, p. 46).

Governments were strongly influenced in their actions by the budding helping professions. In fact, the bureaucratization of public health and welfare reflected the growing specialization of care-givers and their increasing public legitimacy as experts. Although initially lay personnel, the administrators and organizers of asylums, hospitals, clinics, orphanages, almshouses and charitable societies such as the Association for the Improvement of the Condition of the Poor (AICP), Charity Organization Societies (COS) and the Society for the Prevention of Cruelty to Children (SPCC), shared experiences and a communality of outlook that eventually led to their professionalization during the latter part of the nineteenth century. Professional differentiation was rapid, with national associations for medical superintendents, superintendents of the mentally deficient, overseers of the poor and others forming during the 1870–80 period, along with specialized technology, training and ideologies. 'In the past, particularly the 1840s, strong philosophical and moral links held physicians and lay reformers together. . . By the 1860s, the reform impulse had ebbed, and a new medical terminology had evolved that put a wall between the professionals and outsiders' (Bell, 1980, p. 41).

Specialization and differentiation also led to a proliferation of special institutions, such as farms for idiots and the feebleminded, reformatories, schools for the deaf, blind and dumb, and neurological clinics, each institution serving to mark professional boundaries and reinforce professional norms (Scheerenberger, 1983). This trend, which became full-blown after the turn of the century, fore-shadowed progressive ideas concerning the need for individualized problem-identification and treatment and led to a more differen-tiated view of the underclass, but at the same time directed attention away from the most widespread genesis of their problems – poverty and irregular employment.

As Katz (1983) emphasizes, the formation of State Boards of Charities reflected the growing professionalization of care-giving and demonstrated the close interaction and loose distinction between private and public realms during the late nineteenth century. Like today, the voluntary sector often received much of its funding and authority from the state. However, private-sector professionals and the state often locked horns over major policy issues, for example outdoor vs. indoor relief. The professionals, particularly those involved in the scientific charity movement, attacked the abuses of relief by local political bosses, while public officials, never blind to the political advantage of relief-giving and patronage in the form of jobs in the welfare bureaucracies and institutions, also recognized the appro-priateness of outdoor relief, seeing it as means to provide services to lower-class and immigrant populations. This dispute was short-lived, as the professions advanced their power and status by captur-ing the role of relief and institutional managers, while permitting the public to fund their activities (Lubove, 1965).

Spatial segregation and isolation of the dependent classes in institutions and cities

Although the precise spatial distribution of late nineteenth-century institutions, particularly those within major urban areas, has not been documented fully, institutional administrators had developed principles for siting facilities by the early part of the century. Their writings suggest that three factors guided the siting of major facilities such as asylums, penitentiaries and almshouses: locations were to be separated from urban society; provide a therapeutic and productive work environment; and allow institutions to be self-supporting

through on-site industrial or agricultural activities. All three principles worked toward the location of institutions outside cities.

One principle, originating with mental health professionals, was
that institutions ought to be located in small towns, rural areas, or
distant suburbs, as these tranquil settings would be most therapeutic.
Inherent in and underlying this view was the popular image of the
nineteenth-century city as turbulent and unsettling, prompting
undesirable behavior. In addition, it reflected a desire to segregate
and hence control urban dependent populations.

For example, as early as 1811, Dr T. R. Beck provided a concise
definition of 'moral treatment', which in fact opened with geographical principles of isolation: 'MORAL MANAGEMENT. This
consists of removing patients for their residence to some proper
asylum; and for this purpose, a calm retreat in the country is to be
preferred: for it is found that continuance at home aggravates the
disease' (quoted in Deutsch, 1949, pp. 91–2).

Edward Jarvis also suggested that the disadvantages of siting
institutions in urban areas outweighed the benefits. In his 1855
report on *Insanity and Idiocy in Massachusetts* (Jarvis, 1971 edn), Jarvis
stated that:

The position of the Hospital, in the midst of an active and growing city, has
some advantages, and many disadvantages. The busy scenes of life, the stir
of business, the movements of passengers and carriages in the streets, the
rush of railroad trains interest many patients, and stimulate at least the
curiosity of some, and quicken the dormant faculties of others. And there
are some who are benefitted by walking in the public streets, by visits to
factories, shops, and the market-places.

On the contrary, in the acute stages of insanity the excitable and violent
need quiet and freedom from causes of excitement. They are disturbed and
injured by the lively scenes and sounds that belong to the busy haunts of
men. While, therefore, these may be presented with advantage to some
classes of patients in some states of disease, they certainly should be avoided
by others. It is well for a hospital that it have a city within convenient
distance, that its inmates may see its sights and hear its sounds whenever it
shall be profitable for them; but the whole should not be subjected at all
times to the necessity of seeing and hearing them. The officers should,
therefore, be able to shut them out, and the Hospital should not be surrounded by, and near to, the stimulating affairs of city life.

(Jarvis, 1971 edn, p. 179)

A second principle stemmed from both ethics and economics of
institutional management. Rural or exurban locations provided the

opportunity for inmates to work on adjacent farms. This was considered therapeutic for the mentally ill (a form of occupational therapy), but also as a vital element in the 'cure' of pauperism and as a necessary contribution by the able-bodied poor in exchange for food and shelter. For the mentally deficient, labor was an essential part of the educative task, and the so-called 'colony plan' for their care was widespread by 1890. Colonies, sometimes referred to as 'cities of refuge,' trained idiots and imbeciles of various grades in the methods of farming, dairy farming, industrial shops and institutional operations. Most importantly, residents were instructed in the care of their less fortunate brethren.

Perhaps more significant was the fact that officials aimed to make institutions self-supporting, by playing dual roles as agricultural producers and by economizing on land prices. Referring to the optimal location for a 'colony' for the mentally deficient, a prominent nineteenth-century physician claimed that:

a site not too far from some commercial center is preferable. If too near, the institution is subject to so many visitations as to interfere seriously with the household work. If too far off from any large city, transportation becomes so costly as to increase very materially the running expenses of the institution. A distance of from twenty to fifty miles should be reasonably free from either of these objections, and at this distance land is cheaper than it is too near a large city.

(A. Wilmarsh, 1900, as quoted in Scheerenberger, 1983, p. 128)

These factors affected both city and county as well as state decision-makers; thus, even city-run institutions were located in distant fringe zones.

In addition to normative siting principles of facility planners, community fears about the dependent classes would seem to have proscribed their initial placement in community-based facilities. Of course, cities often grew out to encompass once-rural institutions, but their beginnings in isolated places (including islands, in the case of Boston and New York City) indicate the general aversion of the affluent and upwardly mobile to having the dependent in their midst. Ward (1976) implies this aversion in his discussion of prevalent Victorian notions of 'slums' as undifferentiated and dangerous warrens of the depraved and dependent, potential hot-spots of radicalism and anarchy. As the division of labor changed and deepened, as the wage-labor system and unstable economy exposed masses of the population to the risks of casualization and poverty, and as urban residential differentiation reflected the growing social distance and distrust between classes, locational solutions to facility siting problems that promised removal of the offending classes were certain to be viewed favourably by the nondependent majority of urbanites.

By the middle of the century, the question of location had been codified for certain classes of institutions, most extensively for insane asylums (figure 3.1). Thomas Kirkbride, as part of his 1847 treatise *On the Construction, Organization, and General Arrangements of Hospitals for the Insane, with some remarks on Insanity and its Treatment* identified 26 propositions embodying the major structural considerations in a model hospital for the insane. Among these was: 'Each hospital for the insane should be located in the country, not less than two miles from a large town, and easily accessible at all seasons' (quoted in Deutsch, 1949, p. 209). Hence, among the first principles of a 'well-ordered institution' were prompt removal from the community to an institution that was itself separate from the community. As Rothman (1971) points out, no principle was more easily or more consistently enacted than physical separation of clients from community. As a result, almost all asylums for the insane after 1820 were located at some distance (often fairly short) from an urban center.

Nevertheless, the report by Jarvis in 1855 also indicated that an institution's location (in this case, an asylum) had a profound influence on its accessibility to and use by clients in need. He discovered that most asylum inmates came from within a prescribed radius of the institution. Those communities adjacent to it took most advantage of its proximity; those farthest away, the least. Jarvis concluded that the asylum was, to a large extent, a *local institution* (Caplan, 1969, pp. 53–4; Jarvis, 1971, p. 48). Therefore, in his report, he advocated that the proposed new asylum in Massachusetts should be located close to the center of population and communication (and, incidentally, should not house more than 250 patients):

For the convenience of the people who are to use it, it should be on one of the great thoroughfares . . . in a place the most accessible to the whole body of the population of those four counties [to be served]. It should be near to some large town or village, where provisions, mechanics and other aids could be obtained if needed, and near to a railway station, certainly not over two miles from it.

(Jarvis, 1971, p. 185)

FIGURE 3.1   Nineteenth-century principles of asylum location

CHAPTER XIII: Selection of a site

When it has been determined to erect a hospital for the insane, the first object to be attended to by those to whom this important duty has been delegated, is to select a suitable site for the buildings. The utmost caution should be observed in taking this step, on which may depend to no small extent, the future character and usefulness of the institution; for the best style of building and the most liberal organization, can never fully compensate for the loss sustained by a location, that deprives the patients of many valuable privileges, or subjects them to varied annoyances. It is now well established that this class of hospitals should always be located in the country, not within less than two miles of a town of considerable size, and they should be easily accessible at all seasons. They should, if possible, be near turnpikes or other good roads, or within reasonable proximity to a railroad. While two or three miles from a town might be named as a good distance if on either of the first named, the facilities afforded by a railroad might make ten or twelve miles unobjectionable; for it is the time spent in passing and ease of access, rather than distance, that are specially important. Facility of access, is, indeed, for many reasons, a most important consideration. It has been shown by careful statistics that the use made of institutions, and as a consequence thereof, the number of restorations, depend very largely upon the nearness of a hospital to those by whom it is expected to be used or its ease of access by them. Proximity to a town of considerable size has many advantages, as in procuring supplies, obtaining domestic help or mechanical workmen, and also on account of the various matters of interest not elsewhere accessible to the patients. In selecting a site, facility of access from the districts of country from where the patients will be principally derived, should never be overlooked. Under no circumstances should an unsuitable site be accepted because it is offered as a gift to the State. Such a gift can hardly fail to prove costly in the end. A site thus procured often, indeed, becomes of the dearest kind, from its many permanent inconveniences, and the constant expenditures to which it subjects an institution. As these hospitals are for all future time, a liberal expenditure for the proper kind of building, is always a wise investment. The first cost of the building of a hospital for the insane is a matter of small importance to a State, in comparison to the wise and economical management of the institution subsequently.

cont'd

FIGURE 3.1   *(cont.)*

The building should be in a healthful, pleasant, and fertile district of country; the land chosen should be of good quality and easily tilled; the surrounding scenery should be varied and attractive, and the neighborhood should possess numerous objects of an agreeable and interesting character. While the hospital itself should be retired, and its privacy fully secured, the views from it if possible, should exhibit life in its active forms, and on this account stirring objects at a little distance are desirable. Reference should also be made to the amount of wood and tillable land that may be obtained, to the supply of water, and to the facilities for drainage, for enclosing the pleasureground, and also for future extensions of the building.

Source: Thomas S. Kirkbride, *On The Construction, Organization, and General Arrangements of Hospitals for the Insane* (1880), chapter XIII.

It is of interest to note in passing that one of the reasons for rejecting large centrally located facilities for the incurably insane in New York state was a preference for 'additional hospital facilities judiciously distributed to serve all geographic areas of the state' (Grob, 1973, pp. 312–14). Jarvis also made some oblique but prescient observations on the beneficial effects of asylum proximity on the attitudes of surrounding populations; he felt that proximity dispelled fear and prejudice, while distance made mystery (Caplan, 1969, p. 54).

Many dependent people – mostly the poor – were not institutionalized, and even those who were frequently used almshouses only as temporary (often wintertime) refuges. According to most urban historians, residential districts housing the most impoverished (and mostly foreign-born) populations were situated between expanding Central Business Districts and more affluent residential areas serviced by a budding mass-transit industry (Ward 1971). Areas on the fringes of the Central Business Districts (CBDs) were the zones of oldest housing stock, large once-stately houses subdivided into tenements and boarding houses; they were also the sites of newer, large-scale tenement development, constructed to meet the mushrooming demand for low-cost housing accessible to rapidly growing labor-intensive manufacturing and casual-labor markets in the urban core.

At home, the poor and dependent received services from charitable and public agencies. Services provided to the poor and disabled living in tenement districts included material aid (food, clothing, coal), small cash grants and advice on resource and family management. Residential services, such as lodges for the destitute, were also available, and neighborhood churches often provided a range of material and coordinative services. An example of the scope of community-based services available in the larger nineteenth-century cities is provided by Katz (1983), who describes the case history of one Philadelphia family, the Sullivans. Over the course of the Sullivans's troubles, they received food, coal, furniture, clothing and medicine from agents of the Society for Organizing Charity (SOC), who also placed Mrs Sullivan and her children in local lodges for the destitute, found service employment for her and assisted her in securing medical attention for the sickly family. The local parish church supplied groceries, burial services and cemetery plots for two Sullivan children and assisted in the placement of other Sullivan children in orphanages. Municipal Hospital and Philadelphia Hospital supplied ambulance and medical services to the family; it is not clear from the account if such services were publicly funded or not. Lastly, the Society for the Prevention of Cruelty to Children prosecuted the family for neglect, in particular attempting to force Mr Sullivan to remain temperate and meet family support obligations.

The spatial distribution of these services (particularly SOC offices, lodges and hospitals) is not made explicit in Katz's account, or in others available in the literature. Many types of services were delivered to recipients in their homes; for instance, SOC agents would visit needy families and dispense material and monetary support on the spot. Furthermore, they provided coordinative services in the same fashion, meeting clients at lodging houses or hospitals, in order to help them deal with various service providers and acquire needed services. Thus it seems reasonable to assume that most services were fairly localized in the poor districts of the CBD-fringe area – the incipient zone of dependence in the late nineteenth-century city.

TWENTIETH-CENTURY CONSOLIDATION

The Progressive movement of the early twentieth century introduced innovations in the classification and treatment of dependent populations that endured until the middle of the century. Still earlier forms of service delivery remained partially intact as well, rendering this period one of stability and consolidation. In particular, institutional care endured as the most prevalent response to problems of mental illness, retardation, crime, delinquency and dependency among youth and the aged. Following the implementation of progressive reforms prior to World War I, the spirit and drive of the reform movement faltered. Gradual and incremental changes in service approaches during the interwar years still reflected certain basic Progressive assumptions but other Progressive reforms less convenient for officials and administrators to implement were discarded; the old ways persisted. The major exception to this lack of major reform after World War I was the passage of the Social Security Act, at the height of the Great Depression; this Act, however, was the culmination of Progressive struggles initiated much earlier in the century.

The scope of dependency in the twentieth century

Three major events of the first half of the twentieth century had an impact on the scale of dependency and the level of service provision. First, the flow of foreign immigration continued, bringing approximately 19 million people to the US between 1900 and 1930 (Coll, 1969, p. 63). Immigrants facing problems of acculturation and poverty made extensive use of institutional services and the population of asylums and almshouses continued to be disproportionately foreign-born (Rothman, 1980). Secondly, World War I left a legacy of disability that had to be confronted by the medical and social service professions and by government. Over 200,000 soldiers had been wounded and many required extensive rehabilitation and long-term care (Axinn and Levin, 1975, p. 139). Moreover, families of disabled veterans were deprived of a breadwinner and thus relied on voluntary and public relief. Lastly, the depression of the 1930s created widespread unemployment by 1933 and a new type of dependency arose: dependency of middle-class populations.

Information on the numbers and problems of dependent populations improved somewhat during the first decades of the twentieth century, although large gaps in reporting and definitional problems remained. In 1904, the social worker Robert Hunter estimated that the population in poverty was conservatively ten million, while several less conservative studies indicated that approximately 60 per cent of American wage earners were poor and 30 per cent lived in 'abject poverty' (Axinn and Levin, 1975, p. 118).

The poverty population was found largely in the cities. Here immigrants settled and farm families migrated in search of employment but lacked the industrial skill necessary to prosper in the expanding wage-labor system. Also, the rate of industrial accidents and job-related illness rose; during the 1920s it was estimated that 15,000 workers died each year, and one-half million more were injured on the job, leaving mothers and children dependent on the state and private charities for support (Axinn and Levin, 1975, p. 126). Not surprisingly, the majority of recipients of the new Mother's Aid programs being instituted across the country lived in the nation's larger cities (Coll, 1969, p. 80). As late as 1929, the historically high level of poverty persisted; a Brookings Institute study in that year found that 40 per cent of the population had no savings and that 71 per cent earned less than \$2,500 annually – a very modest income for the times. The depression of the 1930s thus exacerbated an already severe problem of income inadequacy and indigence.

Besides growing numbers of urban poor residing outside of institutions, the numbers of institutionalized persons increased steadily. Since the adoption of institution-based modes of treatment, the mentally disabled had probably experienced the highest rates of institutional placement among dependent subpopulations; significant portions of the retarded and neglected children groups, for example, continued to live either with their families, or in foster homes that opened during this period. Nevertheless, institutionalization rates rose across the board. For example, Rothman (1980) reports that between 1922 and 1939, the number of state hospital residents grew from 230,000 to 440,000, 40 per cent of whom were over 50 years of age and 30 per cent of whom were long-term residents (p. 351). The public juvenile reformatory population rose from 25,251 to 30,496 between 1923 and 1933, while juvenile commitments rose from 17,296 to 25,329 during the same period (p. 258). The population of institutions for the retarded also expanded, reaching 68,035 by 1930 (Scheerenberger, 1983). And in 1940, the US Census reported that 70,000 persons resided in sanitoriums and 150,000 children lived in orphanages and in homes for dependent and neglected children (Lerman, 1982, p. 23).

By 1923, more than 352 persons per 100,000 population were confined to almshouses, insane asylums and institutions for the feebleminded – an increase of 17 per cent from the 1904 rate. Increasingly, residents of almshouses and asylums were aged. Almshouse population over 60 years of age increased from 51.2 per cent in 1904 to 65.5 per cent in 1923, but while this institutional population 'aged', a large share of the total institutional population and particularly the elderly in institutional care were sent to mental hospitals. By 1923, insane asylums housed 3.5 times the number in almshouses, a reversal of past trends. The number of elderly in asylums had risen to 700 per 100,000 population – up 26 per cent since 1910 – reaching 1,150 per 100,000 population by 1950.

Progressive treatment theory, enduring institutions and the rise of outdoor relief

Progressive social reformers responded critically to nineteenth-century treatment modalities, attacking custodial and often abusive institutional care for the mentally ill, deficient, poor and criminal classes as inhumane, demonstrably ineffective and expensive (Rothman, 1980). Moreover, they spoke out against heredity as the sole basis of dependency. Some Progressives argued that environmental factors of life in growing urban–industrial centers were critical in creating social pathology. Others, such as Adolf Meyer and the Mental Hygiene movement, were strongly influenced by the budding field of psychology and believed that while environmental forces were potent, individual personality and mind-set, along with family and community interactions, were key variables in determining an individual's risk of dependency.

Progressive theories of dependency and treatment, and by extension, their recommendations for policy change, had three basic tenets (Rothman, 1980). The first was a conviction that each individual was unique and required an individualized diagnosis and treatment regime. 'From their perspective, the Jacksonian commitment to institutions had been wrong, both for assuming that all deviants were of a single type, the victims of social disorder, and for believing that they could all be rehabilitated with a single program, the well-ordered routine of the asylum' (Rothman, 1980, p. 5). Progressives did not necessarily agree on the etiology of dependency; some were environmentalists, others looked to psychological explanations for maladaptation, but in either case they concurred on the necessity for individualized assessment and assignment to treatment setting. A second tenet of Progressive theory was the assumption of harmony between the interests of clients and of the professions, and at a more general scale, between the state and individuals. The 'state as parent' was deemed by Progressives an appropriate relationship between government and polity. Lastly, and as a result of the second principle, was the idea that the state's power could be extended beneficially over various domains of private life, without substantive loss of civil liberties. Since interests of the state and polity were congruent and nonconflictual, the state's assumption of greater powers was not seen as problematical, but instead desirable.

The fact that some of their innovations extended the authority of the state and its potential for disruptive intervention did not inhibit Progressive reformers. Their belief in the state as parent allowed them to equate 'the needs of justice and the aims of therapy, the welfare of the individual and the security of society' (Rothman, 1980, p. 6). If institutionalization for an indeterminate period could perhaps rehabilitate, then custody was justified and un-problematical. In cases (such as retardation) where clients were irreformable, harsh methods were justified in order to stop the propagation of defectives; reformers accepted eugenic arguments and 'were eager to confine the retarded for life' (Rothman, 1978, pp. 81–2), or at a minimum, to require sterilization prior to community placement. The rights of the client were not taken into consideration; rather, professional expertise was the guiding force in determining appropriate therapeutic responses which the state could then carry out.

The Progressive reform programs for criminal justice, juvenile justice, mental hygiene and economic dependency were built on these theoretical principles, along with their basic environmentalist and psychological explanations of etiology. Their innovations called for individualized casework and treatment, necessitating a continuum of treatment settings, ranging from community care to total incar-ceration. Community alternatives were particularly important, because of the general Progressive belief in the role of environment in generating individual problems and the necessity of shaping the everyday environment in order to prevent various forms of dependency. Following the lead of Settlement House workers, reformers of the early twentieth century fought to transform the environmental context via their work in community-based institutions. As the leader of the Mental Hygiene movement put it, psychiatrists had to become 'concerned with conditions at large where the mental disorders are bred . . . Just as bacteriology studies the water supply and the air and food of communities, so we psycho/pathologists have to study more effectively the atmosphere of the community and must devise safeguards in the localities from which patients come, and to which they are to return' (A. Meyer, as quoted in Rothman, 1980, p. 307).

The need for community service alternatives led to proposals for, and later adoption of the probation, parole and juvenile court systems; outpatient mental health clinics and aftercare programs; special education classes in public schools; mothers' pensions and social insurance for the elderly, blind and disabled and unemployed. At the same time, institutions were gravely in need of reform, leading to proposals for special-purpose facilities such as the psychopathic hospital for the conversion of custodial facilities into true treatment institutions. The environmental sources of dependency were also attacked, via what Boyer (1978) terms negative and positive environmentalism. Negative environmental policies sought to curb undesirable products of the social milieu, such as intemperance and prostitution, which were in turn considered root causes of dependency. Positive environmental measures aimed to improve the physical fabric of cities through urban public-works programs and housing reform and eventually city planning.

Some progressive reforms such as mothers' pensions and other forms of social insurance were resisted bitterly and only implemented in weak form after many years of struggle. Lubove's 1965 study of the social insurance movement provides an excellent example of the controversial nature of some reforms that, by advocating a greater state role in the lives of all citizens (not just deviants and dependents), directly challenged fundamental American values of voluntarism. The business sector as well as labor opposed public social insurance proposals as, respectively, a threat to profits and a diminution of the power of organized labor to provide member-services and hence maintain its constituency. Only when business leaders later became convinced of the need for some form of the labor protection were programs such as workmen's compensation adopted. 'Concerned with the growth of unions, strikes, high labor turnover, and the cost of litigation in industrial accidents, late nineteenth- and early twentieth-century employers began to introduce the managerial strategies of welfare capitalism (Katz, 1983, p. 222). The forms of social insurance that were eventually accepted fell far short of advocates' designs, often undercutting original purposes. The support of business, however, and their adoption of in-house protections (i.e., private health insurance, sick pay, etc.), was a critical step on the road to the late twentieth-century Welfare State.

Other progressive innovations were accepted quite readily by public officials and private charities because, according to Rothman (1980), they helped solve administrative problems and were less costly than a simple expansion of previous treatment regimes such as the institution. Moreover, they heightened the power of officials themselves, increasing the discretionary authority of the administrators and the budding human-service professions, and improving their image at a time when caretakers of the poor and dependent were under constant attack concerning the weakness of service provision and social control. Reforms such as parole reduced the prison population and the costs of incarceration; the juvenile court alleviated crowded court dockets and provided judges and psychologists with greater latitude; and the psychopathic hospital allowed doctors to provide quality care for curable patients and escape the negative aura of the state mental hospitals. As was ultimately the case for social insurance, these reforms may have been stimulated by conscience, but were definitely 'convenient' and necessary to officials and service professionals, even if they were not effective in the terms sought by Progressive activists. As Rothman (1980) concludes, in the struggle between conscience and convenience, the latter usually won out.

And they were not, by and large, effective. Psychopathic hospitals designed to treat acute patients in the most medically advanced fashion attracted more and more psychiatrists and the growing numbers of auxiliary mental health professionals (Grob, 1983, chapters 5, 9). But they quickly became overrun with chronic patients, distorting their original purpose beyond recognition. Outpatient services and family care for mental patients, promoted by the Mental Hygiene movement, were undercut by the needs of the state hospital for labor (particularly the labor of the most functional inmates who were best suited to family care) and for scarce public funds. They were also defeated in part because of a lack of support by patient's relatives, most often from the lower classes, who were unable to accept the burden of client care without state compensation. Juvenile 'training schools' were unable to provide adequate formal academic education; vocational training became institutional maintenance; psychological counseling had little relevance; and the children's lives were ruled by rigid, punitive and military principles rather than rehabilitative concepts. Parole systems for both adults and juveniles were 'paper' programs that functioned only to reduce prison crowding, diminish inmates' hostility and the potential for prison riots and minimize costs to state legislators. And community placement for the mentally retarded became embroiled in debates over the potential for the independent feebleminded to propagate a race of subnormal defectives, leading to massive programs of forced sterilization.

Reformers blamed lack of results on meager funding and the failure of program administrators to implement reforms fully or properly. Indeed, programs were badly understaffed, reflecting the continued 'mean-spirited quality of response to the poor and dependent in American history' (Katz, 1983, p. 216). But in addition, the structural problems of programs obviated their success. Assumptions of Progressive theory made reformers blind to the inherent contradictions between custody and rehabilitation, and the conflicts between interests of clients and professions, the state and individuals. Such beliefs in social harmony and the efficiency of the expanded state were shared by Progressive reformers in other policy areas, and, as Katz argues, 'a denial that conflict is a fundamental feature of social life became an enduring tenet of American liberalism during these years' (1983, p. 209).

The central principles of individualized treatment, the legitimacy of the state as parent and the belief in expanded state power were not shared universally by Progressives involved in all policy areas. Their differences, highlighted by Boyer (1978) and Katz (1983), were in some instances deep and have often been overlooked. In the area of child welfare, for instance, 'child-saving' reformers questioned the value of institutions and fought for foster-home care. Divisions were also apparent in the realm of economic dependency. As Lubove (1965) suggests, reformers who sought social insurance had to contend with scientific charity advocates who waged a vicious campaign against mothers' pensions, arguing about the dangers of outdoor relief irrespective of individual circumstances and of the state's expanded power over almsgiving. In other areas, professions supported some reforms while fighting strenuously against others. The medical profession, for example, opposed public health insurance because of its threat to professional power, but at the same time physicians assisted in the fight against unhealthful and unsanitary environmental conditions in tenement districts and pioneered the use of outpatient health clinics, both favorite mainstream Progressive innovations.

Despite internal struggles within the Progressive movement; external struggles between reformers, business, labor, charities and government supervisors; and widespread policy failures, the Progressives left a legacy of social programs that persisted through World War II. At that time, the innovations of parole, probation and juvenile court that had been developed earlier were accepted and intact. Aid to Families with Dependent Children (mothers' pensions), Social Security, workmen's compensation and veterans' benefits had been implemented. The almshouse was deserted. Even programs that were not drastically altered were modified, reordered, or marginally improved.

But the mentally ill and retarded remained largely confined in massive asylums – the lack of community treatment centers illustrative of a major failure of the Progressive movement. Over time, in selected areas such as mental retardation, professionals made an abrupt about-face, dropping eugenic theory and punitive treatment approaches, but facilities remained as inadequate and inhumane as their counterparts of the bygone century. The overwhelming weight and inertia of the philosophy and practice of the asylum also prevented the rapid evolution of alternatives. Despite the improving awareness of mental illness – brought about by the Mental Hygiene movement and the high rates of mental disorder among World War I soldiers (Deutsch, 1944, p. 317) – the mental hospital had become the place of last resort. The decline and ultimate disappearance of the almshouse increased the pressure on the already overcrowded asylum, forcing officials into a dual strategy of expanding hospital size and discharging some patients back into the community. By the late 1930s, nearly 18 per cent of all patients were on parole (Grob, 1983, p. 316).

Professionalization of care and the state as parent

The first half of the twentieth century was a period of rapid professionalization among various branches of human-service workers. During this period, 'friendly visitors,' scientific charity advocates and Settlement House residents became social workers; medical superintendents became psychiatrists; wardens and prison reformers became criminologists; and 'positive environmentalists' became city planners.

As they became more professionalized, the service industries often shifted their primary focus from the identification of social and economic pathology to individual-level problem solving. This was in large part the result of pervasive Progressive ideology, but it also came about as professionals attempted to develop more precise notions of etiology, command more control over their treatment outcomes and hence advance their status and power. The model most often chosen to emulate was medicine; during this time psychiatry moved toward a conduct of practice that closely resembled medicine not only in theoretical approaches to mental illness, but also in terms of service organization. Surgery became a dominant treatment modality and asylums became hospitals. Social work followed suit, switching from a social and economic definition of problems to a psychological one in which internal difficulties of adjustment were at the crux of dependency. Workers in criminal justice, juvenile reform and child welfare similarly relied on the medical approach.

Professional expansion is reflected in the rise of new or renamed associations, the growth of professional schools across the country and moves to license and regulate professionals. The Association of Medical Officers of American Institutions for Idiots and Feebleminded Persons became the American Association on Mental Deficiency; the Association of Medical Superintendents of American Institutions for the Insane became the American Psychiatric Association; the National Conference of Charities and Correction became the National Conference on Social Work; and County Superintendents of the Poor became Public Welfare officials. The American Institute of Criminal Law and Criminology was established, as were the National Probation Association, the American Association of Hospital Social Workers and the American Association of Psychiatric Social Workers. By the first decade of the century, graduate programs in social work had been established and an umbrella group of social-work educators had been founded by 1920. The number of specialized training programs in other areas, such as mental retardation and special education, criminology, clinical psychology and psychiatry, also grew rapidly (Rothman, 1980; Katz, 1983; Trattner, 1974; Scheerenberger, 1983). Finally, state licensing procedures had been initiated in many areas of the human services by 1950.

The growth of the human-service professions spread quickly to encompass public activities, and welfare and related bureaucracies expanded in scope and power. In rapid succession, new bureaus at the city, county, state and federal levels were established to administer public-service and social programs and to coordinate public and private welfare efforts. Increasingly authority and responsibility for some types of human services became centralized. Perhaps the most fully centralized by mid-decade were veterans' programs, social insurance and child/mother welfare. Other functions stayed at the state level, including mental health and retardation and some parts of criminal justice. Jails, juvenile justice and poor relief for indigents remained local responsibilities.

The close links that evolved between the state and professions were, in fact, precisely what early Progressives advocated. The power of the state over individuals, buttressed by the professions and 'scientific' theory, had expanded dramatically since 1900. The ideal of the 'state as parent' had been realized, as public officials and advising professionals decided the fate of wayward juveniles and young offenders, the mentally ill and deficient, prisoners and the poor. For some, state discretionary authority was absolute: indeterminate, involuntary commitment to mental institutions is a case in point. In other instances, state powers were utilized to control and coerce at a greater distance – via the administration of welfare with its eligibility rules and behavioral constraints, for example – but control was exercised nonetheless. By 1950, private philanthropy and welfare capitalism had evolved into Welfare Statism, as the public sector assumed the responsibility of service provision and income supplementation essential to social reproduction, continued state legitimacy and maintenance of the social order.

Spatial separation and segregative control of service clients

Spatial patterns of service delivery remained remarkably similar to those of the nineteenth century. Principles of spatial isolation and segregative control were followed, as institutionalization in remote facilities lingered as the dominant therapeutic treatment mode and as the internal structure of cities became more highly differentiated. Progressive reforms (such as outpatient clinics), which might have tempered this pattern, failed miserably. The success of another Progressive invention – city planning – only exacerbated urban segregation and isolation of the dependent classes.

The workhouse and almshouse declined as outdoor relief gained a foothold after the turn of the century. Almshouses, used primarily for the aged and mentally retarded after 1900, fell into disuse after about 1940 (Coll, 1969; Scheerenberger, 1983). No new facilities appear to have been constructed after the early 1900s. Other large-scale institutions for the insane, mentally deficient and criminals continued to be sited in small towns or rural areas for reasons of institutional economy and therapeutic value (despite the fact that such institutions were demonstrably ineffective at obtaining 'cures'). The exceptions to this locational strategy were acute-care hospitals and psychopathic institutions which were urban based, symbols of the growing power of the medical and psychiatric professions. In the city, patients could be kept under their doctor's surveillance and were close to visiting friends and relatives. Ironically, the urban location of the psychopathic hospital helped to defeat its purpose; easy access prompted physicians to overload urban facilities, instead of placing clients in distant state institutions (Rothman, 1980).

Within cities, noninstitutionalized poor and dependent populations were increasingly segregated in ethnic and racial ghetto areas, located further and further from middle- and upper-class residential neighborhoods. The internal structure of the early twentieth-century city came to be the subject of intense research during the 1920s and 1930s, when Chicago sociologists carried out pioneering work on neighborhood social life and urban ecology. Summarized by Burgess's concentric-zone model, their descriptions of the physical arrangement of land uses and social class in the city indicated a persistence of nineteenth-century patterns, different mainly in degree. The Central Business District had expanded, suburbanization was more extensive, satellite commercial areas were sprouting up and the city had become finely differentiated by economic class. Noting the multitude of urban occupations, Burgess indicates 'how in the city the minute differentiation of occupation analyzes and sifts the population, separating and classifying the diverse elements' (Burgess, 1967a, p. 57).

The zone surrounding the Central Business District, now much further from the core of the city, was termed a 'zone of transition', sometimes called ' "hobohemia" – the teeming Rialto of the homeless migratory man' (Burgess, 1967a, p. 54). It was marked by cheap apartments and rooming houses, inhabited by 'social junk' and threatened by Central Business District expansion. 'In the zone of deterioration encircling the central business section are always to be found the so-called "slums" and "bad lands", with their submerged regions of poverty, degradation, and disease, and their underworld of crime and vice. Within a deteriorating area are rooming-house districts, the purgatory of "lost souls" ' (Burgess, 1967a, pp. 54–6).

Burgess noted that rough indices of social disorganization – disease, crime, disorder, vice, insanity and suicide – were concomitants of rapid urban growth and immigration and the inability of people to adjust to fast-changing social settings. Moreover, physical and social mobility and the stimulation of city life were considered key causal factors. For example, a study of 'girl delinquency' (more accurately, illicit sexual intimacy) found that various levels of physical mobility within the city led to different levels of delinquency, the most serious being the case where the girl delinquent meets a boy from outside her neighborhood in a third location away from either one's home area. This circumstance was termed promiscuity (Burgess, 1967b, pp. 152–3).

The areas of greatest mobility were clearly the poverty-ridden inner zones. 'Where mobility is greatest . . . as in the zone of deterioration in the modern city, there develop areas of demoralization, of promiscuity, and of vice . . . areas of mobility are also the regions in which are found juvenile delinquency, boys' gangs, crime, poverty, wife desertion, divorce, abandoned infants, vice' (Burgess, 1967a, p. 59).

The availability of services in decaying ghetto areas is only hinted at by the Chicago researchers. 'The area of deterioration, while essentially one of decay, of stationary or declining population, is also one of regeneration, as witness the mission, the settlement, the artists' colony, radical centers – all obsessed with the vision of a new and better world' (Burgess, 1967a, p. 56). The image of the slum as a potentially insurgent area remained vivid, but the presence of social services is indicated. Referring to slum areas and the problem of juvenile delinquency, Park also refers to 'new organizations and agencies' that, along with the church, school and courts had been developed to meet problems of slum residents. Such 'new agencies' included juvenile courts, juvenile protective associations, parent – teacher associations, Boy Scouts, YMCA settlements, boys' clubs, playgrounds and playground associations. Slum areas were also most likely the sites of early mental hygiene outpatient and aftercare clinics promoted by Meyer; however, for a variety of reasons, such facilities failed to gain a foothold and could not have been dominant features of poverty-area urban landscapes.

Students of Park and Burges, Durham for example, performed detailed statistical studies of deviance and found distinct social patterns for some disorders. Rates of dependency, delinquency and certain types of mental illness (schizophrenia) were mapped and shown to be heavily skewed toward central, transition-zone areas, as they had been in earlier periods of settlement (Burgess, 1967b; Herbert, 1978).

The Chicago school was strongly environmentalist, attempting to explain human social behavior on the basis of physical organization and spatial interactions in the city. Their findings of causal connection between spatial form and social pathology were consistent with less scientifically based views of Progressive reformers, particularly settlement workers, who advocated changes in the physical structure of the city. Changes were sought initially as a means to restore social order, moral values and community sentiments of an earlier small-town era. Later, the anti-urban bias ebbed, and 'drawing increasingly on experts and hard data, positive environmentalists advocated housing reform, parks, and playgrounds' (Boyer, 1978, pp. 233–4) in order to beautify the city and to reduce the pathological effects of disorderly, unplanned urban growth. By the 1920s, city planning had become a recognized endeavor, armed with the powerful tool of zoning and imbued with theories of good city form and urban aesthetics. In time, they would lose their reform orientation and come to serve the interests of state and capital via programs for downtown renewal, intraurban transportation and exclusionary suburban zoning. And the zone of dependence in the inner city would remain in spite of their efforts.

THE PRESENT CRISIS

In the years following World War II, the nature of service delivery to dependent populations began to change radically across North America. First in the US and then in Canada, human-service professionals rejected the warehousing of mentally ill, physically disabled and elderly populations in massive residential facilities isolated from community life. Instead, they sought community-based service delivery which they argued was more humane, more effective and less costly. These efforts coincided with growing fiscal pressure on state and provincial governments, where policy-makers were only too glad to institute cost-saving reforms. As a result, asylums, penitentiaries and long-term care institutions opened their doors, sending a flood of the disabled and dependent to make their way in the city. By the mid-1970s, many old institutions were empty and closed, as the community-based model of service delivery gained widespread support and popularity. Excluded from affluent suburbs, deinstitutionalized service-dependent clients clustered in inner-city areas. In these neighborhoods, left blighted and abandoned in the wake of postwar suburbanization, shelter was affordable and social and commercial services were nearby. More than ever before, cities became characterized by a zone of dependence, dominated by service clients and their professional helpers.

The scale of postwar dependency

The return of war veterans created a large need for human services to treat their mental and physical disorders and solve their community adjustment problems. It also increased social awareness of the extent of such problems, among the general population. The war itself had contributed to this new perception: of the five million men rejected from the US armed forces because of failure to meet medical standards, approximately 40 per cent were excluded because of mental disabilities; such disorders proved to be the most frequent reasons for premature discharge from the service after induction (Beigel and Levinson, 1972, p.5). The depression era and war years had seen severe underinvestment in health and human services, and in the period following the war, both Canadian and American governments placed a strong emphasis on expansion of service programs and treatment facilities.

The scale of urbanization – and urban disorder – had also increased dramatically since the Depression years, as the mechanization of agriculture displaced rural populations and sent them to cities in search of employment. In particular, the massive interregional migration of Southern blacks into Northern American cities immediately following the war changed the demographic structure of metropolitan areas fundamentally. The adjustment problems of migrants (both black and white) were exacerbated by racial conflict, economic discrimination and spatial segregation of incoming groups in deteriorating inner cities. The public looked toward the human-service professions for a solution to the crises decried in both intellectual journals and the popular press: urban alienation, the cycle of poverty and social disorganization of the family.

At the same time, the human-service professions were expanding rapidly and becoming increasingly specialized. The rise of urban disorder and the plight of the inner cities fueled their expansion. Subfields included not only mental illness, retardation, child welfare and criminal justice, but also juvenile delinquency, marriage and family counseling, child and wife abuse, sexual dysfunction, substance abuse, developmental disabilities, physical handicap. As

McKnight (1977) and others argue, the new professionals sought to define their fields of purview and to gain a clientele largely by convincing potential clients of their 'problems' and need for specialized treatment. This process in effect 'widened the net' of the helping professions, by defining a greater proportion of the population as in need of human services. By the 1960s, human services were no longer confined to what in the previous century had been considered the deviant and dependent classes. Instead, a significant share of middle-and upper-income populations were consuming mental-health, child-welfare, substance-abuse and other social services.

Theory of community treatment and the deinstitutionalization movement

By the middle of the century, a significant shift away from institutional care of the dependent was evidenced. Although the large-scale institution was to continue its dominance for one more decade, changing philosophies, changing professions and changing public attitudes combined to alter patterns of service delivery dramatically.

This shift was first evident in the area of mental health. After World War II, discontent with mental hospitals had become clearly articulated:

There was general agreement that too many patients had become 'institutionalized' and hence were destined to spend the rest of their lives as pitiful guests dependent on public largesse; that brutality and neglect were endemic; that deteriorating physical plants and inadequate care were common; that lethargy, neglect, and overcrowding had reduced mental hospitals to the status of inadequate poorhouses.

(Grob, 1983, p. 199)

During the 1950s two developments revolutionized treatment of the mentally ill and later affected treatment practices in other branches of the human services. The first development (initially introduced in Britain) was the adoption of new psychosocial approaches to the treatment of clients with mental or behavioral problems. The methods were based on principles of social psychiatry, with its emphasis on avoidance of seclusion or of restraint and development of group techniques such as the therapeutic community. The utility of these methods was recognized by professionals dealing with problem children, ex-offenders, substance abusers and the retarded. The second development, particularly vital in the areas of mental illness, retardation and geriatric care, was the introduction of new psychotropic drugs which markedly increased the effectiveness of treatment and symptomatic management of many cases. Drug therapy enabled clients to leave institutions quickly, or prevented the need for institutionalization itself.

Armed with new treatment approaches and drug therapy, the helping professions during the 1960s undertook a crusade to shift the *locus* of care for the service-dependent population away from traditional, large-scale institutions. In many of these facilities, a frightful record of client abuse had persisted without interruption since the discovery of the asylum and the penitentiary. Once again, institutions became the subject of intense criticism by human-service workers, government officials and the media – only this time, the evidence of abuse was revealed to millions of shocked television viewers who amplified the hue and cry against the 'back ward'. The pressure on institutions coincided with the Civil Rights movement, and demands for civil rights soon were extended on behalf of the mentally ill and physically handicapped. Institutions and institutionalization itself were attacked because of the wholesale denial of client liberties that they engendered.

Instead of the 'total' institution, human-service professionals proposed a new method of treatment that was community based. Services provided in small-scale facilities located in rehabilitative neighborhood environments could serve to normalize clients and reintegrate them into the community fabric (Wolfensberger, 1972; Nirje, 1976). Instead of spatial isolation of deviant, dangerous and dependent classes, the modern prescription for client rehabilitation called for spatial integration, engagement in community activities and interaction with the nondependent population in the course of everyday life. Community acceptance and support of clients, along with moderate social pressure to conform to behavioral norms, would speed their return to productive status.

This approach to the problems of service-dependency came to be termed 'deinstitutionalization'. Despite broad usage of the term, its definition in fact was ambiguous, used to mean different phenomena by policy-makers, institutional administrators and scholars. For example, as Lerman (1982) points out, the normative definition of deinstitutionalization used by national policy-makers was stated in a widely-read US General Accounting Office report of 1977: 'the process of 1) preventing both unnecessary admission to and retention in institutions; 2) finding and developing appropriate alternatives in the community for housing, treatment, training, education, and rehabilitation of the mentally disabled who do not need to be in institutions, and 3) improving conditions, care, and treatment for those who need institutional care' (p. 1). In practice, however, deinstitutionalization was measured simply by the reduction in average daily census in traditional public institutions such as state mental hospitals, prison facilities, reformatories and orphanages. From this vantage, deinstitutionalization had started in 1955 and was proceeding at a rapid clip, despite the fact that the total number of admissions to such facilities increased dramatically through 1972 and only a plummeting average length of stay brought the institutional census down. Moreover, the total number of people housed in both traditional institutions and nontraditional community-based facilities such as group homes, halfway houses and board-and-care homes, rose steadily throughout the 1970s (Lerman, 1982). Thus the deinstitutionalization movement was concerned less with reducing the number of people consuming human services but more with transferring clients out of traditional service settings and into nontraditional community-based facilities that could be less restrictive and more beneficial to clients.

State policy contradictions and the professional stance

The community care philosophy was quickly accepted and adopted as policy by the federal governments in both the US and Canada, as reflected in federally funded local service programs first for the mentally ill and later for the elderly, developmentally disabled, retarded and criminal justice populations. For instance, the US National Mental Health Act was passed in 1946, leading to the establishment of the National Institute of Mental Health in 1948 to administer a program of research, training and service activities (Freedman, 1967). Moreover, the shift in scale and location of services, as well as degree of client autonomy, were encouraged by social policies that marked the maturation of the Welfare State in both countries.

At the federal level, comissions of inquiry were established in the US and Canada, to draft plans for the future of health services. In 1955, the US Joint Congressional Commission on Mental Illness and Health criticized the concept of large state mental hospitals and advocated instead the development of services on a local basis. Under the impetus of the Kennedy administration, this philosophy was translated into the 1963 Community Mental Health Centers Act. The primary goal of this Act was to stimulate local communities to assume responsibility for the development of programs for care of their own mentally ill. Hence, federal funds were allocated to the construction and (later) the staffing of a nationwide system of comprehensive 'community mental health centers' (CMHC). Emphasis was placed upon the concept of community-based care since it was reasoned that the large state hospitals had done much to isolate the patient from society, to retard living skills, and to induce a level of disability and dependence over and above that arising from the patient's condition (Mechanic, 1969).

At the same time, Great Society policies of the Kennedy–Johnson administrations created or increased the scope of a variety of redistributive social programs targeted at the poor, unemployed and dependent: Job Corps; Legal Aid; Comprehensive Employment and Training services; Headstart; Neighborhood Health Centers; Foodstamps. The cash-grant programs extended to the disabled and mentally ill during the 1960s were even more fundamental in facilitating deinstitutionalization. Instead of being forced into a large-scale state institution by physical disability, frailty or emotional disorders which prevented employment and led to destitution, dependent persons were provided with the modern version of 'outdoor relief': Aid to the Blind (ATB), Old Age Assistance (OAA), Aid to the Disabled (ATD), and later Supplemental Security Income (SSI) at the federal level and General Assistance at the local level.

These programs permitted state and provincial governments, which had previously been responsible for the welfare of service-dependent population groups, to alter their approach to service delivery radically. State-level policy-makers quickly adopted the community-based care philosophy as it became clear that the switch would reduce state health and welfare costs by precluding massive spending on improvement of mental hospitals and on construction of other large-scale residential facilities. According to their calculus, service-dependent populations would be supported primarily by federal cash grants and Great Society programs instead of state-financed institutions, supplemented by less expensive (and mostly nonresidential) local programs funded by states and local jurisdictions (Bassuk and Gerson, 1978; Rose, 1979; Lamb and Edelson, 1976).

Thus in contrast to the period of fiscal pressure during the 1870s, state and local governments of a century later succeeded in transferring much of the burden of service provision up the governmental hierarchy. Instead of following a course of institutionalization and curtailment of outdoor relief in order to cut costs, updated forms of outdoor relief financed largely by the federal government were instituted in order to achieve cost savings.

But in both cases, these cost savings were garnered at the expense of the service-dependent population. Elimination of outdoor relief during the late nineteenth century had created widespread hardship among the poor and disabled, just as dreadful overcrowding of institutions precluded any therapeutic benefits that they might have offered. In the late 1960s and early 1970s, the marriage of community treatment philosophy and governmental cost-saving strategies led to a golden consensus; a steamroller policy of deinstitutionalization occurred without prior development of community-based service systems or proper preparation of communities that were expected to receive and support the flood of clients. Service-dependent clients escaped the undesirable effects of the total institution, but were left to fend for themselves in the community.

The scale and rate of deinstitutionalization was most pronounced in the mental health sphere. Between 1955 and 1974, America's mental hospital population declined by 62 per cent (Rose, 1979), while the percentage share of patient-care episodes in mental hospitals (as a percentage of all care episodes) dropped from 49 per cent in 1955 to 12 per cent in 1973 (Bassuk and Gerson, 1976). A major portion of the reduction in the number of patients resident in public mental hospitals was accounted for by the movement of elderly patients into nursing homes (Klerman, 1977, p. 623). In addition, a major increase in the volume of service occurred. The total number of inpatient- and outpatient- care episodes in all mental health facilities in 1945 was 1.7 million; by 1973 this had reached 5.2 million episodes. No less than 23 per cent of these episodes occurred in community mental health centers. The major impacts of the mental health program changes were summarized by Wolpert and Wolpert as follows:

Fewer new hospitals are being built and a number have been closed down in recent years; an undetermined but significant proportion of ex-hospital patients have benefited from release; the economic spillover effects of treatment programs and facilities . . . have shifted from the generally remote and rural sites of the state hospitals to more urban locations; and services are more prominently focused upon prevention aspects and the outpatient mode of treatment.

(1976, p. 40)

Although these national trends are evident in most states, there has been considerable interstate variation in specific rates and trends (Smith and Hanham, 1981). In some states the fall was slow and minimal; in others it was precipitous. In California, for example, the number of elderly housed in state and county mental hospitals declined by almost 95 per cent between 1955 and 1977, and the number of persons under 65 years dropped by almost 67 per cent (Lerman, 1982, p. 81) In general, variations over time in public mental hospital patient censuses and release rates tended to fall into several broad categories and be geographically clustered. As Smith and Hanham (1981) show, the patterns of decline in resident totals from 1955–75 included rapid decline from a high base, decline from a lower base, decline from a low base and gradual decline from a high base. Several states, mostly in New England, had more complex patterns of change. With regard to release rates, time patterns ranged from moderate to rapid and consistent increases in release rates; initially rapid increases in release rates but then a later reversal in release policy; and lastly, cautious release rates. Despite this variation, however, virtually all states deinstitutionalized to some extent.

Other branches of the human services followed suit. Between 1950 and 1970, the US census of adult correctional institutions declined 8 per cent; the number of children in homes for the dependent and neglected (mainly orphanages) fell by 64 per cent; and the population of homes and schools for the physically handicapped dropped 21 per cent (Lerman, 1982, p. 62). In the area of mental retardation, clients housed in state mental hospitals were released at the same times and rates as the mentally ill; those in public hospitals specifically for the retarded began to be released to other settings later (during the late sixties), and more slowly. Moreover, interstate variability was pronounced: while Maryland actually increased its census of facilities for the mentally retarded by 4 per cent between 1963 and 1974, Nebraska's institutions for the retarded declined by over 50 per cent.

This deluge of discharged clients produced a surge in the numbers of nontraditional community-based institutions. Between 1969 and 1973 the number of American halfway houses for the mentally ill almost doubled, while the number for alcoholics rose from 120 to 597 facilities (serving 77,250 clients). The US had 8,000 children housed in residential treatment centers located in the community in 1966, but by 1971 there were over 28,000 children in such facilities.

Nontraditional community residential facilities for the retarded also expanded greatly, from 25,000 installations in 1970 (housing 12.8 per cent of the institutionalized retarded population) to 62,400 in 1977 (almost a third of the population).

The share of new community-based facilities organized as private for-profit entities also rose dramatically with the advent of deinstitutionalization. Between 1969 and 1974, for example, the private long-term health care sector absorbed an increase of more than 48 per cent in its mentally disabled population (Rose, 1979). In the area of juvenile corrections, the proportion of total inmates who were detained in private facilities rose from 11 per cent in 1970 to 40 per cent in 1977 (Lerman, 1982, p. 126). Most of the increase in community-based facilities for the retarded was due to the growth of private-sector initiatives. In this fashion, responsibility for the service-dependent population was in part transferred to the private sector (Scull, 1981).

In addition to the expanding private sector, fledgling public and voluntary services including Community Mental Health, Title XX Social Services, centers for the developmentally disabled, and a panoply of other services for substance abusers, ex-offenders, wards of the juvenile courts and the elderly offered a basic framework for client support in the community. But these provisions remained insufficient for the growing numbers in need of assistance. Moreover, a large share of the new community-based services did not conform to the professionals' ideal of being small-scale and offering less restrictive and controlling environments for service-dependent clients. Instead, in many branches of service delivery, facilities remained large (100 residents or more) and highly restrictive, often using drugs to 'manage' mentally ill, elderly and justice-systems clients (Lerman, 1982).

This outcome was clearly not intended by the professionals who had worked so hard for deinstitutionalization and a community-based service system. But like the Progressive reformers, their innovations were accepted and modified by public officials responsible for service delivery only where convenient and cost-effective. The remaining proposals necessary to complete programmatic reform were left to gather dust on the shelf.

The rise of the service-dependent population ghetto

Great Society programs of the 1960s directed resources toward the nation's inner cities, creating a basic network of social support there.

In contrast, the spatial distribution of the new community-based care facilities was not specified by social policy-makers. Instead, the location of facilities was left up to service providers and local governments who controlled land-use allocation. But since deinstitutionalized clients needed to be close to their support services, and since economic constraints and virulent community opposition prevented clients and facilities from locating in affluent neighborhoods and suburbs, both became concentrated in inner cities where many public and commercial services were readily available and where local opposition was weak and fragmented. Eventually, service-dependent population ghettos developed in the most deteriorated sections of central cities: the traditional zone of dependence on the fringe of the Central Business District. As we show in following chapters, these ghettos are now being dismantled as gentrification and urban renewal, along with restructuring of the economy and Welfare State, force more and more service-dependent persons into inadequate support settings and a state of chronic homelessness.

Part II
The rise and fall of the service-dependent ghetto

4

The geography of haunted places

The challenge posed in Part I of this book is daunting. It proposes linking the lives of homeless individuals in today's urban core with two centuries of social welfare evolution in North America. This challenge, and the problems it poses, are unavoidable. Our narrative necessarily measures human lives and mundane routines against the backdrop of great events on a continental scale. In this chapter, we explore how the *longue dureé* of welfare policy ultimately found expression as a service-dependent ghetto in Toronto, Ontario. Four aspects of the *longue dureé* are examined:

1 the growth of social welfare in nineteenth-century Ontario, which gave rise to a collection of welfare services close to the downtown cores of the growing cities and towns (the first expression of an incipient zone of dependence);
2 the specific nineteenth-century welfare policy of asylums for the insane, which provided a second geographical manifestation of the incipient zone of dependence;
3 the twentieth-century growth and restructuring of the Welfare State; and
4 the specific policy of deinstitutionalization for psychiatric patients, which predated the restructuring of the Welfare State but which was rapidly overtaken by these changes in the organization of welfare service provision.

Both the nineteenth- and the twentieth-century narratives reflect a complex interplay of structure and agency, of time and space at different scales of operation. For instance, nineteenth-century welfare reflected traditional community sentiments of self-reliance amongst a largely agrarian society, plus the influence of far-sighted, skillful welfare officers. And in the twentieth century, the reforms of deinstitutionalization were essentially led from the grass roots by a group of caring professionals appalled by the failures of the asylum.

Thus the modern service-dependent ghetto in Toronto, which we describe at the end of this chapter, is a logical outcome of the four interrelated trends outlined above, but also of the actions of those involved in the provision of welfare services and the ongoing restructuring of the Welfare State. In order to interpret such complexity, it is helpful (even essential) to focus on this process in one locale, which in this chapter is the Province of Ontario. In later chapters, we shift focus to the State of California.

SOCIAL WELFARE IN THE NINETEENTH-CENTURY CITY

The origins of the modern Welfare State in Canada have been traced to the rudimentary institutions and practices of social welfare in the eighteenth and nineteenth century (see, for example, Moscovitch, 1983; Splane, 1965; Wallace, 1950). Canadians looked early to their governments to provide the goods and services necessary to support the burgeoning colony, including investment in roads and canals. However, social legislation was provided in a very uneven and *ad hoc* manner. Wallace (1950, p. 384) has argued that, at the time of Confederation (1867), Canadians viewed 'social problems' largely as concerns of the individual, family, community and church rather than as a matter for state intervention. The still largely agrarian society and frontier conditions placed a premium on self-reliance. In rapidly growing Ontario, the development of welfare services began very slowly and was the focus of much fractious debate. However, it was only a matter of time before the explosion of population would place heavy demands on the Province to develop its welfare infrastructure.[1]

Early social welfare in Ontario: 1791–1840

Perhaps the single most important factor that molded the character of welfare provision in nineteenth-century Ontario was the absence of any institution for maintenance of the poor. There is no conclusive evidence as to why the English Poor Law system found no equivalent in Ontario. Given its strong ties to Britain, one might have expected Ontario to adopt some form of the English Poor Law Act of 1601 as a basis for local relief (cf. Allderidge, 1979; Jones,

1972). This Act, and the later Poor Law Amendment Act of 1834, had already formed the basis for colonial provision for the mentally ill in the US (Deutsch, 1949, chapter III; Rothman, 1971), as well as in some eastern Canadian provinces. Splane (1965, pp. 66–7) suggested that the following factors may have played a role in the rejection of the Poor Law system: poverty was not perceived as a likely problem in the new Province; the delegation of poor-law authority to local agents would diminish the authority of the central government; the absence of an Ontario equivalent to the well-ordered English parish system, which would have permitted the levying and collecting of a poor-rate; and the belief that any necessary assistance should come from the British government.

The decision to exclude the English Poor Law system (in 1792) cannot be regarded as a rejection of the principle of aid for those in need. It is simply that the burden of care was shifted onto the individual, family and private philanthropy. However, it rapidly became clear that the abdication of public responsibility could not endure indefinitely. As the early years of the nineteenth century unfolded, a gradual and piecemeal assumption of public responsibility is evidenced, as well as a pragmatic alliance between public and private agencies which was to become an enduring characteristic of social welfare in Ontario.

One vital aspect of everyday life in early Canada was the presence of winter poverty. In Newfoundland, for example, seasonal distress was attributed to 'the absence of employment for the labouring classes during a particular period of the year, when the prosecution of the fishery ceases; and from the fact that the fishery itself was not sufficiently fostered to enable those who prosecuted it to derive their full sustenance from it' (quoted in Fingard, 1974, p. 77).

In the face of seasonality in employment and colonial under-development, attempts were made first to remove the poor from the cities and secondly to provide on-the-spot relief. The former solution was practiced widely: it included efforts to return immigrants to their country of origin; to pass the burden from one town to another; and to transfer the poor from urban to rural areas. However, this approach met with limited success, not least because a large pool of 'surplus' labor was needed in most towns for the summer boom in employment (Fingard, 1974, p. 78).

Contemporary employers and public leaders also promoted individual self-reliance as a solution for winter destitution in urban areas. Savings banks and friendly societies sprang up in the 1820s and 1830s to encourage the poor to 'weather the winter'. However, alternative schemes for poor relief were manifestly necessary. In Nova Scotia and New Brunswick, statutory adaptations of the English Poor Law were introduced, paving the way to the introduction of poor rates and poorhouses. In Québec, shipbuilding as a form of winter relief proved successful. The search for methods of relief for women and children led ultimately to a demand for houses of industry. The Toronto house, established in 1837, operated on a year-round basis but was busiest by far in winter. Voluntary acts of benevolence were also important in these early nineteenth-century towns and cities. These, too, were often seasonal in nature (as, for example, in the supply of fuel and the provision of winter soup kitchens). Many voluntary associations died a 'natural death' with the onset of spring, only to be revived again the following winter if the need recurred (Fingard, 1974, p. 86). As early as the 1820s, several private charitable ventures were established solely to meet the needs of the poor. Through these organizations, demands upon the government for public aid for the poor were forthcoming. Grants to urban-based hospitals were especially common in this early period. Each grant to all kinds of institution was the subject of a separate act of the Legislature.

One important feature of early social welfare in Ontario was the burden that fell on jails as institutions of welfare. They housed many people who had little to do with crime and detention, including lunatics and the poor. This heterogeneous population was undoubtedly a factor in the later, mid-nineteenth century call for special accommodations for prisoners suffering from insanity, for young offenders, etc. As early as 1857, the provision of 'branch' prisons to accommodate these special groups was in evidence. In 1841, Ontario had 13 jails and one penitentiary; by 1867, it had 37 jails and one prison for young offenders (Splane, 1965, p. 157). Apart from efforts to deal with contagious epidemics, the establishment of prisons represented the first provincial undertaking of any magnitude in the field of social welfare.

It is not surprising that the increasing welfare burden was experienced most strongly in the growing urban areas. These were the zones of concentrated industrial and construction activities, the target of immigration waves and the places where the need for relief was experienced most acutely. As local government systems evolved in Ontario, they gradually adopted measures to assist the local poor. However, this was a very slow process and the full development of municipal responsibility had to await much more specific legislation empowering local county authorities in 1849 and 1866 (Splane, 1965, pp. 69–75).

Splane summarized Ontario's early experience in the field of social welfare as follows:

The methods used to meet the needs of the early decades include some sporadic assistance by British authorities where there were acute emergency situations, such as crop failures or epidemics; similar assistance by the province itself, largely through grants to voluntary organizations; the use of gaols as refuges for the poor; provincial support of voluntary organizations when local public action in the institutional field failed to materialize; and the gradual growth of municipal responsibility for assistance to persons in their own homes. (1965, p. 68)

The union period: 1841–67

The 1841 Union of Upper and Lower Canada (the present-day Provinces of Ontario and Québec respectively) into the United Province of Canada gave new impetus to the development of social welfare programs in Ontario. During this period, a systematic structure of municipal government was established, to which was allocated social welfare responsibilities. In addition, a provincial board of inspectors for prisons, asylums, etc., was set up and became the main instrument of welfare administration.

One of the most important factors influencing the growth of social welfare in Ontario in the Union period was the Municipal Corporations Act of 1849. A two-tier system of county and municipality was established. Among the welfare responsibilities delegated to the county was the power to erect a jail, a house of correction and a house of industry. Although the Act did not extend welfare provisions far beyond the institutional care established in earlier legislation, it made possible the first steps away from such care. Another far-reaching action was the introduction in 1859 of a Board of Inspectors of Prisons, Asylums and Public Charities. The inspectors were to have a major impact on the evolution of the prison and asylum system in Ontario. However, they made little effort to bring voluntary organizations under their scrutiny. The Province therefore continued to give financial assistance to the burgeoning private charitable institutions on an essentially pragmatic basis (Splane, 1965, p. 41). This included a reformatory component, which the inspectors believed should be organized under voluntary auspices but with financial support from municipal and provincial governments.

Confederation and after: 1867–1900

The Confederation of Canada was created by the British North America Act of 1867, which contained no distinct philosophy about the appropriate roles of federal and provincial governments in social welfare. With few exceptions, the responsibilities of the new Province were those hitherto assumed by Upper Canada (reflecting the dominant interest in the drafting of the Act). Through this Act, the provinces readily accepted a degree of local autonomy and fiscal responsibility at which they may have balked if they had foreseen the growth of welfare expenditures in the post-Confederation years (Wallace, 1950, p. 384).

The strong bias in favor of institution-based welfare found a sympathetic person in J. W. Langmuir, who was appointed Inspector of Prisons and Asylums for the period 1868–82. Langmuir was a remarkable individual with foresight and a clear understanding of the constitutional and political framework within which he was operating. His assessment of the status of public welfare in Ontario prior to Confederation was bleak:

Previous to Confederation, the accommodation for the treatment of insanity and the care of the insane, was not only in some instances exceedingly bad, but it was entirely inadequate to the wants of the afflicted class, necessitating their detention in private families, or protracted confinement in gaols, until, through lack of proper treatment, their insanity, in a great many cases, became chronic and incurable. No provision whatever was made for idiots so that they had to remain in private houses, no matter how filthy or vicious their habits, or how dangerous their propensities. With the exception of an insignificant grant to a private school, which was struggling for an existence, the education and instruction of the deaf and dumb were entirely neglected by the Government, and the youth of that class were being allowed to grow up in ignorance and moral darkness. The blind were wholly uncared for by Government, both as to education and industrial instruction. While a good deal had been done to improve the condition and discipline of the common gaols, a large majority of them were faulty in construction, defective in arrangement, wanting in the means of classification, loose in discipline, and, worse than all, associated idleness with all its evils reigned supreme within their walls. The Hospitals and Benevolent Institutions were aided by the grant of an arbitrary sum to each without reference to the character or volume of work performed, and without any inspectorial supervision on the part of the Government either in respect to the management of the affairs of the institutions or their structural condition.

Such was the state of this branch of the Public Service prior to Confederation.

(Quoted in Splane, 1965, pp. 48–9)

During Langmuir's term of office, scarcely a year passed without major changes in one or other field of corrections, mental disability, education of the blind and deaf and expansion of financial aid to voluntary agencies (Splane, 1965, appendix 1). His political and administrative acuity was no doubt aided by the relatively strong fiscal status of the provincial government at that time.

Apart from the large expansion of institution-based services which occurred during the post-Confederation years, the role of the province in assisting voluntary organizations also flourished. This expansion occurred mainly under the auspices of the Charity Aid Act (1872) which represented the first legislative attempt to regulate privately operated welfare institutions (Splane, 1965, pp. 56–64; chapter 3). Its effects were to encourage the expansion of existing institutions and the development of new institutions. The example of the Salvation Army is typical of the explosion of activity that occurred in the last quarter of the nineteenth century. From one 'rescue home' in Toronto in 1887, the Army's operations had spread to most major urban centers by 1894 (mostly in Ontario, but elsewhere in Canada also; see Moyles, 1977). Despite Langmuir's preference for public welfare institutions, the Province continued to favor voluntary agencies at the county and municipal level. County houses of refuge and municipal outdoor relief were substantial but fragmented. And, once again, the absence of specific services was reflected elsewhere in the welfare system – the jails. Large numbers of the poor were confined in county jails (Wallace, 1950, p. 387). They numbered 783 in 1869, but had risen to 3,888 in 1877 (Splane, 1965, p. 107).

As the nineteenth-century Confederation matured, it developed an extensive provincially funded institutional system of prisons and asylums. Care of the poor, however, had been delegated to counties and municipalities which themselves relied heavily on publicly subsidized voluntary agencies. At the same time, the rapidly growing provincial population was willing and prepared to make extensive demands on the provincial purse, first for schools and libraries and later for further efforts at poor relief (Wallace, 1950, p. 387). (These demands were paralleled by an increasingly vociferous labor force that obtained significant advances in legislation on trade unions, factory working conditions and workers' compensation.) As a consequence, growing proportions of public funds were directed toward private agencies for social welfare. The Toronto House of Industry, for example, drew an increasing proportion of its operating revenue from municipal sources.[2]

The inner-city zone of dependence, 1791–1900

The history of social welfare in nineteenth-century Ontario is one of first private and then public welfare; the expansion of both sectors; then the increasing absorption of the private by the public (cf. Moscovitch, 1983, p. v). Despite a philosophical commitment to self-reliance, increasing social problems were motivations for the establishment of public institutions (such as jails) and private institutions (such as hospitals). The consequent evolution of social welfare policy was sporadic and piecemeal instead of gradual and continuous. Nevertheless, the achievements of the nineteenth-century legislators were significant. The system which was in place by the opening of the twentieth century formed an integral basis of the modern Welfare State. It was based on a balance between private and public care – a philosophy that evolved organically instead of being enunciated explicitly. The record of achievement was no doubt facilitated by a series of fortuitous events, such as the overall relative fiscal strength of the Province throughout the century, the growth of local municipal autonomy and the felicitous combination of Langmuir's administrative and political acumen. Under his guidance and against a background of strong economic good fortune, the dominant welfare theme in nineteenth-century Ontario was the *proliferation* of both public and private welfare institutions. This resulted not only in increased numbers of welfare agencies, but also in a continuous expansion in expenditures on their services. By 1867, the Province of Ontario bore social welfare costs that were close to one-quarter of its total expenditures. This proportion had risen to one-third by 1893.[3]

The social welfare services that developed in the nineteenth-century city formed the first basic geographical crucible of the service-dependent ghetto. It was composed of the private voluntary-sector agencies that derived an increasing proportion of their budget from public sources. The charitable agencies provided the primary outline of the nineteenth-century geography of haunted places; it was predominantly an *urban* phenomenon and was focused primarily in the older heart of the growing cities.

In the middle of the century, there were six hospitals, three orphanages, three houses of industry and one insane asylum in Upper Canada. Most of these were located in the major urban centers of Toronto and Kingston. By 1870, the number of charitable institutions had doubled and included new centers of urban growth in Hamilton, London and Ottawa. Most of the service expansion occurred in hospitals, orphanages and asylums. By the end of the century, many more specialized institutions (such as homes for the aged and an institute for the blind) had been established, although the general hospital remained the most ubiquitous institution.[4] Toronto, Ottawa, Hamilton, London and Kingston had the largest number of provincially supported institutions, although provincially funded charitable institutions could be found in many smaller towns (Peterborough and Kitchener, for example).

The location of these agencies in the major urban centers is not in itself surprising. What is of greater significance is their geographical concentration in the older parts of the growing cities. The example of Toronto is particularly revealing, since by 1890 it possessed the most developed system of private, provincial- and municipal-sponsored charitable institutions (figure 4.1). The relative concentration of these services close to the site of the earliest settlement in Toronto is noteworthy, although it has to be conceded that the locational factors influencing the decisions of individual agencies could vary widely. For instance, private and municipal-funded agencies in Toronto tended to locate in areas where provincially funded services were lacking. There was also a co-locational tendency in early institutional siting practice; the Mercer reformatory and the central prison were both located on sites adjacent to the provincial lunatic asylum (Martyn, 1982). The Macaulay town/ward area – one of the poorest neighborhoods in the early city – is also likely to have exerted a locational pull. The inner-city *locus* of these various welfare services provided the geographical foundation of the incipient zone of dependence in Toronto. But this was only the first dimension of the modern service-dependent ghetto; the second dimension was associated with the newly emergent institution of the asylum.

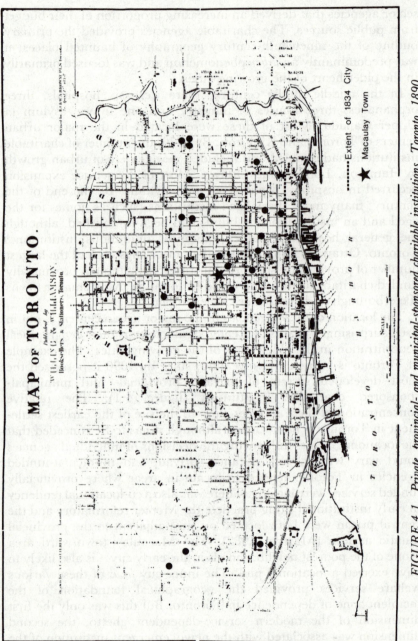

FIGURE 4.1 Private, provincial- and municipal-sponsored charitable institutions, Toronto, 1890

DISCOVERY OF THE ASYLUM IN ONTARIO

Birth of an institution

The first care of the insane in North America was undertaken by the religious orders of New France (now the Province of Québec). Under direct intervention from France, the Hôtel-Dieu of Québec was opened in 1639 'for the care of indigent patients, the crippled and idiots' (Hurd, 1916, p. 446). The tradition of incarceration was transported from Europe by the French colonists of the seventeenth century (Griffen and Greenland, 1981). It was not until 1835 that a converted cholera hospital in St. John (New Brunswick) became the first facility of the British North American provinces to make special provision for the insane (Burgess, 1898, pp. 4–5). Between these two dates, the development of poorhouses and hospitals for the needy was a rather inauspicious and faltering affair.

In Ontario, no specific provision for the care of the insane was made prior to the establishment of the Toronto asylum in 1841 (Hurd, 1916, p. 451). However, the first movement toward provincial responsibility was made in 1830, when an act was passed for the relief of 'destitute lunatics'. This act did not contemplate the erection of an asylum; it merely proposed to legalize payment for the maintenance of lunatics in county jails (Hurd, 1917, p. 120). Prior to this legislation and for many years following it, the insane were routinely assigned to jails, 'all of which were small, custodially unsafe, unsanitary, with no facilities for classification except division of the sexes, and were generally crude and unsatisfactory in all other respects (Lavell, 1942, p. 61).

By the mid-1830s, a rising tide of protest (especially from judicial quarters) focused attention on the plight of the insane. In 1835, the Assembly of Upper Canada appointed a committee to report on establishing a provincial lunatic asylum. The report was submitted in 1836; it expressed strong condemnation of Ontario's continued reliance on jails and advocated immediate erection of a lunatic asylum (Lavell, 1942, p. 63). However, an authorizing grant of £3,000 was not passed by the Assembly until 1839. Further delays in site selection made the need for accommodation so urgent that a temporary asylum was established in 1841 in the abandoned York jail in the city of Toronto. This was the first lunatic asylum in Ontario (Burgess, 1898, pp. 14–20).

The old jail, which accommodated less than 100 patients, was soon found to be inadequate to meet the demands for admission. By 1846, the east wing of the old parliament building (on Front Street, in downtown Toronto) was converted for asylum use, together with a nearby small dwelling-house at Front and Bathurst Streets (Burgess, 1898, p. 22). About the same time, in 1845, work was begun on the erection of a purpose-built asylum, on 50 acres of government ordinance department lands at the fringes of the west end of the City of Toronto. In 1850, the main building was sufficiently advanced to admit its first patients. By 1854, Dr Joseph Workman (the asylum's superintendent) was able to report that the asylum was over-crowded: '376 patients are at present crowded into one-half the space originally intended to be bestowed upon 250' (J. Workman, quoted in Burgess, 1898, pp. 31–2). In order to relieve this congestion at the Toronto asylum, branch asylums were opened rapidly both in the city (the 'University Branch' in 1856) and outside it (Fort Malden in 1859 and at Orillia in 1861).

A striking feature of the early history of asylums in Ontario is the extent to which the 'branch' asylums proliferated, usually in response to overcrowding in existing institutions (table 4.1). In the early days of direct provincial authority, a *de facto* policy-split between the curable and incurably insane was adopted (strongly influenced by the American debate on this topic; cf. Deutsch, 1949; Grob, 1973; 1983; and Rothman, 1971). For example, the branch asylum at Kingston was intended for 'insane criminals and dangerous lunatics only'; at Hamilton, for 'chronic cases of a mild character'; and at Mimico, for the 'chronic insane only' (Burgess, 1898, pp. 38–43). Provincial Inspector Langmuir clearly enunciated this dual policy in his 1875 report: 'I have, therefore, recommended the withdrawal of a part of the chronic cases from the larger Asylums, providing for their accommodation in cheaper structures, where their cost to the State will be diminished, and their home comforts increased, and retaining the large proportion of beds in the Main Asylums for curable cases' (quoted in Simmons, 1982, p. 28).

This practice was put into effect notwithstanding the Province's public stance against separate asylums for the curable and incurable insane. Simmons (1982, p. 20) argues that provincial inspectors accepted the distinction between a 'hospital' for the cure of the insane and an 'asylum' for the care and custody of the dependent. And, since municipalities were apparently loath to develop local

TABLE 4.1   *Asylum growth in Ontario 1850–76*

Year	Institution		Bed capacity
1850	Toronto Asylum established		455
1856	University Branch		75
1859	Malden Branch		235
1861	Orillia Branch		120
1867	Kingston Asylum		118
1868	Arrangement with Dominion Government for an additional 150 beds in Kingston Asylum		150
1869	East Wing Toronto		100
1870	West Wing Toronto		100
1870	Additional space at Kingston		100
1870	London Asylum established		540
1871	Branch Asylum for idiots opened at London Asylum		36
1873	Cottages for chronic insane at London		60
1876	Hamilton Asylum established		200
1876	Orillia Asylum for Idiots re-opened		150
	Total bed-spaces, 1850–76		2,439
1869	University Branch abandoned	75	
1870	Orillia Asylum abandoned	120	
1870	Malden Asylum abandoned	235	−430
	Total Asylum accommodation 30 September 1876		2,009

Source: Adapted from the *Ninth Annual Report of the Inspector of Asylums, Prisons and Public Charities for the Province of Ontario* for the year ending 30 September 1876.

institutions, the Province tacitly approved a policy of building new asylums to meet the burgeoning demand.

The dual system of asylums for the curable and incurable insane was far from popular in practice. The Provincial Inspector's report of 1886 notes the following unease with Hamilton Asylum's role as receptacle for chronic cases:

There are, however, many objections to the establishment of a separate Asylum to be exclusively used for the care of the chronic insane: chief among which is the necessary determination at the time of transfer to such an Asylum, that the insanity of the patient has developed into incurability. This, it must be admitted, is frequently attended with considerable uncertainty, in which case the patient should always get the benefit of the doubt.

Then again, if the cost of maintaining the chronic insane in a separate establishment is to be reduced to a minimum, the Asylum must necessarily have a large capacity – certainly not less than 500 – and to my mind there is something abhorrent in collecting under one roof such a large number of incurable insane in order that they may be supported at the lowest possible rate, and without giving them the comforts, recreations and amusements that necessarily would be extended to curable and incurable alike, if lodged in the same Asylum. Beyond all doubt, the best provision that can be made for the chronic insane is cottages erected upon the ground of the chief Asylums. In this way the number of organizations for the care of the insane is not multiplied, and the maximum of comfort can be given to that class at a minimum cost.

I have, therefore, recomended that this Asylum be made a receiving asylum and that a district of the Province be allotted to it from which the insane will be taken, both under the warrant and ordinary process.

(pp. 106–7)

The dual system of asylums for the curable and the incurable did not last long. Most branch asylums sooner or later became 'receiving asylums', i.e. independent institutions with an assigned territory for intake of patients. Overcrowding remained a problem, despite the proliferation of asylum bed-spaces and many patients continued to be cared for 'in the community' (i.e., at home, or in prison; cf. Hurd, 1971, p. 150; Workman, 1867, p. 45).

Locational principles

Canadian practice in the siting of asylums for the insane tended to follow already well-established American and British practice. Although Toronto's temporary asylum and its extensions were located in the downtown area, the first asylum proper was located on 50 acres of ordinance land on the western periphery of the city known as the 'Government' or 'Garrison Common' (Burgess, 1898, p. 26). The Assembly of Upper Canada was advised that the prospective site:

should be elevated, commanding an extensive prospect of surrounding scenery from which the patients may look down on the surrounding countryside without being too near, so as to be incommoded from the too frequent approach of the imprudent and thoughtless stranger or visitor. It should contain land sufficient to employ the whole number of insane in some interesting and profitable occupation as well as afford each class a large yard.

(Quoted in T. Brown, 1980, p. 113)

In short, the asylum was to be in the country, but not too far from an urban center; to command a pleasant view; and to have sufficient grounds for work and recreation.

The chosen site was three miles west of the city center. It was one of a number of sites which had been considered for the Toronto asylum, but was finally chosen for military strategic reasons. Following the War of 1812, the Colonial Secretary was determined to secure a number of strong-points for any future defence of the city. The construction of a solid and massive asylum on the Garrison Point, just west of the city and controlling the road to Hamilton and the Niagara frontier, seemed to fit the bill. Military considerations (including the availability of land) were therefore, a major factor in the location of the Toronto asylum. Fortunately, Garrison Common seemed also to meet all the other prescribed criteria for an asylum site (T. Brown, 1980, p. 116). There tended to be an air of expediency attending the choice of location of this and many other Ontario asylums (for example, the availability of old jails).

Most of the branch asylums that followed Toronto observed an increasingly familiar set of locational guidelines (Hurd, 1917, pp. 120–98):

1 Hamilton's asylum was located on an escarpment 200 feet above the city (figure 4.2). It was only two miles from the city center, but quite separated from the urban area by topography.
2 Mimico's asylum was centrally located with respect to the provincial population since it was intended solely for the chronic insane. It too had a lakeshore site.
3 Whitby Hospital was just outside the town of Whitby, 30 miles east of Toronto on a railway line. Its lakeshore location possessed great natural beauty, trees, orchards, roads, and convenient railway and water facilities.

It is some measure of the entrenched nature of these asylum locational principles that Dorothea L. Dix, when selecting a site for the Nova Scotia hospital for the insane, chose an 85-acre plot on Halifax harbor two miles from the city (Burgess, 1898, p. 102).

Questions of accessibility were also observed to play a part in asylum location. Facilities intended for province-wide service were

FIGURE 4.2   *Asylum for the insane, Hamilton*

'I next visited the Hamilton asylum. This institution . . . is beautifully
situated, overlooking Lake Ontario at the point of Burlington Bay. The
situation, however, is not altogether advantageous. It is inconveniently
near a precipitious descent [the Niagara escarpment], and the approach to
the asylum is precipitously steep.' (D. Hack Tuke, 1885, 117). The place is
'similar to the eyrie of an eagle, unapproachable and inaccessible'. (Report
of a Provincial Inspector of Hospitals.)

---

located centrally (as at Mimico). In addition, notions of 'districting'
or 'regionalization' surfaced rapidly. The example of Kingston
asylum (then called Rockwood) is representative. Rockwood was
initially intended only for the criminally insane. However, when
Toronto asylum was full, relatives and friends of the insane of
eastern Ontario had to find other accommodation for their charges.
(They might also have wished to avoid transportation costs to
Toronto.) Their subterfuge was simply to have the lunatic committed
to jail as dangerous, whether or not this was true and then transferred
to Rockwood. To prevent this abuse, the provincial inspectors recommended changing Rockwood's status to a general as well as a criminal
asylum:

The inspectors have to remark, with relation to Rockwood, that practically
it has become an asylum for lunatics of every description from the eastern
portion of Upper Canada, as the relatives of the parties, instead of obtaining
the usual medical examination and certificate privately, in order to procure
their admission into the provincial asylum, at Toronto, which is at a great

distance, procure their incarceration as dangerous lunatics in a common jail, from which they are transferred, under warrant of His Excellency, to the Rockwood institution. The board are inclined to recommend that regulations should be made authorizing their reception at Rockwood after the buildings shall have been completely finished, without obliging their relatives to resort to a previous imprisonment in a jail; to convert, in fact, Rockwood into a provincial asylum for the eastern countries of Upper Canada.

(Report of Board of Inspectors of Asylums, Prisons, etc., for 1862, p. 13; quoted in Hurd, 1917, p. 150.)

It would only be a matter of time, of course, before Ontario's asylums – initially sited so carefully on the fringes of urban areas – would be swallowed up by the expanding towns. The Orillia hospital nicely presages its future in a 1923 report: 'The latest undertaking of importance affecting immediately the convenience and comfort of our people has been the construction of the Provincial Highway, directly through our property, shortening the distance to Orillia by half a mile, avoiding all hills and making our community virtually a suburb of the town' (Downey, 1923, p. 180).

The rapid urbanization of the Toronto area absorbed the Toronto asylum almost immediately. Established in 1850 three miles to the west of the city, the asylum, by 1870, had been overtaken by the western limit of the City of Toronto. By 1906, its original 50-acre site had been reduced to 34 acres, prompting its medical super-intendent, Dr C. K. Clarke, to remark:

a large asylum population requires suitable surroundings: plenty of breathing space, in a quiet locality, where fresh air and restful conditions generally are obtainable. At Queen Street West, the antithesis of these requirements is the case. Instead of the desirable two or three hundred acres, 26 acres are enclosed within gaol-like walls [8 acres were just outside the walls]: the days and nights are made hideous by electric cars, on the one side, the railway traffic passes directly by the south wall, where a freight shunting yard is also located. Queen Street, one of the busiest thorough-fares in the city, is directly to the north. The smoke from the many trains and factories in the neighborhood, pollutes the air. A more undesirable site for a hospital could not be selected.

(Ontario Sessional Papers, 1907, no. 41, p. 5; quoted in T. Brown, 1980, 123)

As the final quarter of the nineteenth century began to unfold, the asylum as an institution for care and custody of the insane was well established throughout the populated areas of southern Ontario.

Between 1840 and 1916, 11 hospitals had been erected, accommodating about 7,000 people. All these asylums had been established on the fringes of major urban centers and most were rapidly overtaken by the advances of urbanization.

A crude districting, or catchmenting, of hospital territory to ensure access to the population in need had developed quite early in the growth of Ontario's asylums. This ensured a relatively dispersed pattern of hospital geography throughout the province.[5] It was in these urban-based asylums, with their associated catchments and populations, that the second geographical dimension of the service-dependent ghetto developed. It promised a new overlay upon the first dimension of the inner-city welfare services. The new dimension took the form of a zone of dependence associated with the provincial lunatic asylums. This phenomenon was obviously associated with the tendency for the asylum to draw its inmates from the immediately adjacent population. The tendency was exaggerated as once rural-based asylums were overtaken by the trend toward urbanization and were inexorably 'swallowed up' by the advancing urban fringe. It was in this sense that the asylums became 'local' institutions, essentially serving the population in urban areas adjacent to the asylum. This pattern is strongly reflected in the census of 1871 which describes *inter alia* the distribution by county of 'people of unsound mind'. Not surprisingly, the asylums at Toronto, London and Kingston are associated with heavy rates of insanity (figure 4.3; cf. Jarvis, 1971).[6]

RESTRUCTURING THE TWENTIETH-CENTURY WELFARE STATE

At the commencement of the twentieth century, Canadians were accustomed to state provision of a number of important services, such as education, libraries and parks (Wallace, 1950). In addition, the state had financed much of the infrastructure necessary for the expansion of Canadian industry. However, 'social' legislation was slow to develop, with the exception of some measures involving worker's compensation and the like (Finkel, 1977; Moscovitch, 1983). The more important steps in social legislation were associated with the economic and political turmoil following World War I and the Great Depression of the 1930s. During this period the fundamental legislation that came to constitute the modern Welfare State was put in place. These included unemployment insurance, pensions

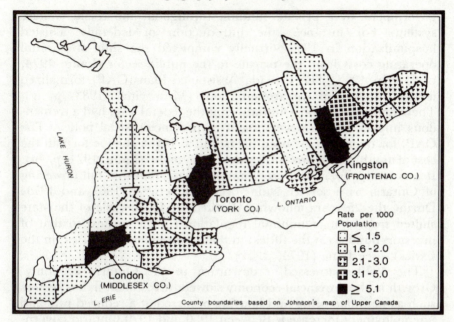

FIGURE 4.3   Province of Ontario, people of unsound mind per 1,000 inhabitants, by county, 1871

and public housing construction (Moscovitch, 1983, pp. iii–iv). The most significant impetus to the development of Canadian social programs was the need to reconstruct and restart the economy after World War II (Finkel, 1977, p. 361). The Province of Ontario is typical of wider trends in Canada at that time. The record in Ontario shows that action on social policy in the period 1946–50 was at a minimum; however, a significant amount of planning went on and its impact would be felt during the 1950s. Typical of this period were the federal government's system of National Health Grants, launched in 1948, and having a 'boom' effect in the 1950s. The early fifties were a period of rapid acceleration in social service provision – including the encouragement of general hospitals to establish their own psychiatric units (Lang, 1974, pp. 15–17). It was a period of intensive capital investment in physical facilities, which paved the way to the most recent wave of social reforms.

The period 1957–62 in Ontario was marked by a sharp rise in federal funding of social policies, continued building and investment in human resources. There was an increasing predominance of government over private funding throughout the social welfare system. For instance, the introduction of federally assisted hospitalization in 1959 virtually completed the shift of hospital operating costs from the private to the public sector (Lang, 1974, p. 21). In 1965, The Canada Assistance Plan (CAP) formalized federal funding of welfare programs (Moscovitch, 1983, p. iv). These and similar policy initiatives at the federal level had a tremendous impact on the development of provincial social policy. The CAP, for instance, has been likened to a 'blank cheque for half the cost of anything the provinces might wish to do' (Lang, 1974, p. 44). It was on this fiscal and programmatic basis that the 'full flowering of Ontario as a service state' occurred between 1967 and 1971. During the 25 years following World War II, the role of the state shifted from that of minimal regulation (in the forties) to that of investor–builder (in the fifties) to that of provider of services (in the sixties) – see Lang (1974, p. 52).

The 1970s witnessed a downturn in the Ontario economy. Growth in the provincial economy slowed, investment in key sectors such as manufacturing and housing occurred at a reduced rate and unemployment increased. Between 1960 and 1970 Ontario government expenditures increased fivefold. By 1975 expenditures reached $9 billion, the annual growth of government expenditures had reached 25 per cent, inflation had topped 10 per cent, and the government debt had doubled in one year to reach $2 billion (Marxist–Leninist Organization of Canada, 1980). These trends prompted serious questioning of government spending, particularly expenditures on social programs. Many were arguing that government spending had absorbed much-needed investment dollars, thereby contributing to inflation. They asked that expenditures on social programs be reduced and money diverted toward the private sector. In 1975 Ontario's Progressive Conservative Government set up the Special Programs Review Committee to 'inquire into ways and means of restraining the cost of government through examining issues such as the continued usefulness of programs' (Ontario Public Service Employees Union, 1980, p. 17). In November 1975 the Committee produced the 'Henderson Report', which was to become the major philosophy behind the Ontario Government's cutback program.

The report offered three solutions to growing state expenditures; these can be classified as *cutback*, *throwback* and *shiftback* measures. Cutback measures involved reducing the numbers and wages of state employees and the levels of social service. Throwback measures involved increasing the costs of services and making the user pay a higher proportion of the costs. Finally shiftback measures involved decentralizing provincial government responsibilities to municipal governments and ultimately to individuals. These three forms of restraint subsequently affected every area of provincial government spending on social services. The recommendations included the elimination of programs, cuts in grants to municipalities, manpower reductions and reductions in social security expenditures. The committee estimated that by 1977–8 this restraint program would have saved the provincial government $3,660 million.

In announcing the 1980 budget, Ontario Treasurer Frank Miller noted that, in 1975–6, government spending accounted for 17.2 per cent of the Gross Provincial Product; in 1980 he estimated this could be reduced to 15.5 per cent. Leaving no doubt about what the cutback program was to achieve and how it had succeeded in transferring more of the Province's wealth to the private sector, Mr Miller stated: 'That 1.7 percentage point reduction translates into $1.9 billion in the hands of the private sector. These are resources that might otherwise have been in the grip of the government had we not had the gumption to implement the restraint program and stick with it' (Ontario Public Service Employees Union, 1980, p. 27).

In practical terms, the pattern of social welfare expenditure reveals the dual impact of restructuring and cutback (table 4.2). The

TABLE 4.2   *Annual compound growth rate of total and selected government expenditures, 1971/2 to 1981/2*

Fiscal years	Growth rates (percentage)		
	1971/2 to 1975/6	*1975/6 to 1980/1*	*1971/2 to 1980/1*
Social development	13.7	9.3	11.2
Ministry of Community and Social Services	23.1	10.5	16.0
Income maintenance	13.8	7.7	10.4
Total Budget	11.8	10.1	10.8

Source: Ontario Welfare Council (1981).

early 1970s indicates an above-average growth in three council welfare sectors: social development, income maintenance and (above all) The Ministry of Community and Social Services (COMSOC). This growth reflects a shift in provincial priorities toward the community-based service sector. However, in the second half of the decade, these same three sectors were subject to some swingeing budgetary restraint. The growth in the COMSOC budget, in particular, was more than halved. Income maintenance expenditures dropped from 4.4 per cent of the total provincial budget in 1975/6 to 4 per cent in the 1980/1 fiscal year. The Ontario Welfare Council (1981) estimated that if income maintenance expenditures had kept pace with the growth rate in the total budget, an extra $77.8 million would have been available for this program.

What has been the fate of the service-dependent populations under these circumstances? Three forms of income maintenance are available in Ontario:

1 General Welfare Assistance (GWA), a program for short-term relief from temporary loss of income;
2 Family Benefits Assistance (FBA), a longer-term program for people in need; and
3 Guaranteed Annual Income System, a supplementary program aimed at special populations such as the disabled (GAINS-D).

The majority of people in the GWA, FBA and GAINS-D fall into the category of blind or disabled (table 4.3). Social assistance recipients have remained a fairly constant proportion of the Ontario population for a decade (table 4.4). Since 1975 the ratio has remained virtually unchanged at 4.4 per cent. However, the total *caseload* of persons receiving assistance under GWA, FBA and GAINS-D increased by 25.8 per cent over the decade and 20.8 per cent between 1975 and 1980. The requirement for long-term assistance increased significantly between 1971 and 1980 in contrast to the requirements for short-term assistance. In comparison with these trends, the number of *beneficiaries* (people who benefit from social assistance programs) has increased by only 2 per cent between 1971 and 1980. The contrast between the increasing caseload and the constant number of people benefiting from the programs reflects changes in the family composition of the welfare household. These households have become smaller with fewer children and other dependents.

TABLE 4.3   *Reasons for welfare dependency, 1979*

Program	Single-parent families	Blindness/ disability	Unemployment	Other
	Percentage dependent			
General Welfare Assistance	23.9	27.4	41.0	7.7
Family Benefits Assistance and GAINS-D	43.1	52.0	0	4.9
GWA, FBA and GAINS-D combined	35.5	42.3	16.2	6.0

Source: Ontario Welfare Council (1981).

All of Ontario's welfare recipients have suffered a substantial loss in their real incomes since 1975. In 1980 the income of a single GWA (short-term welfare) recipient was 11 per cent of the median income; a mother of three on FBA (long-term welfare) had an income of 30 per cent of the median; and a family of four with a disabled father on GAINS-D received an income 33.7 per cent of the median. Incomes of all welfare recipients were well below the poverty line (Ontario Welfare Council, 1981).

The Ontario Welfare Council (1981) examined the relationship between General Welfare Assistance (GWA) and unemployment. It was found that while the upward and downward swings in these rates often coincided, the relationship between the unemployment rate and the number of GWA recipients who requested assistance because of unemployment was not precise. The periodic tightening or loosening of unemployment insurance eligibility criteria has a significant effect on the number of unemployed people who apply for GWA. Since 1978 the federal government has attempted to tighten unemployment insurance regulations despite rising unemployment and this resulted in a heightened demand for GWA assistance. Because GWA is a municipally administered program (the cost of which is shared 50 per cent by the federal government, 30 per cent by the Province, and 20 per cent by the municipality), this shiftback policy placed increasing responsibility on the lower levels of government that are experiencing the tightest fiscal constraints.

TABLE 4.4 Recipients of social assistance in Ontario, caseload and beneficiaries, 1971–80

	Caseload				Beneficiaries				Beneficiaries as % of Ontario's population
	GWA	FBA	GAINS-D	Total	GWA	FBA	GAINS-D	Total	
1971	83,738	71,601		155,339	204,668	167,854		372,522	4.9
1972	82,772	80,108		162,880	181,221	187,721		368,942	4.7
1973	64,634	84,037		148,671	140,413	195,170		335,583	4.3
1974	62,742	89,302		152,044	133,118	199,074		332,192	4.2
1975	69,512	52,633	39,647	161,792	146,584	146,408	56,363	349,355	4.4
1976	66,606	58,838	43,115	168,559	140,364	157,514	60,709	358,587	4.4
1977	64,158	69,133	39,884	173,175	131,200	174,011	55,518	360,729	4.4
1978	70,548	74,303	38,250	183,101	139,698	180,719	52,125	372,542	4.5
1979	73,987	76,114	35,001	185,102	143,949	178,104	46,459	368,512	4.4
1980	80,443	80,935	34,103	195,481	154,701	180,902	44,200	379,803	4.4
Per cent change 1971–80	–3.9	60.7		25.8	–24.4	34.1		2.0	—
Per cent change 1975–80	15.7	53.8	–14.0	20.8	5.5	23.6	21.6	8.7	—

Source: Ontario Welfare Council (1981).

ONTARIO'S COMMUNITY MENTAL HEALTH MOVEMENT

By the end of the nineteenth century, mental hospitals had assumed the form that they would retain until after World War II. In Canada there were 22 asylums in 1920. These institutions continued to expand in size and become increasingly overcrowded. Between 1932 and 1948, the number of psychiatric beds increased from 33,000 to about 42,000. The increased numbers served only to maintain the bed/population ratio (i.e., bed availability grew in proportion to population growth: see Williams and Luterbach, 1976, pp. 15–16).[7] Services could only be provided in grossly overcrowded conditions. For example, the Rockwood (Kingston) asylum in 1948 had 1,217 patients on the books in a hospital designed for under 800 (Heseltine, 1983, p. 10).

As the patient population grew, custodial care and the management of patients became the dominant administrative principle. The decline to custodial care has been associated with a number of factors, including overcrowding, the virtual absence of alternative community facilities and a confusion of authority over admission and treatment regimens (Allodi and Kedward, 1977, pp. 220–1). These difficulties in operation and administration hindered the adoption of many mental health innovations that emerged during the first half of the twentieth century. Chief amongst these was the mental hygiene movement, which was introduced to Canada from the US (Allodi and Kedward, 1977, p. 221).[8]

A second early twentieth-century trend in Ontario was the push for deinstitutionalization of the mentally retarded. In 1929, Superintendent B. T. McGhie of the Orillia institution wrote strongly in support of deinstitutionalization and the need to prepare mentally retarded children for return to the community (Simmons, 1982, pp. 121–31). Orillia introduced a probation program under McGhie's leadership. Such tentative steps toward the community were supported by some contemporary US writers and they became the harbingers of the burgeoning community mental health movement (Grob, 1983, pp. 273–8).

After World War II, significant changes in public attitudes toward mental illness were in evidence. The need to treat disorders of the returning war veterans was coupled with a new awareness of the extent of mental disabilities. In addition, the national government recognized the need to upgrade health and welfare services that were neglected during the depression and war. The new awareness of mental illness prompted the federal government in 1948 to institute a series of National Health Grants. The Mental Health Grant called on the Provinces to assess their mental health needs. The common theme of these individual provincial assessments was the desire to 'expand the existing structure and pattern of services' (Williams and Luterbach, 1976, p. 10). At least 80 per cent of more than 20,000 psychiatric beds authorized for construction between 1948 and 1961 were consigned, as a consequence, to existing mental hospitals (Richman, 1964, chapter 3). (About 1,000 beds were constructed in general hospitals and small psychiatric institutions; 7,000 beds were constructed in institutions for the mentally retarded; and the rest were placed in existing public mental hospitals.) However, this apparent consolidation of the asylum did not proceed without criticism. As Richman and Harris (1983, p. 64) observed: 'Psychiatric care in 1948 was described . . . as the day of the "snake-pit" mental hospital – bars, locks, restraints, "herding", and all the rest; patients and their relatives used the hospital only as a last resort.'

In the face of continuing criticism, the federal government tried to influence the direction of growth in psychiatric services, largely through cost-sharing programs. However, significant changes in provincial practice only came about after a flood of federal and provincial commissions on the status of health services in Canada. Of particular importance in Ontario were the 1959 report entitled *A Proposed Revision of Mental Health Programmes in Ontario* associated with Dr Matthew Dymond the then Minister of Health, and the subsequent Mental Health Act of 1967 (Allodi and Kedward, 1973, pp. 280–1). The Dymond report became the Magna Charta of mental health policy in the province (Simmons, 1982, pp. 163–4). It advocated the establishment of a regionalized mental health service based on psychiatric units in general hospitals, regional mental hospitals (breaking existing hospitals into smaller units of 250–300 beds), hospitals and infirmaries, as well as some form of community care. The American model of a specific 'community mental health center' did not materialize. Instead, Ontario worked toward integrating psychiatric services with public health services and social services. Community mental health care was therefore often provided from psychiatric units attached to general hospitals as well as from a variety of outpatient units. Additional factors providing an impetus to deinstitutionalization in Canada were the splitting of special groups into alternate forms of care (for example, geriatric patients and the mentally retarded) and a new stress on voluntary admissions (Williams and Luterbach, 1976).

The impact of these program developments on the current pattern of care has been immense. In less than 15 years, the number of patients on the books in Ontario provincial asylums dropped by about 75 per cent, whereas the rates of admission doubled and those of discharges almost tripled (table 4.5, figure 4.4). The proportion of readmissions doubled to form two-thirds of all admissions (Woogh et al., 1977). Provincial laws were altered to enable cost-sharing arrangements with the federal government to be made. The general hospital was encouraged to develop psychiatric service units and provincial hospital patients could be transferred to community residential or nursing homes on a cost-sharing basis. In addition, provincial ministries other than Health would share the burden of costs in certain rehabilitation programs. In a very short time, the level of psychiatric care-giving outside the asylum in psychiatric units of general hospitals and in community-based mental health care increased dramatically. Bed capacity in psychiatric hospitals dropped from 16,000 in the early 1960s to 5,314 in 1976.

TABLE 4.5   *Admissions, discharges, and 'on books' population of Ontario provincial asylums for selected years, 1880–1976.*

Year	Provincial population	Admissions	Discharges	'On books'[a]
1880	1,923,228	574	204	2,899
1890	2,114,321	697	262	3,955
1900	2,182,947	793	335	5,877
1910	2,572,292	1,140	555	6,670
1920	2,933,662	2,879	858	7,689
1930	3,431,683	2,469	1,265	10,390
1940	3,787,655	3,224	2,257	15,283
1950	4,597,542	4,334	2,686	18,923
1960	6,236,092	7,820	6,184	19,507
1971	7,703,106	15,712	15,868	8,838
1976	8,264,465	14,112	14,163	5,030

Notes:

[a] Before 1909, the 'on books' total taken as the annual number of patients under treatment.

Sources: *Annual Report*, Ontario Mental Hospitals, 1950–76; Census of Canada, selected years.

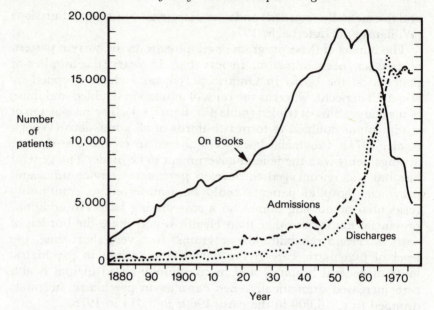

FIGURE 4.4   Trends in psychiatric hospital populations, Ontario, 1876–1976

The effects of deinstitutionalization on hospitals have been profound. In response to the decline in psychiatric hospital inpatient numbers, the government closed several facilities during the 1970s: Goderich Psychiatric Hospital with 204 beds and Northeastern Regional Mental Health Centre (South Porcupine) with 147 beds in 1976; Dr Mackinnon Phillips Hospital (Owen Sound) with 200 beds in 1978; and Lakeshore Psychiatric Hospital (Toronto) with 409 beds in 1979. The patients in these hospitals were discharged to a variety of settings including nursing homes, general hospital psychiatric units and the community (Heseltine, 1983, p. 23). For those hospitals that remained open, the impact was equally startling. In the Hamilton Psychiatric Hospital, for example, there has been a severe reduction in bed capacity; large increases in rates of admissions and discharge; a major reduction in average length of stay; and the appearance of a new systemic pressure in the form of a fluctuating vacancy rate (table 4.6). Allodi and Kedward (1973) describe analogous trends for Toronto's Queen Street Mental Health Center.

The reduction in Ontario's hospital population was achieved partly through the transfer of patients who neither required nor received active treatment. They were transferred to 'residential units' or to

TABLE 4.6   *Average monthly indicators of Hamilton Psychiatric Hospital,*
1960–77[a]

Year	Beds available	Vacancy rate[a]	Admissions	Discharges	On the books
1960	1730	3.25	91	90	2173
1961	1851	7.83	105	111	2178
1962	1583	4.97	129	135	2030
1963	1608	6.64	136	136	2024
1964	1588	7.21	140	146	1843
1965	1586	8.25	163	180	1955
1966	1484	11.20	157	187	1498
1967	1317	11.75	146	168	1343
1968	1127	10.03	162	183	1080
1969	1148	13.88	175	170	1063
1970	1141	14.52	152	168	1065
1971	833	12.51	113	117	810
1972	812	12.81	107	109	789
1973	800	12.39	118	116	773
1974	747	14.47	87	98	698
1975	637	20.77	87	96	676
1976	547	16.53	68	75	502
1977	525	16.62	60	61	456

Notes:

[a] Data are annual figures divided by 12.
[b] Figures are percentages.

Source: Dear et al., 1979, table 3.

'approved homes'. The number of approved homes more than
doubled between 1952 and 1965, but was still insufficient to meet the
demand for bed-spaces. This situation prompted the passage, in
1964, of the Homes for Special Care Act, to provide accommodation
for discharged psychiatric patients. The homes included licensed
lodging homes, nursing homes and residential-care homes
(Simmons, 1982, pp. 186–8). Between 1965 and 1981, about 15,000
patients, 'whose primary needs were accommodation and board',
were transferred from psychiatric hospitals to nursing and residential
homes (Heseltine, 1983, pp. 22–3).

The Homes for Special Care program was one of the very few
efforts specifically directed toward establishing a network of support

services for ex-patients discharged to the community. Progress toward a decentralized system of community-based care was slow and remained focused on the general hospital. Between 1953 and 1976, bed capacity in such units increased from 123 to 1,946 (Heseltine, 1983, p. 26). However, the 1970 report of the Committee on the Healing Arts concluded that outpatient services were still being neglected and that existing inpatient services were geographically maldistributed (Hanly, 1970). Moreover, it seemed that the chronic patient was bearing the brunt of change in the psychiatric services. The mental hospital was becoming the preserve of the chronic patient, while 'easier' patients went to the general hospital psychiatric units. Moreover, many ex-patients experienced acute difficulty in adjusting to their relatively unsheltered community settings (Leighton, 1982; Schmidt, 1965). In 1976, the Ministry of Health responded to increasing pressure to develop community-based resources by establishing the Adult Community Mental Health Program (ACMHP). This was intended to fund programs whose sponsoring organizations were based in the community (including general hospitals). With the development of the ACMHP, the Ministry's concept of community mental health services was broadened to incorporate the provision of a range of local outpatient and support services whose general purpose was to avoid institutionalization of the mentally ill. Significant developments in the ACHMP sector are occurring today in parallel with existing services in the general hospital and the psychiatric hospital. These three sectors together form the basis of Ontario's mental health care system.

The somewhat pragmatic evolution of the Ontario system which we have described in this section was strongly influenced by a number of key administrative adjustments (Heseltine, 1983, pp. 32–3). Prominent amongst these was the introduction of the Ontario Hospital Insurance Plan (OHIP) in 1959. Prior to this date financial assistance for mental illness was available only to inpatients of provincially owned and operated facilities. However, health insurance removed the economic barrier, enabling citizens to choose where they might seek treatment (in principle, at least). In addition, in 1982, the Mental Health Division of the Ministry of Health was reestablished to administer the ACMHP and to develop policy for other psychiatric units. Another important administrative change occurred in 1974, when the Ministry of Community and Social Services (COMSOC) took responsibility for services to the developmentally handicapped, thus paving the way for future delivery of services for the mentally retarded in the community. In 1977, children's mental health services were also transferred to COMSOC (cf. Simmons, 1982).

We have left until last what seems to be a key administrative factor in deinstitutionalization in Ontario (as elsewhere in Canada and the US): that is, the availability of federal funds on a cost-sharing basis as a stimulus to community care. Perhaps the single most important event was the 1966 introduction of the Canada Assistance Plan (CAP). The plan allowed for 50 per cent reimbursement of provincial social expenditures on persons in need. It was associated with a rash of provincial adjustments to take advantage of CAP funds, including the creation of Ontario's Ministry of Community and Social Services (COMSOC). Although initially envisaged as social welfare measures, CAP funds were eventually taken up by large numbers of mentally ill and mentally retarded people (Simmons, 1982, pp. 207–8).[9] These funds were especially important in facilitating the Homes for Special Care (HSC) program, since financial responsibilities for the ex-psychiatric patient could be moved to a different Ministry (other than Health), and be assisted by federal fiscal transfers. As Sylph et al. (1976, p. 235) have argued, the fundamental logic of the Ontario HSC program was economic – trained personnel were saved for those who could benefit; and chronic patients were shifted into the new 'back wards' in the community (Murphy et al., 1972). In 1965, per diem rates paid to nursing-home operators was $6.50 and to residential-home operators $3.00. This compares with the average psychiatric facility per diem rate of $8.00. In addition, although hospital patients did not contribute to their maintenance costs, by 1968 almost half of the HSC program participants contributed to their maintenance from their welfare payments (Simmons, 1982, p. 187).

THE MODERN SERVICE-DEPENDENT GHETTO

The pattern of social welfare provision in the Province of Ontario continues to adjust to the profound changes that have occurred since 1950. The first shock was the radical shift toward deinstitutionalization; the second was an equally significant restructuring of the apparatus and operations of the Welfare State. The net effect of these trends has been a dispersal of many impoverished service-dependent populations (including the mentally ill) from institutional settings to community-based treatment and care. The new community care is characterized by a plethora of political jurisdictions and is currently beseiged by a system-wide retrenchment.

In the case of the mentally ill, the geographical impact of de-institutionalization and restructuring was unanticipated. With the advantage of hindsight, however, we can see that this impact was destined to be felt most severely in the two existing incipient ghettos. First, there was the matrix of city health and welfare agencies, which had historically been established in the inner city. Secondly, there was the psychiatric hospital and its catchment, now essentially an urban-based service. Both these zones have recently been augmented and extended by the addition of new welfare services that have sprung up to meet the needs of the deinstitutionalized. The dominant trends in this modern zone of dependence are the *missassignment* of many service-dependent populations and the *privatization* of service providers, including the proliferation of contract arrangements with voluntary and charitable agencies (Social Planning Council of Metropolitan Toronto, 1984).

Although deinstitutionalization and restructuring provided the necessary preconditions for ghettoization, they were not in themselves sufficient to cause the spatial clustering of clients and services in the modern service-dependent ghetto. The dynamics of supply and demand in the community welfare 'market' are also essential factors. The case of *group homes* in metropolitan Toronto illustrates that service providers, land-use planners and the community have (in different ways) contributed to a very uneven pattern of supply of mental health services. Moreover, the special set of needs among a key service-dependent subpopulation – the chronic patient – leads to specific sets of service demands. The particular variables of supply and demand, when placed against the backdrop parameters of deinstitutionalization and restructuring, have created an inexorable force toward ghettoization.

Operators, planners and community

A group home in Ontario is defined as: 'a single housekeeping unit in a residential dwelling in which three to ten unrelated residents live as a family under responsible supervision, consistent with the requirements of its residents. The house is licensed or approved [in

Ontario] under provincial statute in compliance with municipal by
laws' (Ontario Secretariat for Social Development, 1978, p. 6).

Although group homes are carefully regulated, their operators are
effectively guided by the same market vagaries as apply to other
private providers of goods and services. Chief amongst these are the
conditions that: (a) the service provided (i.e supervised accommodation) must meet the needs of its prospective consumer group
satisfactorily; and (b) the service has very particular operating
requirements that limit the type of accommodation it might utilize.
In the first instance, the operator must provide a service of sufficient
standard to warrant a license, yet be sufficiently economical that it
can be afforded by its clientele. In addition, because clients are
typically poor and immobile, operators seek out home locations that
are centrally located and accessible by public transportation. In the
second instance, operators are faced with a generally limited supply
of properties that are suitable for conversion to group homes. (Few
suburban homes, for example, can be converted to house 10
unrelated adults plus supervisors, together with all the necessary
auxiliary facilities.) Under both constraints – accessible locations
and properties available for conversion – group-home operators
have typically opted for inner-city locations.

Another market factor facing the potential operator is the variety
of zoning restrictions surrounding group-home operations. Local
municipalities in Ontario have the power to permit or to prevent the
establishment of group homes through their zoning laws. Historically,
such homes have not been permitted in single-family residential areas
in most municipalities because they do not fit within the definition of
'family'. Most Ontario bylaws have defined 'family' as 'persons
related by marriage or consanguinity and not more than five
unrelated persons' (Ontario Secretariat for Social Development,
1978, p. 11). Some municipalities have even more restrictive
bylaws. As a consequence, it is not surprising that such municipalities
have effectively prevented the incursion of group homes into their
jurisdictions, while other, more 'permissive' municipalities have
a disproportionate share of group homes.

The situation in Ontario's major cities in 1978 is summarized in
table 4.7. Of the 821 group homes in the province (with 3–20 beds),
301 (37 per cent) were located in the 18 major cities that contained
51.8 per cent of provincial populations. The cities with the most
permissive zoning bylaws were those with the highest concentration
of group homes (for example, Thunder Bay – an urban center serving

TABLE 4.7   *Group home bed-spaces in Ontario cities over 90,000 population, 1978*

City	Population	Homes with 3–10 beds		Homes with 3–20 beds	
		No. of beds (per 1000)	Ratio	No. of beds (per 1000)	Ratio
Metro Toronto					
City of Toronto	678,103	459	.68	944	1.39
East York	104,102	0	0	0	0
Etobicoke	293,464	27	.09	41	.14
North York	550,067	17	.03	17	.03
Scarborough	380,931	29	.08	42	.11
York	139,162	0	0	0	0
Rest of Ontario					
Brampton	104,528	45	.43	100	.96
Burlington	103,728	0	0	29	.28
Hamilton	312,162	109	.35	306	.98
Kitchener	131,801	62	.47	119	.91
London	247,065	75	.30	177	.72
Mississauga	250,399	28	.11	64	.26
Oshawa	105,663	63	.60	107	1.02
Ottawa	305,975	123	.40	292	.96
St Catharines	122,772	15	.12	47	.39
Sudbury	97,618	59	.61	88	.91
Thunder Bay	109,153	134	1.23	231	2.12
Windsor	196,512	30	.15	117	.60
Total	4,233,206	1,275	0.30	2,721	0.64
Total (Ontario)	8,172,212	3,492	0.43	6,836	0.84

Source: Ontario Secretariat for Social Development (1978, appendix 2)

a large, northern population, whose zoning law defines 'family' very loosely as 'one or more persons occupying a single housekeeping unit'; see Ontario Secretariat for Social Development, 1978, p. 12).

The practice of land-use control in metro Toronto is especially interesting. The five suburban jurisdictions in 1978 had very few group homes within their boundaries; most beds were confined to the City of Toronto (figure 4.5).[10] By the early 1980s, some group homes had been established in the outer boroughs, but the City of

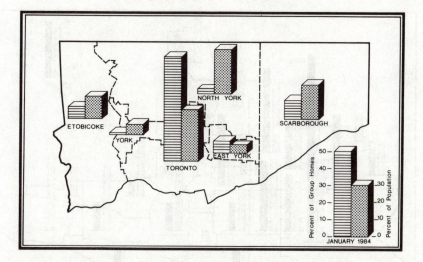

FIGURE 4.5   Distribution of group homes in metropolitan Toronto, by municipality,
1984

Toronto's concentration still dominated. In 1984, one suburban municipality was continuing to block the introduction of a metro-wide revision of zoning laws which would provide for group homes in all residential zones (but see Dear and Laws, 1986).

The geography of group-home provision does not rely solely on the practice of zoning. If we consider the pattern of home location *within* the City of Toronto, an interesting contradiction appears. Within the city itself, with its *uniform* zoning practice, there is an uneven provision of group homes. The pattern of group homes for psychiatric services is especially revealing (figure 4.6). In order to explain ghettoization within a jurisdiction that has a homogeneous zoning law, we must look to the pattern of community opposition to group homes in Toronto.

In a major 1978 survey of community attitudes toward the mentally ill in metro Toronto, Dear and Taylor (1982) clearly established the pattern of accepting and rejecting neighborhoods within the region. Accepting neighborhoods were those with relatively transient populations, high population density, mixed housing stock, few family-based households and lower income. Rejecting neighborhoods were characterized by stable populations, low population density, predominantly single-family housing, a high proportion of families (and children) and higher income levels. In

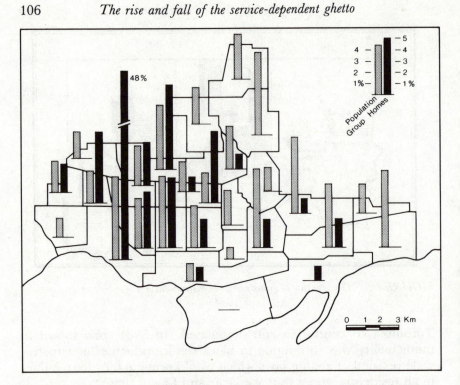

FIGURE 4.6   *Geographical concentration of group homes for ex-psychiatric patients in the city of Toronto, 1982*

many respects these distinctions correspond to the differences between the central city and the suburbs. They confirm the exclusionary attitudes of suburban residents with respect to mental health facilities, which can be documented for many North American cities including Toronto. The 58 census tracts used as sampling units across metro Toronto enable us to draw a map of the 'geography of intolerance' for the region (figure 4.7). It confirms that the distribution of mental health facilities in metro Toronto is concentrated in 'tolerant' areas – i.e., areas of relatively low social cohesion and mixed land-use. The 'intolerant' areas – areas of high social cohesion and relative homogeneity of land use and social composition – typically describe the exclusionary suburbs (cf. Taylor et al., 1984). It would appear that political clout also operates within the City of Toronto to protect certain neighborhoods from the incursion of group homes. A great deal of anecdotal evidence about group home conflicts exists to confirm this impression.

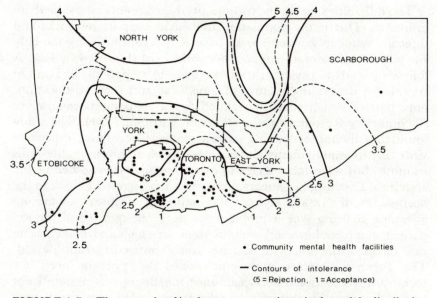

FIGURE 4.7   The geography of intolerance: community attitudes and the distribution of mental health facilities in metro Toronto

Client needs: coping in the community

Deinstitutionalization was a policy adopted with great enthusiasm, even though it was never properly articulated, systematically implemented, nor completely thought through. What has become apparent, since its inception, is the sheer enormity of the task of providing comprehensive community-based care. As Leighton (1982, p. 14) observed with respect to the mentally disabled:

The array of goals, intentions, and activities in the field of mental illness are of such vast proportions that accomplishment is defeated. From the mental hospital movement of the nineteenth century to the mental health center movement of our own time, there have been repeated efforts to achieve goals that were beyond what society could or would sustain. These efforts have had boom and blight properties, with initial enthusiasm and high expectation being followed by disappointment and loss of public confidence, leading to bewildering reversals of policy and the abandonment of mentally ill persons. Commonly, it was and is the chronically ill individual who endures the brunt of these changes.

The difficulties facing the community-based mentally disabled are immense. This is the population that lacks support networks and typically tends to gravitate to an inner-city location, being the only site where rudimentary support networks exist (figures 4.5, 4.6). A follow-up study of psychiatric aftercare of 744 ex-patients in Toronto revealed a depressing picture of loneliness and social dislocation, only part of which could be related to the ex-patients themselves (Community Resources Consultants of Toronto, 1981). The study found that discharge planning was a neglected facet of care, especially since the 'treatment teams' did not place much emphasis on life-skills training, but were more eager to ensure regular psychotherapeutic activities. Discharged patients not surprisingly tended to look to the hospital as the main source of continuing support. Obtaining adequate housing was a problem for over one-quarter of the ex-patients sampled; however, mobility rates were high and an increasing rate of dissatisfaction with housing was expressed as time passed. The Toronto aftercare study emphasized the 'pressing need' for social and recreational services, since loneliness was a significant factor determining community adjustment. Also important were high unemployment rates and stress resulting from financial problems. Unfortunately, the study revealed little about the place of residence of the discharge sample (beyond the facts of tenure arrangements, mobility rates, etc.).

A far more immediate view of everyday life in the ghetto has been provided by Maggie Siggins's (1982) account of ex-patients in the Parkdale area of Toronto, a major zone of group home concentration (figure 4.6). In Toronto, the number of psychiatric beds was reduced from 16,000 to 4,600 in 20 years. Being close to Queen Street Mental Health Center, South Parkdale has become home to over 12,000 ex-psychiatric patients living mainly in about 80 commercial boarding houses.

When Lakeshore Psychiatric Hospital was closed, only $1.15 million of its $13 million annual operating budget was transferred directly to community health care in the area. In 1980/1, the province spent $340 million on psychiatric hospital programs and $14.3 million on community programs. Over 14,000 patients are discharged annually in Toronto, but there are only 250 community-based beds providing special care for the mentally ill, mainly set up by voluntary organizations. The ex-patients are left to fend for themselves. They do so on $258 per month, unless permanently disabled in which case their welfare allowance increases to $364

(1982 rates). Up to 90 per cent of this money goes toward room and board; the remaining $28 a month buys everything else from clothes and transportation to toothpaste. By the end of the month, most residents have run out of both money and personal supplies (Siggins, 1982, p. 10).

In such abject poverty, medication is frequently sold, prostitution flourishes and morale is low. One diary entry, which Siggins (ibid., p. 10) quotes from the *Cuckoo's Nest*, a publication written by and for ex-patients, reads:

Another day is close to ending . . . My pockets, torn and empty; my hands without package or purse seem conspicuously naked amongst the horde of shoppers . . . Yesterday took with it the last two pieces of stale bread. Another 10 days (10 days!) before my cheque comes. It seems I'm always waiting, hanging on till cheque day, which comes and goes so fast, leaving in its wake only a few more slices of bread, and bowls of rice . . . For a moment hunger threatens to overwhelm me, and I realize with shock and shame there are tears blinding my eyes. I fight them back, and fight back also the rage coursing through me. Rage at every misfortune that brought me here, rage at the doctors, the treatments, the pills. Rage at myself, my weakness, my poverty. It's not fair, my God, it's not fair.

Our narrative of the evolution of the modern service-dependent ghetto therefore concludes where it began – with the needs of individuals. The fate of service-dependents in the community has been the conclusive factor in the creation of the new ghetto. As we have seen, these individuals are chronically unemployed, socially isolated, still very much dependent upon the social welfare network and subsisting below the poverty line. In their efforts to cope outside the institution, such individuals have gravitated to an inner-city location. Here, they find relatively cheap accommodation (lodging homes for most, group homes for the few), access to welfare and other service-dependent populations. Since these characteristics are frequently absent elsewhere in the city, it must be expected that the deinstitutionalized, who lack traditional support networks such as the family, will filter toward the ghetto where coping within the community is at least made possible.

5

Anatomy of the service-dependent ghetto

The modern-day service-dependent ghetto has transformed the inner city into a 'coping mechanism' for service-dependent populations, including the recently discharged. Here, in an asylum without walls, the service-dependent are able to link up with a rudimentary social network that provides friendship, support and guidance. What does the ghetto look like? Who lives there? In this chapter, we examine the structure of the modern ghetto in one city. We focus on Hamilton, Ontario a city of just over 300,000 in a metropolitan area of half-a-million people. Hamilton has the advantage of being relatively simple in terms of its physical, economic and social structure, as well as being the site of a well-developed health and welfare network.

The patterns of the Hamilton ghetto are the consequences of almost 200 years of urbanization and Welfare State evolution. The articulation of time and space with structure and agency over this *longue durée* presents formidable synthetic difficulties, not the least of which are adequate data and documentation to demonstrate our line of reasoning. So we focus instead on the *durée*. This suggests a static (or 'snapshot') approach to the present picture of services and the dependent in the City of Hamilton. The broad sketch is then substantiated and illuminated by more detailed studies of specific instances surrounding service provision and groups in need. In this way, the general and specific are merged to explain how the service-dependent ghetto is being created and reconstituted by everyday life in the inner-city zone of dependence.

The chapter begins with a brief overview of the structure and growth of Hamilton in order to place the modern service-dependent ghetto in context. The anatomy of the ghetto is then described in detail, first in terms of the geographical distribution of social services in the city. The growth and intensification of spatial concentration in the lodging-home industry demonstrates the more general dynamics influencing service location. The second aspect of ghetto anatomy is the geographical distribution of service-dependent groups: the mentally disabled, mentally retarded, physically disabled, probationers and parolees and the elderly. Finally, we turn to the specific example of ex-psychiatric patients to illustrate the circumstances under which the groups may be expected to gravitate toward the ghetto for support. While not all groups will have exactly equivalent experiences, we believe that the service-dependent mentally retarded, physically disabled and elderly are likely to report parallel difficulties. The case of probationers and parolees awaits further more detailed investigation.

Welfare in the nineteenth-century city

By the middle of the nineteenth century, Hamilton was a small, compact city. It was dominated by an active commercial core within which specialized retail, wholesale and financial sections were identifiable. Using the first City Directory (1853), Davey and Doucet (1975) have reconstructed the land-use pattern in early Hamilton. Of the 450 establishments in the inner city, 34 per cent were retail, 33 per cent were manufacturing or artisan, 11 per cent professional, 9 per cent hotels and boarding houses, 8 per cent wholesale and 5 per cent financial and administrative. By 1853, an inner core of retail and wholesale, financial and professional activities had been established. Artisan and manufacturing activities had already been excluded and segregated into an outer central area. Between the inner and outer zones, hotels and boarding houses intervened (Davey and Doucet, 1975, pp. 332–3).

It was in the core area of the city that the prosperity and poverty associated with industrial urbanism came together. An analysis of the residential location of selected occupational groups revealed that the core area contained 60 per cent of the city's most wealthy individuals (the top 5 per cent) as well as 64 per cent of its 'statute laborers' (those possessing neither real property nor taxable income). Almost 40 per cent of the statute laborers lived in three cheap hotels and one boarding house on the fringes of the inner core (Davey and Doucet, 1975, p. 340). This juxtaposition was not without its problems, including the ever-present threat of contagious disease and its association with immorality. In one Dickensian fit of outrage, the local newspaper (fearing an outbreak of cholera) chastized the wealthy owners of a large boarding house in the core area as follows:

This house has long been the resort of the lowest and most abandoned creatures of both sexes; the victims of poverty and of vice have both taken advantage of the cheap rents and squalid tenements. . . . The inmates have long been the terror of the neighborhood – and yet this house is situated near the center of the city and is . . . the property of men who are rich and who could afford to allow their barrack to remain idle unless respectable tenants offered themselves.

> (*Hamilton Spectator*, 18 November 1852;
> as quoted in Davey and Doucet, p. 326)

In mid-nineteenth century Hamilton, the poor depended upon the wealthy for charity. Canada was at this time a country of immigrants, encouraged by government policies (such as the provision of free tickets to Hamilton), which persisted throughout the nineteenth century and continued into the twentieth. A city like Hamilton, in the 1850s, could contain as few as one-third relatively 'permanent' residents, the remainder being transients preparing to pass through the city (Katz, 1975, p. 20). During two extraordinary days in 1849, 900 newcomers disembarked. In one early attempt to cope with the flood of immigrants the city opened an 'immigration hospital' near the waterfront in 1847. However, this was quickly closed because of the threat of disease (Weaver, 1982, p. 56).

A more substantial move toward formal provision of social services was prompted by the large number of children abandoned by immigrants. In 1848, the Ladies' Benevolent Society established an Orphan Asylum that received public and voluntary contributions. The Society also established a paupers' hospital and a poorhouse. However, the great expense of this so-called 'House of Industry' caused the City Council to limit eligibility for assistance to those residents who had once enriched their community by 'rate-paying and labor' but who had now fallen on hard times. The city reacted against the burdens posed by immigration (including such hidden costs as the need for extra policing) by urging the government to reduce the numbers of newcomers. In addition, the authorities in Hamilton distributed free tickets and bread in the hope that the newcomers would move on to other towns in Ontario (Weaver, 1982, p. 57).

The establishment of institution-based services for the poor and for children was part of the Ontario-wide diffusion of public charity and institutionalized care which characterized the latter part of the nineteenth century (cf. chapter 4). In 1876, both the Hamilton Psychiatric Hospital (on an escarpment site, away from the city; see figure 4.2) and the Hamilton Boys' Home were established.

The period following 1850 was one of rapid growth and industrial expansion in Hamilton. After 1885, the city core became a specialized commercial district. In Hamilton's first wave of 'suburbanization', wealthy families who once occupied large houses in the core began to move out. Much of the space released by this flight from the city was taken up for commercial uses; but a great deal of property was also converted to rooming houses and multiple-family dwelling units. In addition, an increasing number of property-owners converted to transitional uses in anticipation of speculative gain. The area thus held was far greater than was needed for expanding commercial uses. This led to the development of an area of obsolesence around the downtown zone. The area of incipient blight spread outwards relatively unchecked at a greater speed than the ring contiguous to the commercial core could be transformed into commercial uses (Weaver, 1982).

Thus it was that by the late nineteenth century, a classical zone of transition had been created in downtown Hamilton. This is the district that we regard as the incipient 'zone of dependence', or service-dependent ghetto, in which twentieth-century welfare populations would later become concentrated.

The twentieth-century zone of dependence

At the turn of the century, social conditions in the core and industrial areas deteriorated rapidly, prompting a wave of reform that has since been dubbed the 'city healthy' movement. In 1922, a provincial Act directed municipalities to dedicate more time and resources to public health planning (Weaver, 1982, p. 104). However, the goals of the 'city healthy' and subsequent 'city beautiful' movements (beauty, order, convenience and health) were soon subsumed under the 'city efficient' movement, the aims of which were economy and efficiency. In keeping with this movement's emphasis on the benefits of market competition and minimum government intervention, the City of Hamilton placed its confidence in the private housing market to solve worsening social conditions. It sought to obtain greater housing investment by advertising the profitability of new construction. In a publicity document celebrating the Centennial Year of the City (City Council of Hamilton, 1913, pp. 227–50) it was pointed out that a central property in the heart of the town was bought for $40,000 in 1908 and that in 1913 it could not be purchased for less than $200,000.

However, it was suburban expansion that prompted the wholesale evacuation of the central area. The City Council attempted to attract British capital by pointing to the profits to be made in suburban development:

At present prices, central properties make a good investment and yield 5% after deducting all expenses, and this moreover with a steady increase in the value of the holding itself. Where, however, the largest and quickest returns are made is in the buying of acreage in the suburbs, sub-dividing into building lots, developing the estate by grading and levelling the streets, putting in sewers and sidewalks and selling those improved lots with building clauses suitable to the locality. It is not straining the truth to state that there is no form of investment in existence that shows such a sure and handsome return without any of the risks that usually attend a high rate of profit.
(City Council of Hamilton, 1913, p. 241)

This early period of suburbanization and central city abandonment by the wealthy led to a process of cumulative decline in the core. The narrowing property tax base of the city, together with increasing costs of municipal government affected the quality of services offered in the city. The resulting higher city taxes, together with improved transportation (the advent of the automobile) hastened the evacuation of the less desirable central residential areas (City Council of Hamilton, 1945).

Social problems increased greatly during and after the Depression. By 1942, overcrowding posed a serious problem (City Council of Hamilton, 1945). Thirty-two per cent of the dwellings in the central area were reported as overcrowded. Most overcrowding appeared to result from the sharing of houses by several small families and to the presence of lodgers. Overcrowding was concentrated in the central zone, where the welfare of 1,500 individuals and 20–30 per cent of the homes were endangered. This area also contained from 28–32 per cent of the city's delinquency, desertion, neglect and relief cases.

A survey conducted by the City Council in 1945 provided the first full coverage of housing conditions and amenities for the whole of Hamilton and offered a precise spatial definition of the zone in transition. Three neighborhood types were recognized: sound, declining and blighted. In addition, pockets of slums were also identified. The survey suggests that by 1945, the blighted area in Hamilton had grown to include 35 per cent of the population and 25 per cent of the land area. This area, together with the majority of the slum pockets, was in the northern sections of the city adjacent to the core. Smaller pockets of blight also occurred in areas adjacent to heavy industry. The 1945 inventory of social conditions in Hamilton (City Council of Hamilton, 1945) was used to prepare a plan to guide future development. The plan was completed in 1947 and land-use zoning was instituted in the city in 1951.

A major planned urban-renewal effort subsequently revitalized the downtown core of the city. Several multistory office blocks were built, and these, together with other public buildings, now form the nucleus of a new central business district to the west of the existing core. The future of this new development has been enhanced by the erection in the inner city of high-density apartments, which replaced older semidetached and duplex units. Not suprisingly, the growth in apartment construction at the expense of conventional housing has been a strong stimulus to renting; by 1971, nearly half of all dwelling units were rented, a sharp rise from 34 per cent in 1961.

There is now an acute shortage of housing for certain groups within the city. The local Social Planning and Research Council has noted that many poorer people in Hamilton are effectively excluded from the housing market and that there is still insufficient public housing to compensate, although some effort is being made by the city in conjunction with the Ontario Housing Corporation. Moreover, while most low-income housing is increasingly obsolete, most new housing is not intended for poorer families. For the past two decades, Hamilton's housing market has remained tight. Vacancy rates have seldom exceeded (and are usually far below) the 3–4 per cent rate generally quoted as necessary for the 'normal' rate of turnover in the housing market.

ANATOMY OF A GHETTO: SERVICES

The geography of social services in Hamilton

The spatial distribution of social services in Hamilton is a reflection of the historical growth of the city (figure 5.1). Particularly important in explaining this historical distribution is the pattern of hospital

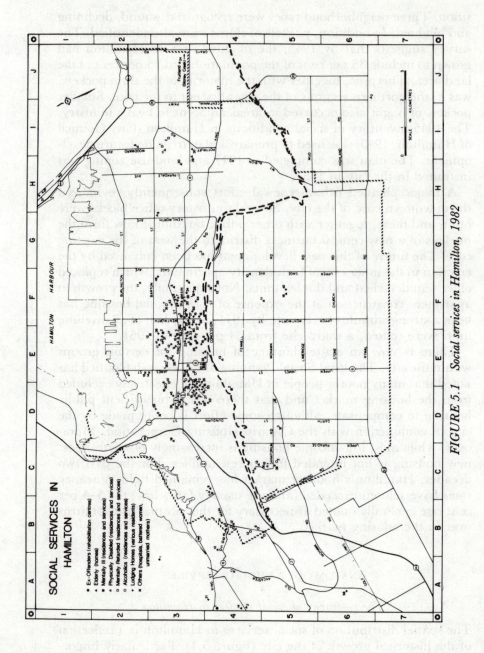

FIGURE 5.1 Social services in Hamilton, 1982

SOCIAL SERVICES IN
HAMILTON

• Ex-Offenders (rehabilitation centres)
■ Elderly (homes)
▲ Mentally Ill (residences and services)
□ Physically Disabled (residences and services)
△ Mentally Retarded (residences and services)
○ Alcoholics (residences and services)
+ Lodging Homes (various residents)
× Others (hospitals, battered women, unmarried mothers)

SCALE IN KILOMETRES

service provision in the city. Hospitals have always been built close to the center of population in Hamilton, or have been rapidly engulfed by the growing city. A primary example of this locational 'pull' is Hamilton General Hospital, which was established in the core area but moved (in 1882) to a more peripheral inner-city location on Barton Street (facility 12 on figure 5.1). Only Hamilton Psychiatric Hospital, opened in 1876, was situated on what could be called a suburban or semirural site (facility 2 on figure 5.1). It was isolated up on 'The Mountain' (i.e. the Niagara escarpment) away from the center of population. After World War II, the expansion of population on the Mountain engulfed the psychiatric hospital and led to the establishment of two new hospitals to serve the suburban population (facilities 10 and 11, figure 5.1). Most recently, another hospital has been established on the west side of the city (in association with McMaster University and reflecting the westward growth of population). A plea for a hospital in the east end of the city has been heard for some time, but no action has yet been taken.

Hospitals are significant in the present context in that they generate ancillary health- and welfare-related activities in their vicinity. Not surprisingly, clusters of social services are located around the city's hospitals (figure 5.1). These clusters include facilities for the elderly, ex-offenders, mentally disabled, mentally retarded, physically disabled and alcoholics. The history of the growth of these facilities has been one of a steady intensification of a geographical pattern initiated in the nineteenth century. Two major clusters of service facilities exist on either side of the downtown business district, one of which is composed primarily of lodging homes. The development of the lodging-home district illustrates the self-reinforcing process of service-facility concentration characteristic of other types of services situated in the service-dependent ghetto. Prompted by deinstitutionalization-driven demand for cheap alternatives to institutional care these facilities have become ghettoized in the zone of dependence.

Locational concentration: the example of lodging homes

Prior to the mid-1970s, lodging homes were essentially an unlicensed business in Hamilton. They were a private-sector phenomenon, mainly devoted to providing accommodation for the poorer segments of the housing market. However, the advent of deinstitutionalization changed all that. Lodging homes grew in number throughout the late 1970s and were increasingly involved in providing shelter for service-dependent populations. This in itself might not have been an issue, except that most of the burgeoning lodging-home industry was concentrated in two aldermanic wards close to the city center (see the pre-bylaw distribution of lodging homes in figure 5.2). This was an area where large houses were available for conversion to homes close to two of the city's five major hospitals. It was also an area where residents were relatively accepting of the newcomers – at least initially.

By 1976, there were 33 licensed lodging homes in Hamilton, plus an unknown number of unlicensed homes. This number had grown to 91 in 1980 and by 1984 it had levelled off to 89 homes. Most of Hamilton's lodging homes entered into an agreement with the Regional Municipality of Hamilton–Wentworth to act as hostels under the General Welfare Assistance Act. Under the terms of this Act, the operators provide more extensive services (for example 24-hour supervision) for 'special needs' clients. The lodging homes

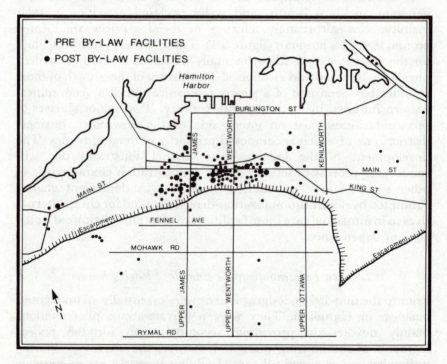

FIGURE 5.2   Residential and short-term care facilities in Hamilton, 1984

that partake of this program are private businesses, owned and usually run by their operators.

The contract lodging homes are funded through the Regional Municipality's Social Services department at a given per diem rate. This rate is set annually by the Regional Social Services committee and is funded 80 per cent by the province and 20 per cent by the region. The province sets a ceiling above which the per diem rate cannot rise if the 80 per cent funding is to continue. In 1979 the per diem rate in Hamilton–Wentworth was $10.50 per day and the provincial ceiling was $13.00 (The local per diem rate has been increased annually at a rate that corresponds roughly with the rate of inflation.) A comparison of per diem rates in various residential care facilities suggests that the lodging-homes option is very attractive from a cost point of view. It is by far the cheapest form of residential care, since it offers only a minimum of service and supervision. Thus, from the Provincial Government's viewpoint, a considerable cost-saving was achieved by placing clients in lodging homes (at a time when the Ministry of Community and Social Services was experiencing severe cutbacks). At the same time, lodging-home operators recognize the opportunity for a steady, profit-making operation funded by the public sector.

The rise of the lodging-home industry in Hamilton should therefore be viewed as a direct consequence of the restructuring of the Welfare State described in chapter 4. This has taken the specific form of a less expensive type of residential care provided increasingly by the private sector. The state reduced the level of care at institutions, and simultaneously developed policies to incorporate highly fragmented and market-specific privatized or voluntary services. These political and legislative changes enabled the lodging-home industry in the core area of Hamilton to develop as a free-market response. The marriage of state and private enterprise provided substantial (if only apparent) fiscal savings to the Welfare State and ever-increasing markets (and profits) to private entrepreneurs.[1]

The effect of restructuring on client groups can be observed in the sociodemographic structure of lodging-home population. A survey of 717 residents conducted in 1980 showed that over half of the lodging-home residents had previously been inmates in psychiatric hospitals; 14 per cent had come from general hospitals (usually elderly people); 9 per cent had been involved in the criminal justice system; and 6 per cent had been referred from organizations dealing with alcoholism. Only 12 per cent had moved directly from private addresses to lodging homes (Beamish, 1981). Interestingly, 26 per cent of this population were not resident in Hamilton before entering this program.[2] More than 30 per cent of the residents were over 65 years of age; and about 34 per cent were under 34 years old. The remaining 36 per cent were spread evenly in the intervening age categories (25–64). At least 77 per cent of the lodging-home residents depended upon direct government transfers as a source of income. Some of the 22 per cent whose income was unspecified may also depend upon government transfers but did not declare this for various reasons. Almost half of the people existed on Family Benefits Assistance (FBA) or GAINS-D (disability) programs, indicating that they were either part of the long-term welfare population or had a permanent disability. Another quarter of the population existed on some form of government pension policy reflecting the sizeable segment of elderly people who live in these homes. Most of these residents subsist on incomes that are below the poverty line and which have shrunk with respect to purchasing power in recent years. In most cases the cost of food and shelter at the lodging home is deducted from the welfare recipients' incomes so that they are left with a disposable income of approximately $60 per month (1984 rates).

During 1975 and 1976, one downtown alderman (Mr Brian Hinkley) noticed that he was receiving an increasing number of phone-calls from irate constituents. They were angered and bewildered by what they perceived as frequent openings of lodging homes in two wards close to the city center. The issue was brought into focus by a tangential occurrence in another neighborhood. There, potential operators of a doughnut store had applied for a license. Following usual procedures, the application was advertised and inspired an intense community opposition. As a consequence, the application was refused by the city. The operator appealed the decision and the court upheld the appeal. It was found that an application for an operator's license could not be refused simply on the grounds that some neighbors objected to the operation.

This seemingly innocuous appeal had a profound effect. It caused an inquiry into the city's licensing procedures. As a result, a formal Licensing Committee was established, whose task it was to rule on matters of fact and not make political judgements. Specifically, the advertising of licensing applications was stopped and the fulfilment of licensing standards (for example health, safety and fire regulations) became a purely technical matter. This licensing inquiry also uncovered considerable information about illegal operations in the city and about the quality of care/accommodation in lodging homes.

The emergent community opposition to neighborhood 'saturation' by lodging homes, together with concerns about licensing and standards, found a combined voice in the 1977 *Report on Lodging Homes, Halfway Houses and Nursing Homes*. Prepared by Alderman Hinkley, this deliberately provocative report drew attention to the problems of the service-dependent in lodging homes. The subsequent firestorm of public concern led to a 1978 conference on community residential services. The conference concluded that deinstitutionalization was a positive step, but that ghettoization/saturation was undesirable.

A new city bylaw was drafted in June 1978. It included much tighter definitions and licensing procedures. A 'lodging house' was defined as: 'dwelling in which four or more persons are lodging for gain, with or without food and without separate cooking facilities, by the week or more than a week and which is licensed as a lodging house'. A residential care facility (RCF) was: 'fully detached residential building occupied wholly by a maximum number of *supervised residents . . . on the premises as a group because of social, emotional, mental, or physical handicap or personal distress* for the purpose of achieving well being' (emphasis added). The bylaw also introduced a distance-spacing requirement; no RCF may locate closer than 180 meters from lot-line to lot-line of another facility. Capacity requirements were also set out. Finally, RCFs were classified as 'permitted uses' in all residential and commercial zones of the city. This condition was introduced because it was the specific intent of the legislation that lodging homes be accepted throughout the city (even though 'fair-share' provisions did not appear as such). Previously the absence of the 'permitted use' designation had frequently caused an application for zoning variance to be made; this application tended to be a significant factor in alerting community opposition.

Appeal, delays and modifications to the legislation ultimately postponed its approval by the Ontario Municipal Board until 1980. The law became operative in 1981. By that time, however, the numbers of lodging homes in the city had peaked. The form of the ghetto had been established (figure 5.2).

In recent years, growth in the lodging-home industry has slowed. In January 1984, the vacancy rate in lodging-home beds was 10 per cent. The region will now license new homes only if an existing home closes or a demonstrable need can be shown. Notwithstanding these strictures, new homes continue to open; 17 have been opened since the implementation of the bylaw in 1981. However, new 'births' are also accompanied by 'deaths' in the industry, with some homes going out of business. There is some evidence to suggest that residents are 'filtering up' into the newer and better-quality homes.

Despite the new bylaw, the new lodging homes continue to adopt a ghetto location (see post-bylaw facilities in figure 5.2). This is largely because the choice of home location remains in the hands of the operator, once formal licensing and distance-spacing requirements have been met. In 1985, for example, 12 out of the 16 new homes opened were located in the core area. This is a reflection of operators' preference to be close to the center of demand, as well as the increasing difficulty of finding properties suitable for conversion outside the core. (Three smaller nursing homes in the region have recently been converted to lodging homes.) Hence, the net effect of the new bylaw has been to reduce the crowding of facilities; but it has not had a significant effect on the core-area concentration of facilities. Instead, there has been an increase in rezoning (to increase capacity in existing facilities) and spot zoning (to allow specific variances in the distance-spacing requirements).

Despite the continuing ghettoization, the more liberal and precise bylaw seems to have had the effect of appeasing community opposition (at least temporarily). Residents in the most impacted zones now seem happier with the situation, although they need no longer be informed of a home's opening. Another factor in the present truce is that home operators have increased their public relations outreach and are more conscious of the need to communicate with the host communities.

However, Alderman Hinkley has warned that if the intent of the bylaw is ignored, then the ghettoization issue is likely to resurface and undermine the lodging-home program. Clearly, while operators retain discretion over locational choice, the ghetto is unlikely to be dismantled. But the provincial government is searching for ways to undertake a more directive role in facility siting (Dear and Laws, 1986). Several suburban jurisdictions around Hamilton are preparing their own bylaws in anticipation of expansion in the lodging-home industry. Meanwhile, the growth of lodging homes, group homes and other facilities into suburban jurisdictions in Toronto is causing opposition in some traditionally exclusionary neighborhoods. And the Ontario Long-term Care Association, with an affiliation representing over 61,000 lodging-home beds in the province, is beginning to exercise its political muscle. The future of the service-dependent ghetto in Ontario cities is, at least for the present, highly uncertain.

ANATOMY OF A GHETTO: SERVICE-DEPENDENT POPULATIONS

The geographical distribution of the service-dependent in Hamilton

The mentally disabled are one of five major deinstitutionalized populations in Hamilton. The others are the mentally retarded, probationers and parolees, physically disabled and dependent elderly. An estimate of the size of each of these populations was derived (see the appendix to this chapter, pp. 258–60), and an index of geographical concentration of each population was calculated for every census tract in the City of Hamilton.[3] The example of the mentally disabled is indicated in figure 5.3. As we delineated in the case of Toronto (see chapter 4), the consequence of deinstitutionalization has been marked concentration of the community-based population in six census tracts adjacent to the central business district.

To what extent do the other service-dependent populations exhibit similar clustering tendencies? In what follows, we provide a brief survey of the history of deinstitutionalization in the four other sectors, together with data summarizing the geographical distribution of each population.

Mental retardation

The historical development of mental retardation services parallels the trends in psychiatric care in Ontario (figure 5.4). Initially care of the retarded was purely custodial; they were segregated from society in large rural-based institutions. However, during the late 1950s, the theory of 'normalization' became popular (Wolfensberger, 1972); the focus of rehabilitation was toward personal life-skills and an early attempt to move the retarded out of institutions and into the community. A number of disturbing examples of the reality of deinstitutionalization became public during 1970 and 1971 and as a result discharge rates actually fell between 1969 and 1972. In response to these incidents, the government commissioned a report on the care of the mentally retarded in Ontario (the Williston Report, 1971). While the report revealed the inadequacies of the government's approach to deinstitutionalization, it nevertheless concluded that 'it

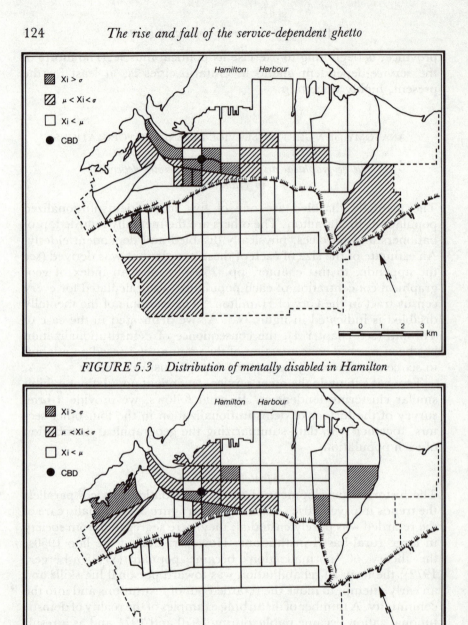

FIGURE 5.3   Distribution of mentally disabled in Hamilton

FIGURE 5.4   Distribution of service-dependent mentally retarded people in Hamilton

is far more economical and humanitarian to give the handicapped the total care he needs in his own community than providing it in an institution' (Ontario Public Service Employees Union, 1980, p. 11). The findings of this and several other reports were used to placate public opposition to the government's policy of deinstitutionalization while simultaneously nurturing the community care ideology. By 1973, discharge rates began to climb again, eventually surpassing their previous peak.

In 1973 the government produced a 'green paper' entitled *Community Living for the Mentally Retarded in Ontario*, a new policy focus enabling care of the retarded to be transferred from the Ministry of Health to the Ministry of Community and Social Services (COMSOC). This transfer was to shift emphasis from institutional to community living for retarded individuals. The proclamation of the Developmental Services Act of 1974 provided the legislative basis for the shift in organizational and fiscal responsibility. What had begun as a piecemeal process of deinstitutionalization became a wholesale restructuring of this sector of the Welfare State.

The restructuring of care for the mentally retarded has been closely associated with the privatization of services. In many instances this has meant the discharge of patients from government-funded institutions into private boarding homes, lodging homes and homes for special care. The provincial government also has shifted large sums of money to private-sector health-care corporations. Recently, the Ontario Association for the Mentally Retarded (OAMR) disclosed that some 2,900 mentally retarded people had been inappropriately placed among the 75,000 elderly people in privately operated nursing homes and homes for special care, after being discharged from provincial institutions during the late 1960s and 1970s. The average cost of maintaining a mentally retarded person in an institution was estimated at approximately $85 per day, whereas the comparable cost to government of a home for special-care bed was $28 (Ontario Public Service Employees Union, 1980).

Investigations of the nature of aftercare and general community life for the deinstitutionalized retarded person indicate that they do not fare much better than the ex-psychiatric patients. For instance, Lambert (1976, p. 17) has observed that: 'Loneliness, isolation, dependency, separateness from other people. . .are the characteristics of the people we studied.' The poor quality of life available to the community-based retarded has underpinned recent successful advocacy group efforts to slow down the Ontario government's closure of retardation institutions, largely on the grounds that the requisite community-based facilities are not yet in place.

Correctional services

During the past decade, Canada had undergone widespread changes in its policies relating to correctional services (figure 5.5). In the sixties, the number incarcerated in Canadian prisons hovered at about 20,000 and rates of recidivism remained high. Of the 4,000 people committed to penitentiaries during 1969 only 20 per cent were imprisoned for the first time. It was apparent that incarceration was becoming less and less effective in fulfilling what are generally presented as its four main aims: rehabilitation, protection, retribution and reduction of the crime rate (Cousineau and Veevers, 1973).

Equally importantly, it was becoming obvious that the costs of maintaining correctional institutions were very high. In 1965, the National Parole Board estimated that it cost about $2,500 a year to maintain a person in prison for one year; in 1968 they revised the estimate upwards to $4,900; and in 1980 the cost was estimated at $12,000 per year (Jobson, 1980). In addition to the direct cost of

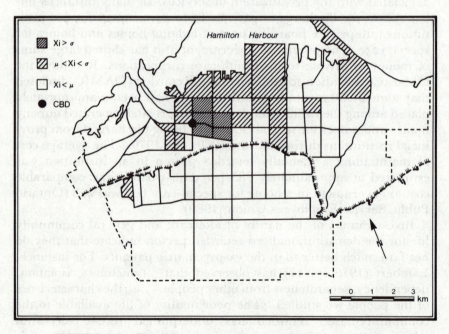

FIGURE 5.5   Distribution of probationers and parolees in Hamilton

maintaining institutions, the indirect cost of supporting the dependents of inmates had to be added. The Parole Board estimated that the cost of supporting dependents on welfare was equal to the costs of incarceration. By contrast, the cost of supervising inmates living in the community was much lower. In 1968, the Board estimated that supervision of a parolee cost between $300 and $500 per year. The cost of probation was estimated at $150 per probationer per year. Therefore, every inmate who could be placed on probation or parole represented a major reduction in the funds required for correctional institutions. In 1968, for instance, the parole of inmates from correctional institutions saved about $9 million plus the funds that would have been required to support 2,500 dependents.

The growing realization that the response to the problem of crime was both ineffective and expensive brought about a major restructuring of correctional services. Eighteen separate acts were consolidated into the 1968 Department of Correctional Services Act. This meant that separate legislation controlling jails, reformatories, industrial farms, parole and regional detention centers was brought together under one jurisdiction. Of special importance were sections of the Act which made provision for temporary absence. Under section 19, 'an official may authorize the temporary absence of a prisoner for humanitarian or medical purposes, or for assistance in rehabilitation.' Section 20 extends the function of temporary absence by providing that 'the Lieutenant Governor may establish Vocational Training Programs under which persons detained in a correctional institution may be granted the privilege of regular employment, obtaining new employment, attending academic institutions or any other program . . . for better opportunity for rehabilitation.' These particular sections formed the legislative basis for the various types of live-in/work-out programs that developed in Ontario.

Alongside these developments, the highly influential '*Report of the Canadian Committee on Corrections* (Ouimet Report) was released in 1969. It concluded that 'unless there are valid reasons to the contrary, the correction of the offender should take place in the community where acceptance of a treatment relationship is more natural, where social and family relationships can be maintained, where resources can be most efficiently marshalled and where the offender can productively discharge his responsibility as a citizen.' After the release of this report, an increasingly community-oriented ideology and policy emerged in the structure of the Canadian correctional services. In response to these legislative changes,

Ontario has witnessed a rapid and intensive growth in the Probation and Parole Services during the 1970s. Successive ministers of correctional services were quick to realize the social and financial benefits that accrued to the programs (Siren, 1979).

Several intermediary types of Temporary Absence (TA) programs emerged in the mid-1970s. The first of these were the industrial TA programs, which operate in conjunction with private industry and provide opportunities for working, learning, earning and development of marketable skills. The other major form of intermediary TA programs are those where Community Resource Center arrangements were contracted with several private agencies. These provide various smaller intermediary residential facilities in local communities where parolees may live in conditions that are closer to those of the community to which they will ultimately return. These programs meant it was possible for the entire range of Temporary Absences, which had previously been confined to institutional boundaries, to occur with halfway houses and similar types of facilities.

McFarlane (1979) calculated that during the month of January 1979, a cohort of 166 extramurally employed industrial TA inmates earned approximately $36,022, saving the cost of their institutional placement and the cost of welfare payments in support of both themselves and their families. During this period, they paid nearly $6,422 toward room and board and contributed nearly $8,950 toward family support. The monetary benefits of these programs to the Ministry of Correctional Services have not gone unnoticed and during the late 1970s the popularity of these programs increased dramatically. Over a 10-year period (August 1969 to January 1979), 128,864 applications for Temporary Absences were received, and 82,811 (64.3 per cent) were approved.

Two of the major strategies that have been followed by the Ontario Government in developing community correctional services have been:

1 the contracting-out of probation and aftercare services to private agencies; and
2 the increasing use of volunteer labor.

The Ontario Government has become increasingly involved in contracting probation and aftercare work to voluntary family-service agencies (FSA). Mounsey (1977) has argued that this was largely a response to the need to curb the expansion of the Civil Service. In return for assuming responsibilities for a caseload, each FSA was paid a fee to cover such items as salary for workers and secretarial staff, travel expenses, office supplies, etc. During this period, many voluntary service agencies were hard-pressed to maintain service and Mounsey (1977) suggested that the government was fulfilling two functions through contracting-out services. As well as reducing its direct responsibilities in the field of corrections, it was helping to develop and strengthen an extensive, but fragmented, privatized and voluntary welfare system in keeping with overall government philosophy. A number of reports had urged that government look toward private agencies for assistance in developing alternative forms of service delivery. The Ouimet Report (1969, chapter 20) included the following recommendations:

What is required is a procedure whereby the voluntary agencies can participate in the planning of correctional services as partners rather than critics. Voluntary agencies should be encouraged to ensure that they are effective, progressive, and creative and that new programs and new approaches to all problems in the field of corrections are not neglected. The capacity of the voluntary agencies for leadership and innovation should continue to develop.

When the Ministry began to expand the probation and aftercare service, it was faced with a dilemma. In order to maintain an effective service it was necessary to reduce average caseload levels per worker to around 35. However, because the overall number of clients entering the service was expanding rapidly, this would have meant a large recruitment of staff and general expansion of the service. This was contrary to the overall government policy of reducing the level of direct service provision and curbing the growth of public expenditures. The solution was found in the increased use of volunteer labor in correctional services. Volunteers are now an indispensable part of the Probation and Parole Service; the extensive growth of community correctional services could not have developed during a period of fiscal restraint had this strategy not been pursued. The pre-1969 Probation and Parole Service in Hamilton, for example, was relatively insignificant. After 1969, however, the changes in the criminal code resulted in the rapid expansion of service. But while the caseload quadrupled between 1969 and 1980, the number of staff only doubled. It was during this period that a very large and active volunteer association was developed, consisting of between 80 and 90 people who work directly with probationers.

Physically disabled

Only a small minority of physically disabled people are gainfully employed in work that closely matches their level of competence (figure 5.6). As a result, most survive on some form of social assistance income. They receive benefits under the GAINS-D section of the Ontario Family Benefits Act. The disabled resemble the welfare population in general: they are chronically poor, but their poverty is compounded by their handicaps.

A survey of 432 service-dependent physically disabled people in Hamilton reveals the plight of the physically disabled. The vast majority of the sample was poor, with 80 per cent having an income below $5,000 per year. Transportation costs consumed about 10 per cent of the respondents' income – about three times what it would be for an able-bodied person. Difficulties with the existing forms of transportation were experienced by 66 per cent of the sample. Approximately one-quarter used some type of specialized equipment, of which wheelchairs and canes were the most common. Finally, the

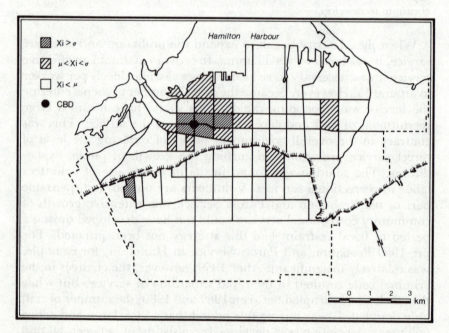

FIGURE 5.6 *Distribution of service-dependent physically disabled people in Hamilton*

majority of the sample (66 per cent) were over the age of 45 and 32 per cent over 65 years of age.

Only a small segment of the handicapped are incapable of work yet few doors, literally and figuratively, are open to them. Those who do manage to work are faced with another problem – high marginal tax rates on disability payments. Individuals on Disabled Persons Allowance can earn only an extra $50 per month before they start to lower their benefits; for every additional dollar they make over the initial $50 they lose $0.75. Similarly, people who find work in special workshops for the handicapped are faced with low wages since these workshops are allowed to pay below minimum wage rates.

There is a variety of special problems, other than those of an economic nature, which face the disabled person in the course of daily life. The most obvious are those caused by architectural barriers which prevent accessibility to buildings, facilities and housing. Because of the combination of low income and lack of suitable housing, many disabled people are forced to live in institutions. Other major problems facing the disabled are the need for specialized transportation and the need for continuing, accessible support services. There are often problems with the availability of specialized transportation and as a result transportation for the disabled is often expensive and problematic. Similarly, support services have been poorly developed and their availability constitutes a major limitation on the residential choices open to the disabled. Most of the cheap housing, institutional living space and services for the disabled are highly concentrated in the core area and, given the particular problems that determine the residential location of the physically disabled, this locational pattern would seem both logical and beneficial. As long as the physically disabled continue to live on inadequate incomes, with only rudimentary support services and a lack of proper accommodation, they will remain a significant segment of the ghetto population.

Elderly

Institutional care for the elderly in Ontario can be broken down into three distinct sectors (figure 5.7). The first of these provides care for the chronically ill elderly in general hospitals and is financed by the Ontario Ministry of Health. The Ministry of Health has experienced major budget cuts since the mid-1970s and these have resulted in the ratio of hospital beds dropping from 4.1 per 1,000 population to 3.5 per 1,000. Coupled with this decrease, increased 'blockages' in the

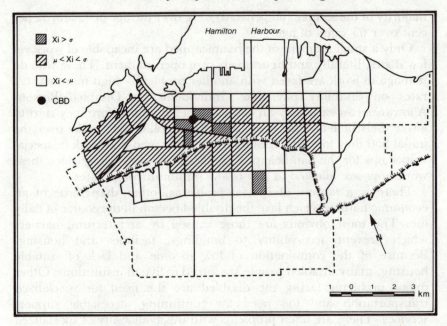

FIGURE 5.7   Distribution of population over 70 years of age in Hamilton

health-care system have resulted in acute shortages of hospital beds (*Toronto Globe and Mail*, 17 September, 1980).

The two other forms of institutional care available to the elderly are Homes for the Aged and Nursing Homes. Homes for the Aged are government-owned or operated by charities and are administered by the Ministry of Community and Social Services. Nursing Homes are privately owned and regulated by the Ministry of Health. Homes for the Aged were initially set up for people who needed residential care, but many accepted also need nursing care. Privately operated nursing homes are reluctant to accept the neediest of clients who require moderate-to-heavy nursing care because this increases their costs.

Provincial policy since the mid-1970s has been to keep community care expansion to a minimum; when expansion does occur, it is always in the area of privately operated nursing homes in Ontario. Almost every nursing home has a long waiting list. Mr John Maynard, Executive Director of the Ontario Nursing Home Association, said that this was important for his industry as: 'there is a guaranteed cash flow – you're never out marketing for customers' (*Toronto Globe and Mail*, 14 March 1981). While these nursing homes are regulated under the 1972 Nursing Act, there is considerable evidence that many nursing homes do not meet these standards. A survey of 50 Ontario nursing homes indicated that 'Nursing homes range in quality from excellent to appalling' (*Toronto Globe and Mail*, 18 March 1981).

In summary, the five major service-dependent groups in Hamilton, when taken together, define a very clear inner-city service-dependent ghetto (figure 5.8). The five populations are concentrated in seven census tracts immediately adjacent to the central business district. Seven other contiguous census tracts contain the majority of the remaining service-dependents. (The two large census tracts to the north-east of the business core, on the harborfront, represent exaggerated concentrations because the population in these essentially industrial areas is nominal. The single tract to the south-west is an outlier, actually on the Mountain adjacent to the large Chedoke Hospital complex.)

DRIFT TO THE GHETTO

In order to grasp how the drift of service-dependent individuals to the inner-city ghetto is motivated,[4] we turn to the views of a representative group of psychiatric hospital patients as they prepare for and begin to experience community life:

When you first get out of the hospital everything seemed rosy for a few days. Then the novelty wore off and you saw how bleak your life looked and you lost all your confidence. It doesn't seem possible to be sufficiently prepared in the hospital for the stresses you have to withstand shortly after leaving. The final days on the ward are directed toward encouraging you to feel strong and confident enough to sever your ties with the hospital community. A realistic appraisal of what lies ahead might very well be incompatible with that goal and might critically reduce the momentum needed to move out. If you knew what you were getting into, you just wouldn't have the courage to leave.

(Quoted in Schmidt, 1965, p. 1)

Once in the community, the problems facing the deinstitutionalized multiply:

Most of the mentally ill are referred to cheap single-room occupancy hotels and rooming houses, found largely in decaying portions of inner cities. They share this space with prostitutes, discharged prisoners, and drug

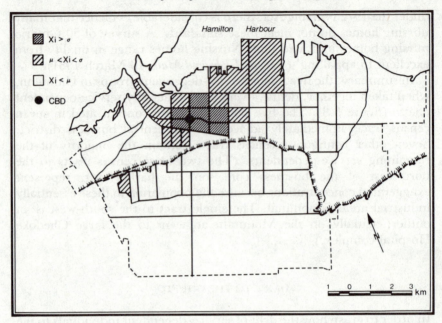

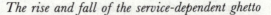

FIGURE 5.8   Distribution of major service-dependent populations in Hamilton

addicts. As the mentally ill are the weakest group, they fall easy prey to the predators of our society who victimize, terrorize and otherwise physically abuse them.

(Reich, 1973, pp. 911–12)

The everyday lives of ex-psychiatric patients reveals an incredible diversity, reflecting varying success in adjusting to the outside world. One ex-patient described his typical day as follows: 'During the week, I get up – go to work from 9 to 5, sometimes grocery shop on my way home, cook supper, and then in the evening I either go swimming or have a game of ball with my friends. Once a week I come to ―― for my appointment. I play my guitar whenever I have a chance.' He seems to be coping very well in the community. Although somewhat dependent on a psychiatric service, he also creates a clear picture of his ability to hold a job, cook, shop independently and to involve himself in recreational activities. He also indicates that he is socially involved with others. Contrast this with an ex-patient who seems to be having trouble coping with community life. It appears that this person has been left to fend for himself.

Many of his needs seem to be unmet. He does not appear prepared to face the day-to-day problems and routines that life entails. Thus: 'I have to get up at 7.30 for breakfast, I go back to bed until lunch, I watch T.V. or walk in the afternoon, and I go to bed after dinner.'

The everyday life of the ex-patient without a job tends to be poorly structured, i.e. lacking in any clear routine or purpose. Passive leisure-oriented activities that do not cost money tend to figure prominently. Large amounts of time are spent eating, walking, watching television and seeing friends. Weekends are spent in much the same way as weekdays, although activity levels drop in response to the diminished opportunities for organized social interaction.

For our purposes, the important question is how one ex-patient can become properly reintegrated while another suffers total collapse. A group of patients interviewed just prior to discharge from Hamilton Psychiatric Hospital (HPH) may provide some clues. Most patients, including those with previous experiences of discharge, viewed their imminent departure optimistically. They did not expect to be rich, but most allowed a clear desire to be employed to override worries about bleak job prospects. Few thought they would have problems in finding housing. They were not ignorant of the hazards of coping in a new environment, but hoped to be able to rely on a professional support network. Most hoped to be active in community social and recreational programs. In short, those who were about to be discharged viewed the process with hopes and fears not unlike those of any individual or family planning a move to new surroundings. Unfortunately, the harsh realities of life for ex-psychiatric patients rapidly erodes their spirits.

The chronic psychiatric patient is, in effect, consigned to permanent *unemployment*. A few subsidized jobs exist; they provide activity, some dignity and a sense of self-worth, which are just as important as the small amounts of money received. But the kinds of difficulties experienced by many find expression in the following reports:

I've worked a long time building up my credentials and now even though I feel I fit in, people still turn me down for employment.

IT [Industrial Therapy] is productive work. Labor is sold on an open market, it's not just useless stuff. IT should pay more [than 35 to 40 cents an hour]. I realize they're saving something on the whole medical system but some people spend their entire lives up there. There are a couple of my friends who were in IT and got so depressed they had to go on antidepressants.

It may help some. It gives some people hope that they may be able to hold a job again. I don't think the staff of —— or —— have any idea of how depressing that kind of work can be. It's almost like back in grade school where you have to ask to get up and go to the bathroom.

My social workers said [I] wouldn't be good for the job – shipping and receiving with a plumbing outfit: [my] social worker didn't want any failures. He wants me to go back to school but I want to work. I don't think spelling is required for the job I want. I would rather work and try it out. [My] social worker feels that because I was in the hospital, I'm not fit to work.

[I feel I fit in] at IT to a point. I find it a bit depressing because you're working with people who've been there for 10 or 12 years. I'm eager to get out of IT and get some vocational training.

I think jobs are the key to better mental health.

I would feel useful if I had a job.

The poverty that results from unemployment and limited welfare checks imposes severe restrictions on choice of *housing*. 'Choice' in housing is often reduced to selecting one of a number of indifferent single-room occupancy units, usually in a downtown area, as these comments indicate:

It's hard to find a place to live – people avoid me.

[I] don't like the neighborhood: [it's a] slum, people are always fighting: [the] area is really rundown.

I couldn't find a place to live, —— Housing Agency turned me down three times in a row.

Poverty-stricken and unable to afford anything but the cheapest housing, the ex-patient might anticipate support from the professional *aftercare* support network. This, however, often fails by doing too much or too little.

I feel sometimes I need psychiatric attention but I don't know where to go to get it. I'm afraid they'll just put me in the hospital.

[The] psychiatric attention [I get is] not adequate. I feel funny after medication. They only cut down on medication; they don't explain anything; they keep secrets.

I don't want any more medication, that's all they *do* is give me medication.

I feel I'm being taken advantage of because of my situation. [I] took 35 or 40 shock treatments. I cooperated with the doctors when I didn't know what they were doing to me. People always see me as a psychiatric patient when I want to be normal and respectable.

The drift to the ghetto in search of informal support networks is often accelerated by the professional care-givers. In a follow-up study of 495 discharged from HPH between 1 April 1978 and 31 March 1979, Dear et al. (1980) found that 70 per cent were actually discharged to destinations in the core area. The discharged population was confined predominantly to nine census tracts close to the central business district and included a significant number (12 per cent) of people who had lived outside Hamilton prior to admission to HPH. Many outsiders seem to remain in Hamilton after discharge. The discharged population is highly mobile, but most make changes of address within the ghetto, which acts almost as a 'reservoir' for potential clients for readmission to the hospital (Dear, 1977).

The *social networks* of the discharged mentally ill in Hamilton tend to be much smaller than those of the nondisabled. The mentally disabled have fewer ties with kin, fewer friends, less interaction with friends and relatives and fewer different sources of friends, as their comments show:

I feel terribly lonely, like I'm forgotten by everyone.

I don't like going home [to my family] because as soon as I get there, everyone goes out and leaves me there alone.

Since I was ill, I've lost out on the finer things in life. I used to enjoy going to the opera, the ballet . . . but haven't been able to in a long time.

[I'm] not accepted in the community because of my sickness.

In summary, the experience of discharge can effectively dash the hopes and optimism of many patients as they reenter the community. They face severely limited (usually downtown) housing opportunities; they are frequently referred upon discharge to core-area accommodations and services that are often found to be unsatisfactory and ineffective; and they are forced to turn inward in the face of diminished social networks. In their search for 'community', those ex-patients (who have not already been referred there) gravitate toward the zone of dependence. It is almost self-evident that the impetus behind ghettoization is the search for a wider support network. The inner city has become a coping mechanism where ex-patients can find help in the search for jobs and homes, can locate other support facilities, begin or renew friendships, start self-help groups and operate newsletters. Although still far from constituting an optimal setting, in the absence of any better alternative the ghetto is functional for Hamilton's ex-patients. It is a spatially limited zone where access to different kinds of support is made possible through geographical proximity.

It may be worth recalling that the role and significance of the service-dependent ghetto was not anticipated by the architects of deinstitutionalization. The inner-city zone of dependence simply became the unwitting target of the movement (cf. chapter 4). The implication of the present chapter is that the fates of dependent and discharged populations might have been much worse if it were not for the rudimentary support network made possible by the ghetto. However, just as we may be willing to concede the positive side of the ghetto, others are already beginning to dismantle it. And the assault on the ghetto appears to pay little or no heed to the service-dependent population's view of the ghetto. A coping mechanism that was unintentionally created by deinstitutionalization may now be destroyed by equally unintentional agents in the urban landscape.

6

Dismantling the community-based human-services system

In the preceding chapters we have seen how service-dependent populations have become ghettoized in a particular urban setting. In many North American cities, the ghetto still flourishes as an integral component of the social and physical landscape. In other cities however, a new stage in the historical evolution of the ghetto is already unfolding. In this chapter, we turn attention to the case of San Jose in California, where a rapid and catastrophic destruction of the service-dependent ghetto was recently achieved.

The City of San Jose is located in Santa Clara County, California. There, the goal of downtown gentrification and revitalization is in direct conflict with the goals of community-based service for dependent groups, and the removal of this population and their support facilities is seen by local officials as necessary for successful gentrification and renewal. In cities like San Jose, where new regional economic growth patterns encourage the downtown renewal process, private market mechanisms and public programs may work to oust low-income, service-dependent clients. State fiscal limitations and social spending cutbacks at all levels of government have accelerated facility closure, service removal and client dispersal. Service-dependent populations are unwelcome in central cities no longer willing to shoulder more than their share of clients and they are ringed by suburbs crying 'not in our neighborhood'; they may be the 'boat people' of North America's cities.

In this chapter, we examine the development and decline of San Jose's community-based service system and downtown zone of dependence. These findings raise questions about the prospects for human-service delivery, which are taken up in detail in the following chapters.

BACKGROUND OF DEINSTITUTIONALIZATION IN CALIFORNIA

Like other states in the union, California built its first insane asylum during the nineteenth century. As Lerman (1982) argues in his brief history of the California experience, this asylum and the institutions that followed it, served multiple functions and populations from the outset. Not only were the mentally ill committed there, but also the mentally retarded, the aged, drug/alcohol abusers, mentally disordered offenders and particularly the poor and indigent. Thus the early state hospital system provided a mixture of 'relief, care, custody and protection' to its clientele (Lerman, 1982, p. 102).

The system quickly became overcrowded; since the state paid the costs of institutionalization, counties and cities had no incentive to provide extensive outdoor relief or institutions of their own, such as almshouses. By 1910, overcrowding had become severe, leading the state to adopt some of the new Progressive reforms sweeping the country: parole of offenders; psychiatric parole; support of local hygiene clinics offering preventative services; establishment of two psychopathic wards; and a sterilization program for parolees.

These 'reforms' eased the crowding problem but by no means solved it. By the 1930s, crowding was still severe. Under the leadership of an innovative mental health practitioner, Dr Aaron J. Rosanoff, California undertook a program to reduce crowding and to dampen the growth in state hospital populations via the addition of 4,000 new beds. This included the construction of two neuropsychiatric units (at the University of California at Berkeley and later at Los Angeles); development of 'family-care' homes for one to five patients in the community; increasing the number of parolees in 'extramural care' from 2,500 to 5,000; and the parole of more patients to private institutions that would be licensed and reimbursed by the state (Lerman, 1982, p. 82–3).

In essence, Rosanoff's program was the beginning of a community-based service system. By the early 1940s, 5,000 patients had been paroled to extramural care, supported by a cadre of trained social workers stationed in the community. Many professionals in the state mental health hierarchy firmly believed that much greater reductions were possible; Rosanoff himself considered that a reduction of 62 per cent in the state hospital population could be achieved (Lerman, 1982, p. 83). Mental health leaders in the state thus seemed both professionally and ideologically prepared for deinstitutionalization.

By the end of World War II, the growth in institutional population had slowed but the total population had not declined. Further measures to depopulate the hospitals were held in abeyance and instead a $90 million hospital construction program was initiated (cf. the Ontario postwar experience reported in chapter 4). Under the influence of the Veterans Administration (acknowledged leader in institutional psychiatry in the postwar period), and financed by the 1946 Hospital Survey and Construction Act (Hill–Burton Act), California built 29,300 state psychiatric beds. Since existing state hospitals were eligible to receive Hill–Burton funds, over 19,000 of these beds were added to exurban state mental hospitals (Lerman, 1982, p. 86).

The beds were filled faster than they could be constructed and certified. By 1958–9, there were over 37,000 California residents housed in state hospitals. However, the passage of federal programs for the elderly in 1960, which provided nursing-home care and home-health services, allowed aged patients to leave the state hospitals (which were ineligible for these federal funds) and return to community-based facilities. Also, the adoption of federal programs for the disabled, elderly and poor (Aid for the Totally Disabled, Old Age Assistance, Old Age Security and Disability Insurance, Medicare, Medicaid and Title XX Social Services) allowed potential clients to remain outside of state institutions (cf. chapter 3). The leadership in the state's Division of Mental Health was sympathetic to a policy of deinstitutionalization and acted to take full advantage of the federal programs in order to reduce state hospital populations.

Their eagerness for deinstitutionalization was only surpassed by a zealous California State Legislature, which at one point attempted the closure of the entire state hospital system. Beginning in the late 1950s and accelerating in the 1960s, liberal social policy-makers in the state expanded on federal Great Society mandates and provided the fiscal incentives for the switch to community-based services. The state sought to expand the rights of service-dependent groups, particularly the mentally ill and to create state-funded community services to augment federal programs. The Short–Doyle Act of 1957 and the Lanterman–Petris–Short Act of 1968 shifted responsibility for the care and treatment of dependent groups to local communities via a 90 per cent state funding of approved local programs. Programs eligible for state funds included:

1 inpatient services for the mentally ill;
2 outpatient mental health services;

3 partial hospitalization;
4 emergency services;
5 consultation and education services for both professionals and the general public;
6 diagnostic services;
7 rehabilitation services;
8 precare and aftercare services including foster-home placement, home visiting and halfway houses;
9 training; and
10 research and evaluation of local programs.

The Lanterman Act of 1969 also set up a network of regional centers for the developmentally disabled. Counties could purchase state hospital care for the mentally ill, developmentally disabled and elderly under the 90/10 per cent formula of state/local payment responsibility; since the cost of state hospital services was so expensive relative to community-based care this provision served as a powerful incentive for local program development (Lamb and Edelson, 1976).

In addition to these programs, the state channeled drug and alcohol abusers to the mental health system via the 'Deukmejian option'. This program allowed 'public inebriates' to be treated in 36-hour detoxification instead of being jailed as criminals. Also, many juvenile offenders were transferred from institutions to community care facilities during the 1970s and community-based social adjustment programs for ex-offenders were initiated by the State Department of Corrections (Sundeen and Fisk, 1982).

By 1977, the total population confined to state hospitals was less than 6,000 persons. The long-sought abandonment of the total institution had finally been accomplished.

DEVELOPMENT OF AN ASYLUM WITHOUT WALLS:
SAN JOSE, CALIFORNIA

In San Jose, a service-dependent population ghetto emerged following the state's rapid release of institutionalized clients (Wolpert and Wolpert, 1976; Aviram and Segal, 1973). As elsewhere, mental patients and other dependent populations were released into a system of community care that many critics felt was untried and poorly organized (US General Accounting Office, 1977). Local services and aftercare programming were insufficient for chronic and severely disabled residents (Kirk and Therrian, 1975). Little coordination existed between services and professional expertise in reintegrating clients into residential settings was limited (Rose, 1979).

Little attention was paid to the spatial distribution of clients or services. Because many clients were received by private residential-care facilities, governmental control over their location was limited. The 'steamroller solution' of deinstitutionalization created a ghetto in aging downtown San Jose following the closure of nearby Agnews State Hospital (in 1971). Board-and-care facilities for ex-convicts, ex-drug addicts and alcoholics, Job Corps workers and juvenile wards of the court existed alongside over 1,000 discharged mental patients and their programs in the downtown area near San Jose State University.

The development of the ghetto in downtown San Jose was encouraged by metropolitan development patterns in Santa Clara County acting in conjunction with the state policy of deinstitutionalization. The growth of Silicon Valley in the northern part of the county; the condition of central city housing markets; and local government land-use policies all played significant parts in the agglomeration of human services and clients in downtown San Jose.

Economic development of Santa Clara County

Prior to World War II, Santa Clara County was an agricultural center, ranked as one of the 15 most productive agricultural counties in the nation (Saxenian, 1981). But the war generated rapid industrial development and population growth in the county. In particular, it spawned fledgling aerospace and electronics industries. Massive postwar government spending for research and development fueled the high-technology industries, whose plants clustered near Stanford University. Research and development activity expanded rapidly during the 1950s and 1960s, and this area became the nation's largest high-technology center. Popularly dubbed 'Silicon Valley', the area was notable for its concentration of semiconductor firms (Saxenian, 1981).

The impact of high-tech growth on Santa Clara County was dramatic, with population doubling once between 1950 and 1960 and once again between 1960 and 1970. The regional economy boomed and the employment base grew 156 per cent between 1960 and 1975 – three times the national growth rate (Saxenian, 1981, p. 63).

The county's rapid growth was accompanied by striking shifts in the pattern of urban development. The region's manufacturing employment became heavily concentrated in the north-western cities of the county, particularly Palo Alto, Sunnyvale, Mountain View, Santa Clara and Cupertino. During the 1960s it became clear that these cities had not allocated sufficient land for housing development. Instead, they had opted to devote vacant land to light industry, which increased the tax base faster than housing developments. San Jose, located to the south, became a 'bedroom' community for the northern job center as early as 1950, tripling in population size by 1960. Backed by a pro-growth coalition of 'landowners, realtors, roadbuilders, contractors, developers and members of the financial community' the city aggressively pursued an expansionary course of community annexation, rapid suburban home development, federally funded freeway building and the construction of large suburban shopping centers (Saxenian, 1981, p. 72). At the same time, the city became the locus of the county's blue-collar electronics workers, minority populations and low- and moderate-income families, because of the availability of modest and affordable new housing.

Yet at this stage in the county's development, San Jose's inner city not only failed to enjoy the bounty of regional growth, but suffered in its wake. The rapid suburbanization of population and commercial services in the postwar period left downtown San Jose behind. Unable to compete with suburban shopping malls, the demand for downtown commercial space plummeted and retail activity dwindled. The commercial core became severely dilapidated. Similarly, the central-area housing markets filtered downward, failing to compete successfully with the new, low-cost suburban tract homes south of the city center. Even the city and county administrations left the core, representing an official abandonment of the territory to marginal uses.

The downtown housing market

Throughout the sixties, demand for central-city homes fell relative to other parts of the city and county. The area was 'soft' and susceptible to the entry of less desirable land-uses and occupants. By 1970, median home values and rents in the central area were as much as a third lower than city-wide averages, and unlike the city as a whole, the central area housing stock was primarily multiple-family units (US

Department of Commerce, 1970). The rate of demolition exceeded new construction; between 1970 and 1975, the city added 32 per cent of its dwelling stock while the central area lost significant numbers of units (US Department of Commerce, 1970).

The central-area housing market declined further after a 1968 reversal in San Jose State University housing regulations. Prior to this change, students had been required to live in University-approved housing units located close to campus. The new regulations granted students the freedom to reside in housing units of their choice. In conjunction with the construction of new dormitory facilities on campus, this regulatory change altered student resident patterns. The stately fraternities, sororities, student rooming houses and apartments around the downtown campus were deserted by their student occupants in rapid succession.

These changes in central-area/University neighborhoods led to a rapid concentration of community care facilities there. The area offered an eminently suitable supply of residential stock for service-dependent populations and a new clientele for rooming-house operators eligible to receive payments on their behalf. Since clients typically received Aid to the Disabled, operators of a small family home for six could expect monthly payments that were more steady and compared favorably with previous student rental payments (Wolpert, Dear and Crawford, 1975). These operators were by and large untrained in the delivery of support services to rehabilitating clients and provided mainly custodial care to home residents.

Suburban development policies

The establishment of a facilities 'hub' in the downtown section of San Jose was also a symptom of the budding 'no-growth' movement gaining momentum in Santa Clara County's suburban jurisdictions. Many severely restricted the extent and type of residential development and most excluded residential services for the elderly, handicapped and mentally ill via zoning ordinances that prohibited these uses or required them to obtain use permits in order to operate. Efforts to provide public housing opportunities in these communities were also singularly unsuccessful. Citizens regularly defeated local referenda (necessary under Article 34 of the State Constitution), to construct subsidized housing for poor, elderly and disabled households.

The City of Saratoga exemplifies the stance of suburban Santa Clara County jurisdictions toward development in general and toward the entry of service-dependent populations. Despite intense South Bay development pressures, the city remained high-income, white-collar and small. Housing prices were higher and poverty taxes were lower than any other Santa Clara County jurisdictions (see table 6.1). This was accomplished with the help of a virulent no-growth policy. The General Plan of 1974, replete with objectives concerning the maintenance of Saratoga's 'rural character,' scenic beauty and environmental quality, detailed development plans that underscored the desirability of low-density, single-family housing. Infrastructure capacity was restricted in order to keep growth at a minimum. Numerous regulatory hurdles stood in the prospective developer's path. Development fees were high and most of the city's developable land was zoned for one unit per acre.

Moreover, the city's residents consistently voted against project proposals for housing for the elderly, vociferously sounding their opposition to such projects at City Council meetings. Municipal zoning ordinances explicitly prohibited community care facilities of most types and by 1975 only one small family home for children (with two residents) and three group homes for adults had been sited and licensed in Saratoga. The city had completely excluded small

TABLE 6.1   Profile of Saratoga, California, 1976

Population	29,000
Mean household income	$27,630
Percentage minority	5
Percentage white-collar workers	77.8
Mean housing price	$94,000
Mean house size	2,154
Mean age of housing stock (years)	14
Development fees per unit built	$1,496
Percentage of developable land zoned for large lots	45
Total planned number of dwelling units	2,875
Total acres of developable land remaining	2,387
Mean density of planning development (units/acre)	1

Source: Wolch, J. R., and Gabriel, S. A. 'Local Land Development Policies and Urban Housing Values', *Environment and Planning A*, 13: 1253–76 (1981).

family homes for adults, large family homes for both adults and children, adult day-care centers, vocational rehabilitation facilities, services for the mentally retarded and social rehabilitation clinics (Santa Clara County Planning Department, 1976).

Saratoga's approach was typical of Santa Clara County municipal zoning ordinances. As shown in table 6.2, a majority of cities either prohibited such facilities or required them to obtain conditional use permits. The existence of the use-permit process virtually insured exclusion, as homeowner groups were quick to protect their turf and organize to defeat siting requests. Such exclusionary tactics channeled potential providers into less restrictive areas. San Jose, for example, imposed no restrictions on the right of small board-and-care facilities (small family homes) to operate in residential neighborhoods during the late sixties and early seventies. In fact, many facilities only required city business permits, a fire clearance and a building inspection in order to operate.

Board-and-care clients were not only excluded from most Santa Clara County jurisdictions, but from the surrounding counties of Alameda and San Mateo as well. Not prepared to handle deinstitutionalized populations, these counties actively placed reentry clients in Santa Clara County facilities located in downtown San Jose. In 1973 a special study conducted by the California State

TABLE 6.2   *Zoning regulations affecting community care facilities in Santa Clara County, 1984*

| Community care | Number of cities in which use is: | | |
facility type	Permitted	Prohibited	Use permit required
(1) Small family homes	5	10	0
(2) Large family homes	2	9	4
(3) Group homes	0	15	0
(4) Small family day homes	3	4	8
(5) Large family day homes	2	9	4
(6) Adult day-care centers	1	7	6

Notes: Rows (1) and (4) homes for six persons for less, rows (2) and (5) for six or more persons and row (3) homes for both children and adults.
Source: Santa Clara County Planning Department, *A Report on Zoning and Non Medical Facilities in Santa Clara County*, San Jose, CA, (1976).

Department of Health, indicated that approximately one-third of all board-and-care clients living in the San Jose area originated in other counties. Some of these were local and nonlocal Veteran's Administration (VA) clients placed there by the VA Hospital in Palo Alto, only one-third of whom had been Santa Clara County residents to begin with. The study concluded that:

Conservators from several of the Bay Area counties have found the area adjacent to San Jose University a convenient resource for placement . . . In addition, some of the county mental health programs and county welfare departments in the Bay Area counties have apparently found this to be a primary resource for residential placements. Some operators, also, have directly contacted state hospitals, county conservators, county welfare departments, and other placement agencies to recruit residents for their homes.

(California State Department of Health, 1973, p. 22)

By the mid-seventies, an uncoordinated, fragmented and diverse set of services for a variety of service-dependent groups had evolved in downtown San Jose. Job Corps; Community Mental Health centers; Lanterman–Petris–Short and Short–Doyle mental health programs; neighborhood health centers; vocational rehabilitation services; drug/alcohol treatment centers; employment centers; and a spate of voluntary services providing food, clothing and emergency shelter, all concentrated downtown near the University. The downtown/University zone offered proximity to the expanding transient and dependent populations, suitable low-cost housing and building stock for organizations providing human services, and escape from homeowner conflict and opposition in the suburbs.

THE SERVICE-DEPENDENT POPULATION GHETTO MID-DECADE

A 1972 survey of the San Jose State University area indicated that over 1,800 individuals were residing in 140 board-and-care facilities or rehabilitation programs, representing 83 per cent of all board-and-care capacity in the city in an area housing only 15 per cent of the city's population (California State Department of Health, 1973, p. 12). Only one-half of this capacity was licensed. The residential facilities augmenting the board-and-care homes were Job Corps Centers (four); Alcoholic Halfway Houses (13); Drug Abuse Facility (one); Boarding Homes for the Aged (11); and Homes for Felons (one). About half of these facilities housed 10 or more residents. The majority (59.9 per cent) of residents were supported by public assistance alone (Aid to the Disabled), another 22.5 per cent received a combination of Social Security, Veterans Compensation, Public Assistance and/or had some private resources. Many (29.5 per cent) had no contact with aftercare agencies, while the remainder had either monthly, quarterly or annual contact and review. Of all residents interviewed, almost three-fourths were mentally ill and were receiving psychotropic medications.

A wide array of nonresidential support services was available to board-and-care clients and to those living autonomously in the neighborhood. The services included guidance, adjustment and therapy clinics, physical medicine, family health clinics, advocacy, community education, information and referral, vocational training, sheltered workshops, transportation, employment training, socialization and recreation services.

A 1975 profile indicated a worsening situation (table 6.3). In the area around the University, the population had declined since 1970, as had the proportion of students. The zone was the site of demolitions and very little new construction. Most of the housing stock was multifamily rental units, with rents well below city average. Approximately 1,243 households were receiving Aid to Families with Dependent Children, over 900 relied on county medical assistance and 600 availed themselves of one of several Title XX Social Services, representing a far higher dependency rate than the city average. A special 1975 census indicated that the group-quarters population was estimated at 1,135 in the three census tracts adjacent to the University, housed in 88 facilities – almost half the community care capacity in the city (Santa Clara County Planning Department, 1975).

In the University zip-code area, 6,449 persons received Old Age Security and Disability Insurance and 2,927 relied on Supplemental Security Income for the Aged and Disabled, representing 31 per cent of the city's SSI recipients (US Department of Health, Education and Welfare, 1976). Community care facilities had begun to require state licensure in 1973, but by 1975 there remained large numbers of facilities unlicensed by either the state or county. Nonetheless, the state recorded 34 facilities in the zip-code area, representing 1,012 licensed beds and almost two-thirds of the city's licensed capacity (California State Department of Health, 1975).

Analysis of the larger 15-city County of Santa Clara indicated that the San Jose ghetto was the only concentration of service-dependent

TABLE 6.3 Profile of the San Jose Ghetto, 1975

	Census Tract 5009	Census Tract 5010	Census Tract 5013	City
(1) Population, 1975	4,352	3,475	3,719	551,224
(2) Change in population 1970–5	–9%	–5%	–7%	+20%
(3) Median income, 1975	$2,932	$2,238	$5,566	$12,361
(4) Percentage of households in poverty, 1975	33%	35%	22%	9%
(5) Percentage student population, 1975	67%	21%	41%	18%
(6) Change in student population, 1970–5	–23%	–9%	–5%	–2%
(7) Percentage of labor force unemployed, 1975	9%	9%	7%	6%
(8) Change in dwelling units 1970–5	–25%	–1%	–13%	+32%
(9) Proportion renters, 1975	97%	88%	66%	34%
(10) Percentage in group quarters, 1975	43%	5%	32%	2%
(11) Percentage AFDC recipients, 1975	7%	17%	10%	7%
(12) Percentage handicapped, 1975	8%	15%	3%	4%
(13) Change in AFDC recipients, 1970–5	2%	1%	6%	0
(14) Percentage receiving medical assistance, 1975	7%	6%	12%	2%
(15) Change in percentage receiving medical assistance, 1970–5	6%	5%	11%	1%
(16) Percentage receiving Foodstamps 1975	12%	21%	13%	9%
(17) Percentage receiving Title XX Services, 1975	8%	15%	3%	4%
(18) Rooming houses, 1973	10	13	65	153
(19) Residential-care beds, 1975	193	135	807	2,728
(20) Beds/1,000 population, 1975	44	39	217	5
(21) Licensed residential-care facilities, 1975	3	1	22	84
(22) Licensed beds, 1975	69	24	521	1,094

Notes: Rows (1)–(11) from Santa Clara County Planning Department, *Special Census, 1975,* San Jose, CA. The source of 1970 population and housing data is US Department of Commerce, Bureau of Census, *Census of Population and Housing, 1970,* Washington, DC. Rows (12)–(17) from unpublished data of the Santa Clara County Planning Department. Rows (18)–(20) from untabulated data from Santa Clara County Planning Department, *Special Census, 1975.* Rows (21)–(22) from California Department of Health, Facilities Licensing Section, *Directory of Community Care Facilities 1975,* Sacramento, CA.

population groups and was the human-service facility 'hub' of the county (figure 6.1). As shown in table 6.4, Supplemental Security recipients, welfare recipients, community care facilities and community-based institutionalized populations (particularly adult) were concentrated in San Jose.

THE WAR ON THE GHETTO

By 1972 opposition to the expanding service-dependent population ghetto was growing and becoming publicly articulated. A moratorium on board-and-care facility licensing was enacted by the San Jose City Council, in a measure that prohibited the issuance of fire permits by the Fire Marshal (Ordinance 16265, San Jose City Council, June 1972). In 1975, an amendment to the city's zoning ordinance was adopted, which identified districts in which community care facilities (by type) would be permitted by right, by use permit, or prohibited. Residential facilities had begun to require

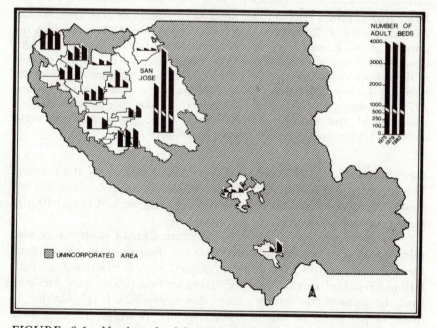

FIGURE 6.1   Number of adult community care beds, Santa Clara county, 1975–82

TABLE 6.4   *Concentration of county public assistance and community care services in San Jose, 1975*

	Percentage of county total located in San Jose
Public assistance	
(1) Supplementary Security Income recipients	63.2
(2) Cash-grant recipients	65.1
(3) Medical Assistance Only recipients	58.4
(4) Foodstamps	63.2
(5) Title XX cases in service	60.9
Community care facilities	
(6) Residential facilities (beds) – for children	49.2 (26.2)
(7) Residential facilities (beds) – for adults	69.6 (42.2)
(8) Nonresidential facilities (capacity)	84.0 (88.0)
(9) *County population*	47.2

Notes: Row (1) from HEW, 1976, *Social Security Beneficiaries by Zip-Code, San Francisco Region, 1975,* Washington DC. Figures include data for unincorporated areas. Rows (2)–(5) from unpublished data of the Santa Clara County Department of Social Services. Figures are for incorporated areas of the county only. Rows (6)–(8) from California Department of Health, Facilities Licensing Section, 1975, *Directory of Community Care Facilities, 1975*, Sacramento, CA. Row (9) refers to base population of both incorporated and unincorporated county areas: unincorporated areas contain 11.3 per cent of total county population.

state licensure in 1973 and they were also licensed by the county. Under persistent community pressure, the county licensing agency closed 20 substandard facilities while bringing an additional 40 into their program of inspection and licensure.

Several reports on 'impaction' in Santa Clara County were also released. A state report indicated that the 'failure of the city to zone areas for board and care homes, coupled with restrictive fire regulations, resulted in the total exclusion of board and care facilities from all areas of the county except downtown San Jose' (California State Department of Health, 1973, p. 6). It suggested that local residents blamed community care facilities for ruined businesses, lowered property values and economic decline of downtown San Jose and pointed out deficiencies in human-service delivery. Licensing procedures, required qualifications for home operators and community aftercare programming were inadequate, and shortages in placement, follow-up and social service programs were major service system shortcomings.

The exclusion of residential facilities in other areas of the county was documented in a county planning department report three years later. This report documented the uneven distribution of community care facilities and the variance in their local zoning treatment. It suggested a 'fair-share' system of allocating facilities to local jurisdictions within the county as a means of overcoming the ghettoization problem (Santa Clara County Planning Department, 1976).

Local elected officials complained to the county and the county complained to state officials that San Jose had become a 'dumping ground for social problems'. The Advisory Commission on the Developmentally Disabled of the Santa Clara County Board of Supervisors informed the State Department of Health of 'this County's intention of discouraging the recruitment and establishment of new residential facilities in Santa Clara County' (Santa Clara County Board of Supervisors, 1976–9, p. 4). In addition, the local media provided continual coverage of the ghetto and its problem residents.

But while these declarations and actions added to the groundswell of sentiment against the service-dependent ghetto, the expediency of siting public and private facilities in the ghetto neighborhood, and conflict both between the state and local jurisdictions and between cities, worked against a more equitable distribution of social services and clients. Moreover, public, private and nonprofit human-service agencies operated in an uncoordinated, fragmented fashion and failed to consider the cumulative impacts of their decisions to site services downtown.

Local economic pressures for change

Only when the spillovers of rapid county development finally reached the inner city, catalyzing private gentrification and public redevelopment, did the ouster of services facilities and their clients take hold. The job/housing imbalance – that is, the contradiction between fast employment growth and increasingly restrictive suburban housing development – became the foremost planning problem of the South Bay region. This imbalance set into motion changes in downtown San Jose that were reinforced by larger shifts in political priorities and social spending cutbacks at all levels of government.

The job/housing imbalance problem

The imbalance between the number of jobs created for Santa Clara County and its available (or potentially available) housing stock was widely documented during the late 1970s. The trend toward imbalance began in the postwar years, accelerating to become such a critical issue that housing shortages deterred high-tech expansion and instigated calls for industrial growth controls.

The figures in table 6.5 portray the dimensions of the imbalance problem. The county's cities drastically reduced their allocation of land for housing, permitting instead more industrial development and down-zoning residential areas. In 1965, for example, local

TABLE 6.5   *Imbalance between jobs and housing potential in Santa Clara County, 1980*

City	Job expansion based on local zoning	Housing-unit expansion based on local zoning
Campbell	500	200
Cupertino	5,120	4,980
Gilroy	7,000	4,875
Los Altos	0	238
Los Altos Hills	0	322
Los Gatos	350	395
Milpitas	29,700	3,648
Monte Sereno	0	35
Morgan Hill	21,700	6,475
Mountain View	18,620	3,600
Palo Alto	3,000	1,300
San Jose	123,475	45,786
Santa Clara	23,940	2,826
Saratoga	270	2,271
Sunnyvale	12,350	1,680

Source: Santa Clara County Manufacturing Group, *Vacant Land in Santa Clara County: Implications for Job Growth and Housing in the 1980s*, San Jose, CA, (1980).

government general plans provided for 978,000 housing units but by 1975, that figure had dropped to 561,000, a 417,000 decrease (43 per cent). Between 1966 and 1975, 17,000 acres had been developed for 75,000 units for an average density of 4.7 units per acre. During the same period, however, the allowable number of jobs per acre of industrial land rose from 20 to 30–35 – a 75 per cent increase. By 1977 the job/housing discrepancy was striking: a 102 per cent increase was scheduled for jobs, but only a 43 per cent increase in housing units (Saxenian, 1981).

Restrictions on residential development were caused in part by the proliferation of no-growth ordinances designed to protect property values, social composition and the suburban environment (Wolch and Gabriel, 1981). Growth-management plans and development fees regulated the level, timing and type of development permitted. This no-growth movement spread from traditionally exclusive enclaves (like Saratoga) to other cities including San Jose, where moderates gained control and slowed the pace of suburban expansion (Lane, 1978). In 1978 San Jose charged the highest fees for single-family dwelling units constructed in the county: $4,626. Los Altos Hills and Saratoga led the way with respect to subdivision exactions for amenities and community facilities: $10,750 in fees per subdivision in Los Altos Hills and $11,855 in Saratoga, compared to $2,925 in San Jose (Association of Bay Area Governments, 1980).

Limited housing development was also related to the reduction of its tax base advantages for local governments resulting from Proposition 13. With imposition of the tax limitation, most housing projects generated a negative cost/revenue impact on local tax bases and many cities consciously slowed the pace of residential development (Gabriel, Katz and Wolch, 1980).

Local development plans and policies, job expansion and changing household demographics accelerated the upward spiral of county housing prices. While county population grew about 10 per cent during the 1970–5 period, the household formation rate rose 21.5 per cent because of the increased prevalence of single- and two-person households. This growth in demand for housing put further pressure on home prices. Median county home prices rose faster than anywhere in the state or nation. In California during the year 1977 median home prices rose 32 per cent ($47,000 to $62,000) but in Santa Clara County the increase was 40 per cent, starting from a higher base ($52,000 to $73,500). Between 1970 and 1975, prices increased 92 per cent and between 1971 and 1977 they rose 151.4 per cent (Saxenian, 1981).

These price increases far outstripped growth in personal income. During the same 1971–7 period, median family income rose only 42.5 per cent. HUD identified 68,200 low-income households in the county as requiring housing assistance in 1977–8, which together with an additional 100,000 low-income families not requiring housing aid, indicated the threatened economic position of a full 43 per cent of the county's population (Santa Clara County Housing Task Force, 1977).

Gentrification and redevelopment in downtown San Jose

This crisis in housing affordability led potential homebuyers and redevelopers to inner-city San Jose. The growing number of high-wage, white-collar jobs in the Silicon Valley area exhausted the supply of housing in north county, and residents looked southward in their search for shelter and lower home prices. Between 1970 and 1975, Palo Alto housing prices rose 73.3 per cent while San Jose prices only rose 47 per cent, indicating that demand for housing in San Jose was lower than in the north-county cities. But between 1975 and 1979, this situation had changed and a southward shift in demand was evident: home price inflation in San Jose matched that in Palo Alto (Saxenian, 1981, p. 95).

The new residents were attracted to central San Jose because of the architectural quality of the older homes, its accessibility to major highways north and its affordability. This trend was reflected in increased rates of alterations and additions to existing units and high rates of infill development – a third of all new units in San Jose was built on 'developed' (i.e. serviced and built-out) areas in 1981 (San Jose Department of City Planning, 1980; 1982).

The southward expansion of new jobs and the potential for gentrification provided the basis for major downtown redevelopment plans by the City of San Jose. Economic, planning and design consultants developed extensive plans for renewal of the city's obsolete core, to include massive office construction, a convention center, a stadium, a hotel, residential complexes and a major new thoroughfare. Their plans were big: the consultant report on San Antonio Plaza, the major development in the project area, is worth noting:

During the 1960s and 1970s, San Jose was at the southern end of the rapidly growing Silicon Valley. Because of its location at the periphery rather than at the heart of this economic engine, San Jose serves as a bedroom community to employment centers in the Palo Alto to Santa Clara corridor. During the 1980s as land to the north of San Jose is largely absorbed, the new growth will be to the south and east. As a result, downtown San Jose becomes the logical geographical center of this expanding Silicon Valley.

Our market analysis indicated downtown demand for 250,000 to 300,000 square feet of new office space per year . . . Over a ten-year period from approximately 1983 to 1993, (the consultant) forecasts the potential for 1.2 to 1.6 million square feet of office space for San Antonio Plaza. Office construction is therefore the economic engine driving redevelopment of downtown San Jose and San Antonio Plaza.

Although up to this point in time San Jose has grown along the traditional suburban low-rise housing patterns, there is now strong developer interest in higher density projects in the core area . . . (the consultant) forecasts a demand for 160 to 180 units per year for a residential complex in the San Antonio project, or 1,600 to 1,800 units over a decade.
(Economic Research Associates, 1980, p. 1–2)

The glossy Center City Development Plan ultimately prepared by the city was remarkable in that few of its sketch plans identify the State University, although streets and other landmarks are shown. Furthermore, the text of the plan only mentions the University once. The institution is not integrated into any of the renewal plans, even though the redevelopment areas are immediately adjacent to it.

Like a renewal plan of the 1950s era, the San Jose redevelopment plan overlooked the existing residents of the University area. Instead, the plan targeted these neighborhoods for rehabilitation and occupancy by faculty, high-tech workers and other professionals. This 'oversight' is easily understood in light of the politics of San Jose redevelopment and the concerted efforts of renewal advocates in the City Council, the business community and among homeowners, to overcome the service-dependent population ghetto.

Political action against the Ghetto

By the close of the decade, both gentrification and downtown renewal had begun to affect the service-dependent population ghetto. A strong political coalition of San Jose City Council representatives, the Santa Clara Board of Supervisors and various local businesses and community groups pursued a policy of ghetto dispersal. According to public documents, our interviews with coalition leaders, and their public pronouncements and actions, the coalition had three primary objectives:

1 downtown renewal;
2 prevention of additional human-service facility siting in the core area; and
3 elimination of at least some portion of the existing services located there.

The coalition's original stance toward services was straightforward: close down or move facilities for poor, mentally ill, retarded, disabled or justice-system clients and thereby force such populations out of the downtown area where they jeopardized urban redevelopment chances. In pursuit of these objectives the coalition employed systematic means including administrative reforms, community action groups and development of technical evidence supporting facility removal. For example, the coalition-controlled University Area Task Force was created to report on the ghetto area and its problems, inform the community of the severity of local impacts and provide technical evidence on which to base recommendations for facility removal and promotion of neighborhood rehabilitation (San Jose Department of City Planning, 1978). The coalition also focused attention on isolated incidents of violent crime by ex-offenders or ex-mental patients and on controversial facility sitings, in order to sway public sentiment and polarize the community.

The coalition enjoyed substantial success in its battle against the ghetto. During the 1977–82 period, the following coalition-backed actions were taken by the City of San Jose or Santa Clara County:

1 *Facility relocation*: Multiservices Center; County Forensic Services; Vocational Learning Treatment Center; All Cooperating Together (Emergency Psychiatric Services); Downtown Alcoholism Center; Linden Health Clinic (Low-cost Health Care).
2 *Facility closure*: San Jose Psychiatric Hospital Unit; Goodwill Industries Vocational Training Center; Santa Clara County Mobile Emergency (Psychiatric) Services; Drop-in Alcoholism Center; Urban Food Coalition; University Alternatives (Ex-offenders at San Jose State University).
3 *Attempted closure*: Job Corps; Alcoholics Rescue Mission.
4 *Elimination of Duekmejian option*: (thereby criminalizing more of the service-dependent population).
5 *Prevention of facility siting*: Prerelease facility for offenders; public inebriate reception center.

In addition to these concrete actions, in some cases prompted by budgetary cutbacks, the board of Supervisors and City Council have put persistent pressure on the state to adopt legislation designed to

1 place responsibility for collection and dissemination of information concerning the geographic incidence of service facilities with the state;
2 place responsibility with the state to distribute facilities to all socioeconomic areas;
3 encourage exclusionary communities to accept their fair share of the service-dependent population; and
4 permit service authorities to take facility densities into account when making licensing and permit decisions in order to prevent overconcentration.

This last objective was achieved when the state allowed Santa Clara County (along with two other counties) to use concentration measures as licensing criteria. At the local level, the coalition's approach was to move forward aggressively with downtown redevelopment plans, encourage gentrification by attracting state and federal funds for rehabilitation, prohibit any further service facilities or residential homes in the University area, and then wait for increasing land values and attrition to drive existing residents and facilities out.

The coalition was not overtly 'anti-services'. Their claims of core-area impaction were justified and their general recommendations for state legislation echoed reforms suggested by human-service professionals at all levels of government and in all branches of service. Nonetheless, the power of the coalition to remove services far exceeded their ability to enact programmatic reforms of service-delivery policy or create new service opportunities elsewhere. They were not inactive because of this limitation; rather, they shifted the burden to other communities, other agencies, other levels of government. The ghettoized community-based service system built up in the 1960s and 1970s would be incrementally dismantled regardless of the availability of alternatives to care for those displaced.

State and federal social-policy shifts

The actions of the downtown coalition to dismantle the service-dependent population ghetto coincided with shifts in political attitudes concerning the role of government in society and in the lives of dependent populations. State and federal changes in fiscal policy and service-delivery strategy in the late 1970s and 1980s imposed significant cutbacks in human services and jeopardized client well-being.

Proposition 13

California's tax limitation movement culminated in 1978 with a successful referendum to limit property taxes to 1 per cent of 1976 market value, thus reducing local government revenues by $7 billion (Stumpf and Terrell, 1979). Later, a second successful referendum limited growth in local government spending to 4 per cent annum. These measures, which limited not only revenue from property tax sources but also restrained local governments from raising revenue from other sources, had dire consequences for local government service delivery. And since the state was forced to provide 'bail-out' funds to local jurisdictions, its own service programs were also reduced. The state Title XX budget was cut 5 per cent in 1979; alcohol and drug-abuse programs were cut by $1.8 billion and $91,000 was trimmed from elderly nutrition programming (Stumpf and Terrell, 1979). These cuts, along with local reductions in human-service spending, resulted in a 6.5 per cent real cut in 1979 county human-services budgets, including a 7 per cent cut in General Assistance funds; a 20 per cent reduction in Title XX Social Services; a 9 per cent cut in mental health services; an 8 per cent cut in substance-abuse programs; and a 31 per cent reduction in revenue-sharing for social service programs (Stumpf and Terrell, 1979).

In Santa Clára County, losses were sizeable. Ninety-six human-service worker positions were eliminated and $42 million was cut from the human-services budget. Contracts to nonprofit service providers fell by 18 per cent and fees were instituted to overcome revenue shortfalls in several areas. A mobile emergency crisis-intervention unit that operated in the downtown San Jose district was also eliminated and a key coordinative service – informational and referral – was closed.

Federal budget impacts

Despite the rhetoric of a 'social safety-net', Reagan Administration cutbacks in service programs since 1980 were substantial, further weakening community-based service resources (Palmer and Sawhill, 1982). Overall, an estimated $12 billion in constant 1980 dollars was excised from the federal social-program budget in 1982 (Salamon and Abramson, 1982). This was accomplished by tightening eligibility rules, reducing cost-of-living increases for public-aid recipients and eliminating programs. The results for social services in 1982 included a 43 per cent drop in Title XX funding; a 35 per cent cut in child welfare programs; a 27 per cent reduction in programs for the elderly; a 42 per cent cut in rehabilitation funding; an 83 per cent drop in community services monies; and a 38 per cent reduction in other social services – in all, a 38 per cent cut in total spending (adjusted for inflation) from 1981 levels (Palmer and Sawhill, 1982). Mental health funds were reduced 19 per cent during the 1980–2 period and regulatory changes in Medicare and Medicaid implied reductions in health care services to low-income and indigent groups; 1982 budget revisions specified an additional $2 billion reduction in AFDC and Foodstamp outlays and changes in SSI 'income disregards' effectively reduced the income floor for many recipients. Along with these reductions, new federal guidelines for the states permitted local governments to discontinue targeting human-service assistance to SSI and AFDC recipients; slash reporting requirements; eliminate planning and public participation requirements; and allow states and localities to forego use of federal income eligibility rules of all programs (Palmer and Sawhill, 1982).

The private voluntary sector, originally expected to fill the gap created by federal budget cuts in social spending, instead suffered reductions in service-delivery capacity because of its financial dependence on governmental grants, contracts and subsidized fees-for-service. Voluntary agencies were expected to lose 60 per cent of their federal support by 1985 and $2 billion in 1982 alone (Salamon and Abramson, 1982). In order to offset the losses of the voluntary sector, private giving would have had to increase three- to fourfold; to offset both public- and voluntary-sector losses, private donations would have had to rise almost 100 per cent or eight times faster than their historical rate (Salamon and Abramson, 1982).

Impacts of federal cutbacks on Santa Clara County were swift and deep. During 1981/2, the Social Services Department lost 363 positions, 200 of which were social workers. In-home support services for the aged, blind and disabled were cut, with 24 per cent of all cases terminated and 52 per cent of all cases experiencing a reduction in service by late 1981 as eligibility rules and need criteria became more stringent. New AFDC regulations were expected to affect 12 per cent of recipients, 43 per cent of whom were likely to be terminated, the remainder suffering payment reductions. Terminated cases would also lose access to Foodstamps and Medi-Cal (California's version of Medicaid). The nominal value of Foodstamp coupons was to drop by 5 per cent, cash-grant cases by 6 per cent and social service cases by 14 per cent (Santa Clara County Department of Social Services, 1981; 1982). The 1982/3 County Budget painted a picture of continuing austerity, reflected in a 20 per cent reduction in social service program funding, a 34 per cent reduction in General Assistance monies and a 19 per cent cut in alcoholism services (table 6.6).

GHETTO DECLINE AND THE PROSPECTS
FOR SANTA CLARA'S SERVICE-DEPENDENT POPULATION

While results of local political–economic pressure and social-policy shifts are only beginning to be observed, a marked decline in licensed community care facility capacity has already occurred in San Jose's service-dependent population ghetto (figure 6.2). As shown in table 6.7, there have also been substantial reductions in this area's welfare and Title XX caseloads. The net loss in service capacity and welfare suggests that service-dependent populations are either being dispersed to non-ghetto community care homes, misassigned to inappropriate services, reinstitutionalized, or are not receiving services at all.

The extent of these changes is unclear. Not only do clients move freely through various service settings without any record of their mobility, but the level of population in need of services, while by all accounts growing, is changing to an unknown extent.

Intra-county dispersal

While out-of-county placements and independent migration rates are unknown, one indicator of client dispersal is the shift in community care capacity within the county. Unlike the city, which lost beds (particularly in the ghetto), the county gained 177 community care beds between 1979 and 1982, indicating some dispersal of the service-dependent. The increase did not occur in any one location, suggesting that no new service-dependent population ghetto is in the process of formation in Santa Clara County. Beyond quantitative measures, the expectation of dispersal is reinforced by 1978 state legislation prohibiting local jurisdictions from zoning out

TABLE 6.6 *Recent changes in human-services program budgets in Santa Clara county, 1982–3*

Program	Approved 1982/3 expenditures ($)	FY 81/2 changes (%)	Comments
(1) Social Services Administration	52,280,061	2	Since 1978/9, 500 positions cut; 225 cut since 1981/2
(2) Income Maintenance Administration	31,626,000	4	
AFDC	15,968,000	12	
Medi-Cal	6,268,000	13	
General Assistance	566,000	−64	
Nonassistance Foodstamps	3,864,000	22	
Refugee Assistance	4,090,000	64	
Staff Development	666,000	−63	
(3) Social Services Programs	20,232,000	−20	Since 1979/80, 32% decline
Title XX	11,536,000	−5	Since 1979/80, 10% decline
Children's Shelter	1,411,000	−19	
In-Home Support	3,043,000	−39	Since 1979/80, 53% decline
Optional Services	422,000	−24	Since 1979/80, 68% decline
(4) Categorical Aid payments	156,411,000	−3	
General Assistance	4,599,000	−34	
County Supplemental Assistance	55,000	−72	
AFDC	135,638,000	4	
(5) Drug Abuse Programs	2,734,542	23	Since 1978/9, staff cut by a third; contracts now in budget instead of going direct to contractors; effective budget therefore reduced
(6) Alcoholism Services	3,686,479	−19	
(7) Mental Health Bureau	24,955,338	−2	
(8) Health Services Administration	15,930,842	−17	Since 1981/2, 18% staff cut

Source: Santa Clara County, *Annual Budget*, San Jose, CA, (1978–83).

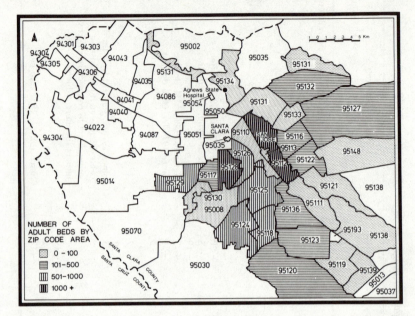

FIGURE 6.2   Number of adult community care beds by Zip Code, northern Santa Clara county, 1982

small community care facilities for six or fewer persons via outright exclusion or use-permit strategies. However, this imposition of the state's power over local land-use decisions may be short-lived: since the law went into effect, legislation has been introduced annually to revoke it.

Misassignment

Misassignment occurs as clients are transferred from one system of institutional settings to another typically less appropriate to their needs. Anecdotal evidence suggests that misassignment of dependent populations into the criminal justice system is becoming more frequent, as service reductions are accompanied by increased vagrancy, erratic behavior and petty crime (Urmer, 1975; Lamb and Grant, 1982). Moreover, new state budgets have targeted the prison system for significant expansion, one justification being that the penal system has become increasingly responsible for the mentally ill (cf. chapter 7). Misassignment to medical facilities is commonplace despite the lack of psychiatric or social services available in

TABLE 6.7   *Dismantling the community-based human-service system: evidence from San Jose, California*

	Indicators of service-dependent population ghetto size	Percentage change in indicators from earlier years
Community care facilities		
(1) Number of facilities	59	−13
(2) Number of beds	863	−20
(3) Supplemental Security Income recipients (SSI)	2,889	−1
(4) Old Age and Survivors Assistance recipients	5,819	−10
(5) AFDC recipients	1,142	−8
(6) Foodstamps recipients	1,164	−32
(7) Medical assistance only	888	−9
(8) Title XX Service cases	214	−65

Notes: Rows (1) and (2) include small and large family homes, group homes and day care for adults, social rehabilitation and vocational rehabilitation facilities located in Zip Code 95112, in 1982. Percentage change figures measure the difference between 1979 and 1982 levels. The data is derived from California State Department of Social Services, Community Care Licensing Division, *Directory of Community Care Facilities in California*, 1979 and 1982, Sacramento, California. Row (3) for Zip Code 95112, in 1979. Percentage change figures measure the difference between 1975 and 1979 levels. The data is derived from HEW/HHS, *Social Security Beneficiaries by Zip Code, San Francisco Region, 1975, 1979*, Washington DC, 1976 and 1980. Row (4) for Zip Code 95112, in 1980. Percentage change figures measure the difference between 1975 and 1980 levels. The data is derived from HEW/HHS, *Social Security Beneficiaries by Zip Code, San Francisco Region, 1975, 1980*, Washington DC, 1976 and 1983. Rows (5)–(8) for Census Tracts 5009, 5010, 5013, 1980. Percentage change figures measure the difference between 1975 and 1980 levels. The data is derived from unpublished files on AFDC, Foodstamps, Medical Assistance Only and Title XX recipients compiled by the Santa Clara County Department of Social Services.

those institutions (Scull, 1981; Rose, 1979). It has been estimated that the chronically mentally ill comprise 44 per cent of the nation's nursing-home population (US Department of Health and Human Services, 1980).

In Santa Clara County, some of the loss in community care capacity seems to have been replaced by skilled-nursing beds, although there are no data on client transfer between types of institutions. Between 1979 and 1982, the service-dependent population ghetto lost 20 per cent of its community care beds and the city lost 4 per cent (123 beds), while between 1978 and 1981 skilled-nursing facility capacity in the city grew by 5 per cent (123 beds), all in non-ghetto locales. The county gained only 82 skilled-nursing beds, indicating a loss in some noncentral cities, leaving San Jose with 48 per cent of total county capacity (California State Department of Health, 1978, 1981).

Reinstitutionalization

Expanded utilization of the state's large-scale institutions for dependent populations is unlikely in the short term. The failure of state hospitals for the mentally ill and physically disabled to meet federal and professional standards for accreditation means that these institutions are ineligible to receive federal reimbursement for services. Since per diem costs for state hospital care greatly exceed community care costs, the fiscal disincentive for using state hospitals without reaccreditation is substantial. In the longer term, however, higher rates of institutional placement are almost certain to occur, as we show in chapter 7.

Besides the state hospitals, county psychiatric institutions serve the more severely dependent. In Santa Clara County, public psychiatric hospital capacity has remained constant for some time. The facilities are always full but due to increased demand for inpatient treatment, lengths of stays are declining. Administrators suggest that incoming client populations are in greater distress, stay shorter periods of time and are released in less satisfactory condition to an unstable community support system. Destabilization in the community results in more frequent admissions and recidivism seems to have increased.

Nontreatment

Nontreatment typically means either homelessness or residence in cheap residential hotels with perhaps only SSI support. Very little is known about the extent to which service-dependents 'disappear' to autonomous, marginal living situations. In Santa Clara County, as across the nation, the rate of homelessness increased as recession and service cutbacks diminished personal resources and access to treatment. Recent reports on skid-row populations, for instance, reveal that a large proportion of the homeless have been released from large institutions, and/or are mentally or physically handicapped. The homelessness problem, as we discuss in chapter 7, has since reached crisis proportions.

The urban future

The prospects for the county's service-dependent populations are bleak. At best they face the status quo, which although inadequate is still preferred by many clients to the total institutions of the past (Dear et al., 1980). Alternatively, they receive insufficient or inappropriate support, or at worst no support at all. These changes in service delivery seriously jeopardize the ability of dependent persons to function in the community and may be expected to erode their already precarious quality of life. Nevertheless, programs to aid displaced service-dependent populations are not a topic of public debate or sustained policy-making; options for new or reinvigorated service systems are not being pursued; nor are local planners yet attempting to design and implement urban land-use policies that could ameliorate either ghettoization or displacement.

San Jose is but one city. Is this process of service-dependent ghetto decline being replicated in other cities? We suspect so, although the outcome is not likely to be universal. Neither ghettoization nor gentrification and renewal are unique to San Jose. As we have illustrated in earlier chapters, studies of service-dependent populations have illustrated a common pattern of ghettoization of clients and facilities in such cities as Washington DC (Trotter and Kutner, 1974); Toronto (Dear and Taylor, 1982); Hamilton, Ontario (cf. chapter 5); and Philadelphia (Wolch, 1980). Examples of gentrification and revitalization are more common, as indicated in the multicity studies by Lipton (1977), James (1977) and Clay (1978). The detailed dynamics of the process clearly vary from place to place, but the major trends documented in Santa Clara County have been experienced widely: federal spending cuts triggering reductions in public and voluntary human services (Salamon and Abramson, 1982; Palmer and Sawhill, 1982); restrictive suburban land-use controls increasing the costs and constraining the supply of peripheral housing as illustrated for the San Francisco Bay area by Frieden (1979) and Dowall (1985); late 1970s housing-price escalation documented for California (Grebler and Mittlebach, 1979) and other parts of the US (Sternlieb et al., 1980); and the entry of major service employers and their white-collar labor force into the urban core as the national economy is restructured (Fainstein and Fainstein, 1982; Sawers and Tabb, 1984; Cohen, 1979; Noyelle, 1983).

Like San Jose, many cities have responded to the newly perceived potentials of downtown by pushing ahead with renewal projects. The ghettoization of service-dependent populations in central cities, often near the CBD and skid-row zones, suggests that these efforts to revitalize old urban centers will involve conflict not only with low-income occupants, but also with dependent populations. The losers in this struggle will likely be the service-dependent. Except when professional goals and client needs coincide, many service-dependent groups are effectively disenfranchised, without the political voice to express their demands. At both federal and local levels, their needs fall through the cracks as social choices and priorities are redefined in the new political–economic environment of the 1980s. In the process, the promising 'solution' of deinstitutionalization and community-based care may be scuttled, to be haphazardly replaced by alternatives that are less desirable, less appropriate and less humane.

The local consequences of deinstitutionalization and community-based service delivery were simply not anticipated by state-level social planners (and legislators) who controlled service policy, until after the Pandora's box was opened. Nor did they appreciate that local governments, with divergent and conflicting interests in land use, were in fact implicit and indispensable partners in the community care experiment. Afterwards, the firm control of land use by local jurisdictions and the fragmentation of government responsibility for service-delivery systems (mental health, criminal justice, developmental disabilities, etc.) prevented the formulation of plans to improve the situation. Local social welfare workers reacted to the flood of clients as best they could, having little choice but to place them and their support facilities in 'soft' inner-city zones as planners in exclusionary suburbs defended 'their' turf from encroachment by service-dependent populations. Now, as they advocate urban revitalization, land-use planners may play a role in fostering ghetto decline and the development of more deleterious service patterns for service-dependent groups.

7

Homelessness and the retreat to institutions

The professional and public commitment to community-based care philosophy that has guided human-service delivery policy for the last three decades may be waning, just at a time when such commitment is needed to make the necessary adjustments to the deinstitutionalization process. Some experts now acknowledge, albeit reluctantly, that community care is an ideal that may never be fully realized in practice. Community service advocates, spurred by genuine concern over the worsening plight of the dependent populations, are enjoying a renewed public interest in their efforts. Yet simultaneously, there are significant signs of retrenchment from community care theory and practice. The emphasis on provision of shelters as an expedient response to the burgeoning problem of the homeless, the growing concern about upgrading or expanding jails and state mental hospitals and the increasing number of mental health professionals who are aligning themselves with the 'new asylum movement', all presage a shift in human-service policy toward *reinstitutionalization* of service-dependent populations.[1]

The future prospects for the service-dependent population have thus altered dramatically. As suggested in chapter 6, the evolving outcomes for dependent individuals include misassignment to inappropriate settings such as jails and nursing homes and homelessness, which ironically has been instrumental in raising public consciousness concerning the dependent but has simultaneously fueled pressures for their reinstitutionalization.

How real is the threat of reinstitutionalization? In this chapter, we assess the growing plight of the mentally disabled in the US, arguing that this group has joined the ranks of prisoners and the homeless in ever-greater numbers. The heart of the question revolves around the public and professional response to misassignment and homelessness. To explore this issue, we document the experience of the mentally disabled in California. Responses to misassignment and the crisis of homelessness there are complex, but have to date generally been characterized by efforts to expand institutional capacity (in both traditional hospital and nonhospital settings); to increase the degree of social control over the mentally disabled; shift the intergovernmental, sectoral and spatial pattern of responsibility for the mentally disabled. All three signal a movement towards reinstitutionalization. A fourth type of response has been increased advocacy by the community mental health movement, culminating in successful litigation and legislative initiatives designed to redress present inadequacies of California's mental health care programs. The mixed character of responses raises a question as to whether the retreat to institutions, spurred perhaps by a small but zealous vanguard, presages a far-reaching philosophical and ideological realignment among professionals and the public or a temporary set-back for the community care movement.

EVOLVING OUTCOMES:
SHRINKING HOUSING SUPPLY, MISASSIGNMENT AND HOMELESSNESS

Since its implementation three decades ago, deinstitutionalization of the mentally disabled has failed to live up to the expectations of politicians, professionals, the public and the disabled themselves. Although legislative initiatives creating a system of community-based mental health care centers represented a positive step toward improving and protecting the rights of the mentally disabled, what emerged were 'awkward' and 'underdeveloped' systems. For a number of reasons, these were unable to provide the long-term care and support services needed by the chronically ill (Nickerson, 1985a). As Lamb (1984), points out:

With the advantage of hindsight, we can see that the era of deinstitutionalization was ushered in with much naivete and many simplistic notions. . . The importance of developing. . .supportive living arrangements was not clearly seen, or at least not implemented. Community treatment was much discussed, but there was no clear idea as to what it should consist of, and the resistance of community mental health centers to providing services to the chronically mentally ill was not anticipated. Nor was it foreseen how reluctant many states would be to allocate funds for community-based services.

(pp. 900–1)

Among the most frequently cited factors responsible for the apparent 'failure' of deinstitutionalization was the lack of financial support for community mental health networks. In many cases mental health funds continued to be targeted to state facilities while cities, already financially burdened, tried to cope with the influx of ex-patients. Lacking sufficient resources, localities found it nearly impossible to construct community care systems that provided the full range of cash and in-kind income supplements, health care, mental health and rehabilitation services needed by this group (Nickerson, 1985a).

Community mental health programs were also plagued by lack of planning and coordination. As Bassuk (1984) notes, community centers failed to coordinate their activities with state institutions. Furthermore, state hospitals provided treatment and services under one roof, whereas no analogous entity was created to oversee the numerous services required by clients living in the community (Lamb, 1984).

Finally, the concept of deinstitutionalization was flawed by the notion that serious, chronic mental disorders could be minimized, if not totally prevented, through care provided within the local community. The community care paradigm was never sufficiently validated, despite its emergence as the conceptual and ideological basis for mental health policy nationwide (Lyons, 1984, p. c4). Consequently, community mental health centers failed to address fully the needs of the mentally disabled, particularly those with chronic illnesses. Rather, programs offered by outpatient clinics emphasized counseling and other therapies aimed at people suffering from anxiety or mild depression, those whose mental problems were not incapacitating and those who showed the most 'promise' for recovery (Nickerson, 1985b).

As we have documented in San Jose and Hamilton, inadequacies in the community-based service network, coupled with urban social and economic conditions, channeled the mentally disabled (along with other service-dependent populations) to decaying central-city areas. Housed in group homes and board-and-care facilities, as well as transinstitutionalized to nursing homes, ex-patients typically subsisted near the poverty line, and – often heavily medicated – 'shuffle[d] to oblivion' (Reich and Siegal, 1973). Nonetheless, most clients preferred to stay out of large-scale institutions, even though they remained unaccepted by and inadequately cared for in the community.

By the late seventies and early eighties, their prospects had changed. Pressures to gentrify and redevelop the urban zone of dependence had begun to push mentally disabled and other service-dependent residents and their support facilities out (Wolch and Gabriel, 1984). Suburban housing price escalation, spurred by the no-growth movements of the seventies, along with continued regional and central-city job expansion, had led middle-income households to inner-city neighborhoods. There, new residents joined city politicians to revitalize their downtowns and improve sagging local tax bases, in an increasingly successful attempt to dismantle the meager community-based service network. At the same time, however, pressure on state hospitals to keep patient counts to a minimum, plus policies to protect client rights by limiting powers of involuntary commitment, foreclosed on a retreat back to state mental hospitals.

Urban renewal and gentrification in the inner city, coupled with cutbacks in social services in the urban core, have forced mentally disabled persons to seek shelter and treatment in increasingly less adequate community settings. Although few studies have attempted to track their mobility systematically, many mentally disabled persons have been found living in single-room occupancy hotels or flophouses, which offer only the most meager of living accommodations and limited access to needed social services. Others have dispersed to adjacent communities that have yet to mount significant opposition to their presence (US General Accounting Office, 1983). A number of trends, however, indicate loss of housing opportunities, increasing misassignment to inappropriate treatment settings and growing rates of homelessness among the mentally disabled.

Loss of housing opportunities

The plight of mentally disabled residents of congregate living quarters seems to have grown substantially worse, primarily as a result of heightened competition for a shrinking supply of adequate facilities. Competition for adequate community living situations has grown because of demolition of facilities in the path of redevelopment and reconversion of properties back to family residential use (Wolch and Gabriel, 1985; Leaman, personal communication, 1985). Moreover, although not well documented, continued neighborhood opposition to group care facilities has frustrated attempts to establish new community care capacity.

On the demand side, the mentally disabled along with other service-dependent groups face growing competition from low-income service workers. Squeezed by a general shortage of low-income housing and attracted to the core area by expansion of service-sector employment opportunities there, low-wage service workers have been reduced to such shelter options as single-room occupancy hotels and boarding houses. Although low-waged, such workers nevertheless can typically outbid the mentally disabled reliant on minimal state housing allowances.

In addition to competition from low-wage laborers, changes in relative payment schedules for retarded vs. mentally disabled has led to provider preferences for retarded clients. In 1977, for example, California began increasing reimbursements for the board and care of retarded adults, while holding down levels for the mentally disabled; the disparity is now almost $500 per month ($945 for retarded adults vs. $503 for mentally disabled) (Jacobs, 1985d, p. I:3). As a result few home operators are willing to take in the mentally disabled, particularly the most severely disturbed who require extensive supervision.

Increasing competition has effectively forced mentally disabled residents out of higher quality board-and-care homes. Many reside in substandard facilities; one-third of the 22,000 licensed board-and-care homes in California, housing 150,000 people, are considered substandard (California State Commission on California Government Organization and Economy, 1983). Others have wound up in run-down apartments and rooming houses and in unlicensed facilities offering little supervision or activity programs, frequently in brutalizing conditions (*Los Angeles Times*, 20 June 1985, p. I:33).

Dimensions of the misassignment phenomenon

Misassignment of the mentally disabled has been recognized as a problem since in the mid-1970s, although rates seem to have been increasing dramatically. Misassignment is a predictable outcome given the shrinking resources and growing need for specialized community-based services for the mentally disabled, particularly the chronically ill. A common destination of the misassigned are skilled-nursing facilities, which offer custodial care and limited health care but no mental health programming. In 1977, 350,000 out of 1.3 million nursing-home residents nationwide were diagnosed with either a primary or secondary level of mental disorder; in 1984, the

National Institutes of Mental Health estimated that the number had increased to 750,000 (US General Accounting Office, 1977; Ahr and Holcomb, 1985; Nickerson, 1985a). In Massachusetts, for example, a survey found that the number of former mental patients residing in nursing homes ranged from 30 per cent to 90 per cent of facility clients (Nickerson, 1985a). Many of these individuals were released from state hospitals, bypassing the community mental health system to 'follow the beds'. Others have undoubtedly been placed in such facilities because of the absence of more appropriate community settings.

The lack of adequate community supports has also led to incarceration of the mentally disabled within the criminal justice system for crimes more indicative of their mental health disabilities than criminal intent. Recent reports suggest that this type of misassignment has reached alarming proportions (Boodman, 1985). Nickerson (1985a, p. 1) quotes a care provider: 'As one mental health professional put it, "mentally ill persons. . .are thought to be too dangerous to be accepted for treatment [at community health centers] but not dangerous enough to be committed [to mental hospitals]. . .the criminal justice system [has become] the system that can't say no". . .they are becoming the. . ."poor man's mental hospital".' In Virginia, for example, at least 12,000 mentally ill persons were estimated to have been jailed annually due to the lack of appropriate community-based residential and psychiatric facilities (Boodman, 1985). This problem is exacerbated by pressure on state hospitals to keep patient counts to a minimum, by policies that protect client rights by limiting involuntary commitment and by society's limited tolerance of the behavior patterns manifested by the mentally ill.

Prisons and jails are now being deluged with mentally disabled persons drawn particularly from the ranks of the homeless. In California, this trend has exacerbated an explosion in the in-carcerated population brought about by the imposition of stiffer sentencing laws and the Administration's 'law and order' stance. Like criminal justice systems in many other parts of the country, the state prison system population has doubled since 1982, now standing in excess of 50,000 persons and is severely overcrowded (by 64 per cent) (*New York Times*, 30 October 1984, p. C1; Paddock, 1985, p. I:16; *Los Angeles Times*, 21 December 1985, p. I:2). In Los Angeles County, the daily jail population jumped from 9,000 inmates in 1980 to the current total of 17,000: 6,000 more than the design capacity of local facilities (Paddock, 1985, p. I:16). While estimates of the mentally disabled proportion of the criminal justice population are scarce (pending state legislation calls for a study of this very issue), state officials acknowledge that poor community living opportunities and the homelessness crisis have resulted in a dramatic upsurge of mentally disabled in the criminal justice system (Richard Mandella, California State Department of Mental Health, Chief, Forensic Services, personal communication, March 1985).

The crisis of the homeless mentally disabled

In some respects, an even more disturbing outcome of deinstitutionalization is the recent and widely publicized increase in the number of homeless mentally disabled. Definitions of homelessness itself vary; the condition is most simply defined as the absence of a stable residence, where one can sleep and receive mail (Robertson, Ropers and Boyer, 1984). This is a relatively broad definition that would include living in a single-room occupancy unit (SRO) as equivalent to having a 'home'. Other definitions of homelessness emphasize the lack of shelter plus a dimension of disaffiliation or social isolation (Bachrach, 1984b). Ellen Bassuk (1984, p. 43) has drawn attention to the complexity of arriving at a simple definition by observing that: 'There is usually no single, simple reason for an individual's becoming homeless; rather homelessness is often the final stage in a lifelong series of crises and missed opportunities, the culmination of a gradual disengagement from supportive relationships and institutions.'

The homeless population is notoriously 'fugitive' and thus difficult to count. National estimates for the US vary widely (table 7.1). A 1984 survey by the Department of Housing and Urban Development suggests that the most likely figure lies between 250,000 and 350,000 per night. This would imply that nightly demand for bed-spaces exceeds the supply by 140,000 (US Department of Housing and Urban Development, 1984). These estimates have been severely criticized by human-service professionals. In contrast to the Department's low estimates, the National Coalition for the Homeless puts the 1985 figure at 2.5 million homeless, up 0.5 million since 1982 (*Los Angeles Times*, 17 February 1985: I:1).

Most analysts agree that numbers of homeless have been increasing, largely due to an expansion in the homeless mentally disabled, thereby radically changing the composition of the homeless population (Bassuk, 1984). For years, the homeless population was typified by the familiar skid-row transient: male, alcoholic, averaging 50 years of age. Now young persons are found among the homeless, as well as women and families. The youthful population consists mainly of so-called 'chronic drifters', frequently diagnosed as schizophrenic or as suffering from affective and personality disorders and substance abuse, but who have never been institutionalized (Bachrach, 1984a; Nickerson, 1985b). Bachrach also cites 'the existence of impoverished and highly stressed social networks, revolving-door utilization of the mental health service system, revolving-door involvement in the criminal justice system, high prevalence of physical illness, and a high degree of resistance to traditional treatment interventions,' as characteristic of many homeless mentally disabled persons (Bachrach, 1984b, p. 12).

Media accounts reveal the extent to which the crisis of the homeless mentally disabled has reached into communities nation-wide. In Boston, for example, most guests at homeless shelters are young (in their thirties) and have a history of mental illness (Nickerson, 1985b, p. 12). In St Louis, roughly half of the clients using homeless services were judged to be mentally disabled, showing symptoms of paranoid ideation and psychosis (Morse et al., 1985). A staggering 97 per cent of all guests at a homeless shelter in the Washington DC area were found to suffer from some form of mental disability (Huguenin, 1984).

Increasing numbers of the homeless mentally disabled have had little or no contact with state hospitals or the ostensible 'safety net' of the community mental health system (Lamb, 1984; Bachrach, 1984). Drastic cutbacks in public spending for social services and the absence of fully developed, coordinated and funded community-based pro-grams for the chronically mentally disabled have exacerbated the crisis. The most important manifestation of crises are twofold, represented in a paradox of inadequate shelter for the homeless, plus underutilization of at least some portion of those shelters that do exist. In Chicago, for instance, where there were an estimated 12–25,000 homeless persons in 1983, there were only 1,078 beds available in 30 shelters. In Los Angeles in 1985, an estimated 90 per cent of the city's 35,000 homeless have no possibility of finding shelter on any given night (Robertson, Ropers and Boyer, 1984, p. 62). However, at the same time as news media stories reveal overcrowding in shelters and the necessity for shelter operators to turn people away on a nightly

TABLE 7.1   *US City size and percentage homeless*

City by region	Number of homeless[a] (1984)	City population[b] (1980)	Rate per 1000 population[c] (low-high)
North-east			
Baltimore	8,000–15,000	786,775	10.17–19.07
Boston	2,000–8,000	562,994	3.55–14.21
Brockton	250	95,172	2.63
Buffalo	500	357,870	1.40
Cleveland	400–1,000	573,822	.70–1.74
Elizabeth	300	106,201	2.82
New York	36,000–50,000	7,071,639	5.09–7.07
Philadelphia	8,000	1,688,210	4.74
Pittsburgh	1,500	423,938	3.54
Rochester	400–500	241,741	1.65–2.07
Springfield	570–780	152,319	3.74–5.12
Syracuse	450	170,105	2.65
Washington DC	5,000–10,000	638,333	7.83–15.67
Worcester	2500	161,799	15.45
South-east			
Atlanta	1,500–3,000	425,022	3.53–8.23
Birmingham	291	284,413	1.02
Jacksonville	150–300	540,920	.28–.55
Miami	4,000	346,865	11.53
New Orleans	700	557,515	1.26
Norfolk	100–300	266,979	.37–1.12
Orlando	400	128,291	3.12
Richmond	2,000–4,000	219,214	9.12–18.25
Midwest			
Chicago	12,000–25,000	3,005,072	3.99–8.32
Denver	1,500–5,000	492,365	3.05–10.16
Detroit	2,000–8,000	1,203,339	1.66–6.65
Minneapolis	900	370,951	2.43
Salt Lake City	600–1,000	163,033	3.68–6.13
Tulsa	1,300	360,919	3.60
North-west			
Portland	1,000–2,000	366,383	2.73–5.46
Seattle	500–5,000	493,846	1.01–10.12

TABLE 7.1 *(Continued)*   US City size and percentage homeless

City by region	Number of homeless[a] (1984)	City population[b] (1980)	Rate per 1000 population[c] (low-high)
South-west			
Fresno	600	218,202	2.75
Los Angeles	22,000–30,000	2,966,850	7.42–10.11
Phoenix	500–6,200	789,704	.63–7.85
San Francisco	4,500–10,000	678,974	6.63–14.73
San Jose	1,000	629,442	1.59
Tucson	3,000	330,537	9.08

Notes:

[a] US Department of Housing and Urban Development, 1984, table 1.

[b] US Department of Commerce, Bureau of the Census, 1980.

[c] Apart from the intrinsic error in estimates of the homeless population, the calculation of the rate of homelessness is significantly impacted by the choice of population base. In this table, *city* population is used to compute the rate. However, different rates are obtained if county or SMSA statistics are used as the base. For example, for both county and SMSA in Los Angeles, the homeless rate drops to 2.94–4.01 (compared with 7.42–10.11 in the table). In New York, the SMSA-based rate of homelessness is 3.95–5.48; for the county base, 25.21–35.01. For this sample of cities, there can be no consistent preference for city, county or SMSA figures. This, plus the inherent unreliability in the homelessness figures, has led us to the arbitrary choice of city-based estimates for this evidence.

basis, some shelters frequently report underutilization. The Department of Housing and Urban Development Report estimates that, nationally, shelters are often only utilized up to 70 per cent of their capacity. This estimate must be treated with caution, however. A more recent (1985) survey of 23 shelters with 1,500 beds in Los Angeles reported an average vacancy rate of only three beds per night per shelter – an overall vacancy rate of 4.6 per cent (Los Angeles County Community and Senior Citizens Services Department, 1985, p. 47). One main reason for underutilization appears to be the operating procedures and living conditions of many shelters. These include intrusive intake procedures, degrading in-house routines, filthy and unhealthy conditions, restrictions on length of stay and the ever-present threat of violence (Bassuk, 1984; Baxter and Hopper,

1982). In addition, many shelters have restrictive admission policies (for example men only; no mentally disabled; battered women only; Los Angeles County Community and Senior Citizens Services Department, 1985).

Homelessness in California has grown dramatically since 1980, according to both formal and informal estimates. The most recent count of the unsheltered population stands at 75,000 (Jacobs, 1985d). State mental health officials corroborate findings of the few research reports that have been done, as well as informal estimates of service operators: approximately 20 to 40 per cent of the homeless in California are mentally disabled; if drug and alcohol abusers are included (many of whom suffer mental disabilities), the proportion is considerably higher (Jacobs, 1985d; Robertson, Ropers and Boyer, 1985). Los Angeles in particular has become a 'mecca' for the homeless. Dubbed the 'homeless capital of the nation', Los Angeles County is estimated to have up to 30,000 homeless (US Department of Housing and Urban Development, 1984). Local estimates indicate that a high proportion of the homeless population is mentally disabled, either ex-patients released from state mental hospitals, or part of the 'young chronic drifter' population (Lamb, 1982).

PUBLIC OUTCRY AND PROFESSIONAL PRESSURE: THE CALIFORNIA RESPONSE

Research on community-based care problems in California in general, and in Los Angeles County in particular, enables a preliminary assessment of the response to mounting public and professional pressure to ameliorate the crisis of the mentally disabled. California is frequently a 'bellwether' state, at the forefront of social policy trends and so examination of the California case may be indicative of future events in other areas. The current mood in California is not optimistic; as one mental health leader indicated, 'it will take a long time and many more restorations to get the [California] program back to where we were in the mid-1970s. And we were not in good shape then' (Elpers, in Jacobs, 1985c, p. 11).

As detailed in chapter 6, California released large numbers of mentally disabled clients from its state hospital system during the 1960s, established county-run community-based services and altered involuntary commitment laws that inhibited hospitalization. Local governments were not prepared to establish comprehensive mental health treatment programs, many were not particularly committed to the notion of community-based care, and coordination between the state hospital system and fledgling local programs was minimal. Most significantly, state funds were inadequate. Subsequent fiscal policies at all levels of government exacerbated the situation; in particular Proposition 13 and the Reagan Administration social spending reductions 'sent the system into a tailspin' (Anderson, 1984, p. 215). Federal cuts have not been offset by increased state or local spending; during his first year in office, Governor Deukmejian vetoed $30 million for mental health, following the trend of curtailing mental health budgets set by his predecessor Brown. During fiscal year 1985 Deukmejian has requested increases in state funding for mental health, but state financial support will still be less than before he took office, even if increases are appropriated (Jacobs, 1985a, p. I:1).

What have been the results of this haphazard transfer of care of California's mentally disabled to the community level? And what have been the major elements in the political response to the mounting problems of the state's mentally disabled population? Our work has uncovered: deteriorating living conditions for the mentally disabled in the community; mounting incarceration of the mentally disabled; and increased homelessness. Although just emerging and not yet well documented, several responses in the direction of reinstitutionalization of the mentally disabled can be identified, as well as efforts to strengthen the community-based service system. These responses include:

- public policy initiatives to increase and protect state and local institutional capacity;
- public policies to strengthen social control measures;
- state and local policies and community opposition movements, to shift the intergovernmental, sectoral and spatial division of responsibility for the mentally disabled; and
- renewed advocacy efforts designed to correct the problems created by deinstitutionalization as implemented over the past two decades.

Institutional capacity

State and local governments are seeking to expand the institutional capacity available to handle the mentally disabled. These efforts include:

1 construction of and increased funding for shelters for the homeless;
2 the upgrading of the state mental hospital system and expansion of local inpatient facilities; and
3 expansion of criminal-justice beds, along with segregation of mentally disordered offenders.

Together, these policies represent an effort toward reinstitutional-ization of a growing proportion of the mentally disabled.

The construction and expansion of existing shelters for the home-less has occurred across the state, especially in urban areas deluged by the hungry and homeless. While these shelters are designed as temporary or transitional lodging, residents frequently have extended lengths of stay, or rotate in and out of shelters on a continuous basis. As a result, these facilities have become yet another way in which the mentally disabled are institutionalized and hence spatially and socially isolated.

In an effort to increase the number and capacity of shelters, new state legislation has been initiated to supply emergency shelters for the homeless and for veterans and to develop transitional housing. The initial state augmentation proposed for shelters was $20 million. Public shelter capacity in Los Angeles County, which stood at about 1,500 bed-spaces as of spring 1984, received a boost with the con-struction of a 19,000 square-foot, 138-bed 'temporary' plywood shelter, built by union volunteers in the skid-row zone of Los Angeles. There have also been various initiatives to construct new additional shelters in the cities of Santa Monica and West Hollywood, as well as in San Pedro and San Fernando Valley districts of the City of Los Angeles (Los Angeles County Department of Mental Health, 1985; *Los Angeles Times*, 28 June 1985, p. II:4; Clayton, 1985, p. I2).[2]

California has also led the way in funding increased resources for the state mental hospital system, in an effort to upgrade staffing levels and improve seriously deteriorated physical facilities. The Deukmejian Administration has committed itself to spending $133 million over the next five years (1985–90) to accomplish this goal. Programs are being designed to permit the hospital system to meet national professional standards and be reaccredited for receipt of federal reimbursements; but no specific long-term commitment has been made to community-based service delivery – a pattern similar to that found in other states (Jacobs, 1985b, p. I3:2; Boodman, 1985, p. A16; Nickerson, 1985a, p. 22).

Efforts to upgrade the state mental hospitals have been supported by the state's psychiatric workers' union, which is concerned with state hospital safety problems (Hernandez, 1985, p. I24:3). Re-accreditation is also the objective of many mental health professionals influenced by the 'new asylum' movement in psychiatry. Advocates of this movement see an upgraded state hospital system as a necessary and valuable resource for the most severely disabled. Proponents point to the number of acutely ill and often dangerous persons who require a more 'structured' environment, particularly some severe chronic schizophrenics (Lamb and Lamb, 1984; Krauthammer, 1985; Lamb and Peele, 1984; Rosenblatt, 1984; Boffey, 1984; Talbott, 1984). A long-term asylum may be a necessary and humane option: 'the snake pit was probably better than lying on a grate in the middle of a New England winter' (*Los Angeles Times*, 18 February 1985, p. I:5). According to some leading psychiatrists, 'the goal [in the case of the chronically disturbed] would be to provide the patient with a comfortable and friendly asylum' (Bassuk, 1984, p. 45). Involuntary placement in asylums admittedly may infringe on client rights; an 'asylum means taking people away to be cared for, whether they like it or not. That means taking control – and that means violating their rights, as currently defined' (Krauthammer, 1985, p. A15a). But some suggest that the only solution to the problem of rights violation is to limit the rights in question (Lamb, 1984).[3]

Plans to upgrade the system do not increase the bed capacity of the state hospital system, but increasingly the quality of care may reduce existing disincentives for utilization of these facilities. Moreover, long-range plans for the mental health system, still in the initial design stage, include proposals to increase hospital capacity and to expand community-based service capacity. Instead of the 2,200 short-term care beds now in place in the state mental hospital system, a new model plan for mental health service system development (dubbed the 'California Model') calls for increasing that number to 3,900; and instead of the current 1,800 long-term rehabilitation beds in existence, the plan suggests the need for more than 10,000 (Jacobs, 1985b).

In addition to targeting funds for improvement of the state mental hospital system, California has adopted a renewed policy of transferring responsibility for the mentally disabled to the county level, this time with some additional resources. The new state budget calls for a 14 per cent ($40 million) augmentation in local mental health programs, to be allocated to individual counties for the buy-out of state hospital beds (according to initial proposals) as well as a 4 per cent cost-of-living increase for local programs. The majority of the funds, however, are to be used by counties in developing state-approved community programs that can range from long-term hospital beds to independent living arrangements and day-treatment services (California Legislative Analyst, 1985).

While seemingly supportive of community-based services, there is some indication that local discretion in the utilization of augmentation funds will lead to the development of more extensive inpatient facilities. This may result from professional pressures for more acute-care beds, as well from community pressures to remove the mentally ill from their midst. In Los Angeles County, for example, the Director of County Mental Health proposes to use most of the $13.8 million state allocation to build new or support existing residential capacity: for psychiatric beds ($5.1 million); to support shelters for the homeless ($857,461); for children's inpatient beds and services ($2 million); and for mentally ill in the jails ($791,251) (Los Angeles County Department of Mental Health, 1985). This leaves approximately $5 million for other services. After deducting cost-of-living adjustments and administrative services, community-based out-patient, outreach and other support programs are left with only $1.5 million – or about 11 per cent – for the community-based system. This is still a substantial increase over initial proposals by the Department made earlier in 1985.

One of the factors underlying this emphasis on beds is the vocal opposition of many local politicians and community leaders to any further reductions in state hospital bed capacity and their demands that the indigent mentally disabled be removed from the streets. During the 1985 hearings on the state mental health budget, for example, the Department of Mental Health advised that 399 beds at a hospital in the Los Angeles vicinity be 'bought out' by counties. These beds would be closed and the funds redirected to counties on the basis of local proposals to meet mental health needs via alternative, community-based service provision. This proposal was vehemently quashed by legislators, led by a state senator from the Los Angeles area. Policy-makers questioned whether proposed community-based programs had demonstrated the ability to substitute for state mental hospital beds. Moreover, they emphasized that political pressure from business and community leaders to curb and control the homeless population was so strong that proposals to reduce the state's capacity to isolate the mentally disabled from society would be soundly defeated (William De Risi, California Department of Mental Health, Division of State Hospitals, personal communication, March 1985).

Lastly, the state response to the exploding prison population is to build more bed capacity. The Deukmejian Administration has won voter approval for a $1.2 billion bond issue to add capacity for 19,000 inmates by 1989. In addition, abandoned facilities will be drawn into service, instructional and recreation rooms (day rooms, classrooms and gymnasiums) in existing prisons may be used for temporary bed-spaces and minimum security facilities will be upgraded to house a wider range of offenders (*Los Angeles Times*, 2 September 1985, p. I:4). In addition to building more beds, the criminal justice system is increasingly attempting to segregate mentally ill offenders and transfer them to state mental hospitals (*Los Angeles Times*, 2 September 1985, p. III-4; California Legislative Analyst, 1985). The Department of Corrections budget request for 1985-6 includes funds for additional state mental hospital bed-spaces – a 250 per cent increase in contracted space since 1982-3 (California Legislative Analyst, 1985, p. 999).

Increasing social control

In addition to policies related to institutional capacity, state administrators and legislators have initiated policies that dramatically increase the degree of social control over the mentally disabled, particularly offenders. These initiatives are designed to reduce the prison overcrowding problem by transferring mentally disordered prisoners to the mental health system and to prevent the release of potentially violent offenders at the end of their terms. Furthermore, pressure to revise basic commitment laws (Lanterman–Petris–Short Act) is growing and likely to result in legislative action. Local officials' organizations such as the League of California Cities and professional groups including the Los Angeles Psychiatric Association, are behind such initiatives (Jacobs, 1985a, p. I:1).

Two bills currently under discussion in the State Legislature are indicative of the new efforts to alter involuntary commitment procedures as they affect mentally disordered offenders. Although they have been amended and weakened during legislative debate, both bills have similar agenda: to circumvent indeterminant sentencing laws and to require state hospital treatment of mentally disordered offenders coming out of the criminal justice system. One Senate Bill (1054), as originally drafted, would have blocked the release of as many as 300 prisoners per year. According to this bill, a new condition of parole would be acceptance of mental hospital treatment unless the State Department of Mental Health certifies that the offender will not be a danger to the health and safety of others while on outpatient status and will benefit from outpatient status. Once an outpatient, treatment would be compulsory; failure to submit to treatment could result in immediate return to state hospital. The other Senate Bill (1296) is similar. It introduces special provisions for one-year commitment of mentally disordered violent offenders after their sentences have been completed, without court hearing. This essentially extends their incarceration in either prison or state mental hospital until they are deemed 'sufficiently improved'. In the absence of any improvement in condition, commitment can be extended, subject to court hearing, every year. Again, once on parole, parolees are subject to compulsory treatment and to the threat of return to prison or hospital should they refuse such treatment.[4]

Shifting the problem

The crises of homelessness and the jail population explosion have in many ways become 'political footballs', with responsible parties attempting to deflect the problem to one another and thereby avoiding the burden of solution and/or failure. These concerted efforts to foist the 'knotty problem' onto others include attempts:

1 to alter the intergovernmental division of responsibility for the mentally disabled;
2 to change the sectoral division of labor between mental health and criminal justice departments; and
3 to shift the spatial distribution of caring responsibilities among urban districts and communities.

At the level of intergovernmental relations, California has clearly followed a policy of reducing state provision of services, instead providing counties with funds and administrative support to develop 'local' systems of mental health care. This is also, however, a way to situate the burden of failure at the local level and to insulate the Deukmejian Administration from attacks on the state's mental health program. At the same time, local governments faced with major budgetary dilemmas due to soaring relief costs have begun to attack the state for lack of attention and action on the homelessness question and for past failures in mental health policy. For instance, Los Angeles County blamed over half of its $37.5 million deficit on expansion of homelessness and poverty relief program costs

(Vollmer, 1985a, p. II1). Over half of the continually increasing number of relief requests are from the homeless (Vollmer, 1985b, p. II6). In response, the Los Angeles Grand Jury charged that the state is 'shirking its responsibility' for the homelessness problem by requiring localities to provide relief programs but not providing funds for them (Connell, 1985a). In their report to the County Board of Supervisors, the Jury also claimed that the state has sent the mentally disabled back to counties but failed to send sufficient funds to meet their needs (Connell, 1985a). Politically, this has been a (successful) strategy to pressure the state to expand its local funding for the homeless.

Ongoing struggles between the State Departments of Mental Health and Corrections reveal the sectoral dimension of problem shifting. Because of differences in professional orientation and the political pressures to which each unit is subject, there have been several attempts to transfer responsibility for care of mentally disordered offenders between mental health and criminal justice. The Department of Mental Health favors the development of a continuum of treatment settings for mentally disordered offenders within (and by) the criminal justice system, given their growing numbers in prisons and jails. In contrast, the Department of Corrections is under severe pressure to expand prison capacity and relieve overcrowding. Transfer of mentally disordered offenders to state mental hospitals is an attractive way to help alleviate the pressure for new prison construction. The Mental Health Department response, on the basis of both theory and practice, is to reserve the use of asylums for the noncriminally insane (Richard Mandella, personal communication, March 1985).

Lastly, business groups, residential communities and local governments have all attempted to shift the problem of hosting facilities for the homeless and mentally disabled to other locales. The Los Angeles case is particularly revealing. The homeless population there is concentrated in 'skid row', directly east of the central business district. Here, single-room occupancy hotels, emergency service agencies, temporary employment agencies, missions and public parks provide support and space for the population. This concentration is the historical legacy of explicit strategies by the City of Los Angeles and its Community Redevelopment Agency (CRA) to 'contain' the homeless via spatial segregation and isolation. However, as in other service-dependent ghettos, attempts are now being made to dismantle 'skid row'. Currently, CRA plans for the central business district expansion are impeded by skid row, leading to an effort to 'move' skid row further east.

In response, a new association of eastern downtown businesses (mainly light industry) has been established to fight this move and to demand concessions from CRA. The association claims that it is unable and unwilling to bear even greater burdens of proximity to the ghetto. As a result, CRA has doubled security forces in the area (Ackerman, 1985, p. 1). The CRA also compromised on the issue of relocating its 'temporary' shelter and promised to make the relocated shelter 'temporary' – it now has a one-year life (Connell, 1985b). The councilman for the skid-row district reportedly has no intention of allowing a 'total concentration' of homeless shelters there and has proposed the creation of an 'outdoor home' for street people in Saugus, a distant semirural part of the city's fringe (Connell, 1985b).[5]

As the problem of the homeless has become increasingly visible, it has begun to impinge on better-off neighborhoods hitherto unaccustomed to the sight of homeless persons. In Santa Monica, a mounting homelessness problem has been blamed on the state and the City of Los Angeles; both are seen as failing to provide adequate services for the homeless, who are then encouraged to migrate from downtown Los Angeles to Santa Monica. Waiting for others to take action, the city has not proposed concrete local solutions or programs to meet the needs of the homeless.

Advocacy efforts to avoid reinstitutionalization

Pressure for reinstitutionalization and tighter social controls on the mentally disabled have put community mental health advocates on the defensive. Amid accusations that deinstitutionalization was a failure, community mental health leaders have attempted to show that the policy itself was not misguided, but its implementation was faulty. In addition, advocates have been active in resisting local efforts to target augmentation funds for inpatient facilities, insisting on more funds for community-based residential alternatives and outpatient services (*Los Angeles Times*, 28 June 1985, p. II:4). Along with the American Civil Liberties Union, they have also fought changes in involuntary commitments and treatment procedures for mentally disordered offenders and succeeded in substantially weakening proposed legislation (Jacobs, 1985c).

Progressive efforts to reform and support the community-based mental health system have also been advocated by community mental health organizations and parent associations. As a result of their input, legislation has been passed which seeks to augment the community-based resource pool dramatically. The bill provides for additional funds for the homeless mentally disabled, isolated elderly and the mentally disabled in jail; increases payments to board-and-care operators for the mentally disabled; establishes local treatment programs for those mentally disabled jailed for minor offenses; doubles the number of therapy sessions allowed under Medi-Cal (California's version of Medicaid), now limited to two per month; and launches a model program to monitor potentially dangerous mentally ill offenders after their release from prison to make certain they receive adequate treatment in the community (Jacobs, 1985c). This legislation (the Bronzan–Mojonnier Assembly Bill 2541) has met with remarkable success, although funding was not appropriated at the .level necessary to fully implement the bill's proposals.

Other proposed bills are also encouraging. For instance, Senate Bill SB 667 would require that homeless persons who are detained under the provision of the Lanterman–Petris–Short Act receive special attention at the time of discharge, instead of simply being released. A second Senate Bill (822) requires the Department of Mental Health to set up $1.5 million pilot programs in three large urban counties to provide case management services to homeless chronically mentally disabled persons. Amendments to the 1957 Short–Doyle Act in a third Assembly Bill (2381), provide additional financial incentives for new and more innovative programs at the county level and streamline relationships between counties and the state (Bronzan, 1984).

In addition to legislation, the development of a model continuum of mental health care has begun, although it is still in the research and financial analysis stages and has not been officially endorsed by the Department of Mental Health. (This is the 'California Model' referred to earlier.) The proposal, developed by a group including legislative staff, county and state mental health officials, professionals and patient and family advocate organizations, describes a continuum of mental health care that should be available in each community. The mix of services specified in the model makes concessions to demands for more institutional capacity, as mentioned earlier; however, community treatment facilities are heavily emphasized. Preliminary cost estimates suggest that such a model system would require a doubling of mental health expenditures, to $1.8 billion. While not likely to become official policy in the immediate future, the California Model does provide a well-articulated vision of an adequate community-based mental health system (Jacobs, 1985b).

In other parts of the US, positive steps are also underway. For example, Massachusetts has planned to spend $10.8 million in 1985 for expansion of income, medical and mental health care to homeless persons in the community, while also allocating $13.6 million in programs to prevent homelessness (including rental assistance and utility payments; Henshaw, 1984, p. I36:4). New Jersey is committed to spending an additional $7 million on mental health centers and residential development projects for the mentally disabled; Bergen County has used these funds to build scattered-site facilities in upper- and middle-income areas (*New York Times*, 31 May 1984, p. I:26:4). In western Massachusetts, a model community-based care plan similar to other plans in Madison, Denver and Rockland County, New York, offers a rich continuum of services (Goleman, 1984, p. III 1:4)). Lastly, all across the country, public interest lawyers have gone to bat for the homeless and mentally disabled, putting barriers in the way of reinstitutionalization and obtaining increased and improved services in the community.

Perhaps the single most important intervention was the announcement (in early 1986) of the Program for the Chronically Mentally Ill. Under the joint auspices of the Robert Wood Johnson Foundation and the US Department of Housing and Urban Development (HUD), the Foundation will provide $28 million in grants and low-interest loans to eight of the 60 largest US cities. HUD will provide rent subsidies to help the selected cities to obtain appropriate housing; and the Social Security Administration (SSA) will work to ensure the effectiveness of the disability determination process. The Program will seek to develop community-wide systems of care, including health, mental health, social services and housing opportunities. Its ultimate purpose is to help the chronically mentally disabled to function more effectively in their everyday lives and to avoid inappropriate institutionalization.

BACK TO BACK WARDS?

To some, reinstitutionalization seems like a simple solution to the problems of deinstitutionalization such as homelessness. But activity and treatment programs geared to the needs of long-term patients can easily be set up in the community, and living conditions, structured or unstructured, can be raised to any level we choose – if adequate funds are made available.

(Lamb, 1984, p. 904)

Is widespread reinstitutionalization likely to become the new policy dominant? Seen in historical perspective, such a direction seems entirely predictable. In chapter 3, we argued that public workhouses developed as an early form of support for indigent populations. The insane and other disabled groups accumulated in prison basements since there was nowhere else to put them. One of the first great advances in social welfare was to recognize the need for a separate asylum for the dependent, away from the other deviant prison populations. As a consequence, large asylums were built in remote locations to contain the mad, aged, chronically ill and the mentally deficient. A culture of expansionism saw such institutions proliferate in many countries. Ultimately, the asylum came to dominate the landscape with its own peculiar geography of haunted places.

We contend that history is now repeating itself. Although public workhouses are rare, such a workhouse was opened in Sacramento, California, in 1983. One could receive assistance only if one lived there, surrendering any residence and could work there only in the absence of an alternative job (Stoner, 1984). It seems highly unlikely that workhouses will again become the preferred mode of social assistance; however, prisons have once again taken up the role of custodial care that they held in the eighteenth and nineteenth centuries. It has been estimated that about one-eighth of California's prison population is 'severely mentally ill' (*Los Angeles Times*, 18 February 1985, p. II-6). And in Canada, a pilot project to separate the mentally disabled in prisons from the regular inmate population was announced recently (*Toronto Globe and Mail*, 18 September 1984, p. 9).

The historical parallels do not stop there. We have once again begun to build (or convert existing structures to) relatively large-scale, isolated 'asylums'. In New York City, a shelter for the homeless was built recently on an isolated and uninhabited island. Its operating capacity was originally 180, but during 1985, it sheltered in excess of 800 persons daily. Many New York homeless are encouraged to take a bus to Camp La Guardia, a rural-based, 970-bed facility in upstate New York (Baxter and Hopper, 1982). Finally, we once again seem to be embarking on a period of institutional expansionism, as indicated in the California case.

Our studies of prospects for reinstitutionalization in California reinforce predictions based on these historical parallels. Some encouraging program developments aimed at strengthening the community-based services system are underway; but these are to some degree overshadowed by ominous signs of renewed professional emphasis, societal willingness and increased legal authority to isolate the mentally disabled in new institutions. While less is known about the situation of other service-dependent groups, it is possible that the backlash against community-based care will filter down to affect patterns of service provision in other sectors, just as the idea of deinstitutionalization of the mentally disabled came to be advocated throughout the human services.

Our belief in the continuing relevance of deinstitutionalization and the merits of community care underlie the final chapters of this book. In them, we address the issue of planning and strategy in support of an effective community-based human-services network.

Part III
Public policy for the city

8

From homelessness to deinstitutionalization: closing the circle

Homelessness is a symbol of that part of the deinstitutionalization process which failed. As pointed out in the academic literature and the popular press, gross inadequacies in the quality and availability of primary support services face those now residing outside institutions – from the mentally disabled to ex-offenders and the retarded.[1] A combination of factors now threatens a return to the institution. Yet we believe that deinstitutionalization was, and is, a worthwhile goal. In the closing chapters of this book, we outline planning principles that could move us *from homeless to deinstitutionalization* – that is, to complete the process of evolution in social welfare policy by *delivering* on the promise of deinstitutionalization.

The problems experienced during deinstitutionalization were twofold. First, most if not all of the major participants in the program (clients, professionals, communities, planners) were ill-prepared to implement deinstitutionalization or to cope with either its anticipated or unforeseen consequences. Clients accustomed to the total institution had difficulties coping in less protected settings, often lacking in vital supports. Professional experience with community care was limited and ambiguities arose not only in diagnosing individual needs, but in referring clients to proper service modalities (Test, 1981; Group for the Advancement of Psychiatry, 1978). Both these problems were exacerbated by the rigid professional boundaries between elements of the service system (Hobbs, 1975; Fincher, 1977). Professional expectations of what community care could accomplish for the chronically dependent may also have been too high; and in not recognizing that rehabilitation was an unrealistic goal for many service-dependent persons, the basic needs and rights of chronic clients were neglected in favor of more 'promising' individuals (Lamb, 1981; Lewis, 1982; Rose, 1979; Scull, 1981). Some communities unfamiliar with the problems and support requirements of service-dependent groups reacted to protect themselves from perceived threats, while others unable to resist became saturated with clients and facilities (Dear and Taylor, 1982; Wolpert and Wolpert, 1976). And local planners, who maintained a commitment to integrated social and physical planning practices, were without political support, institutional mechanisms, or program resources to solve the problems created by deinstitutionalization.

Secondly, the roles and routines of these human agents (initially constrained by inadequate and inappropriate funding) were rapidly overtaken by the maelstrom of socioeconomic and political events – the economic and social welfare restructuring – which struck in the seventies and eighties. Funding occurred at levels far below those needed to support the kind of comprehensive service network required for successful client rehabilitation or even maintenance in the community (Estroff, 1981). Mandated eligibility requirements for various programs created distorting incentives which resulted in the inappropriate use of services (US General Accounting Office, 1977; Rubin, 1981). The system of private board-and-care homes which developed in the US largely in response to the availability of federal funding (principally Supplemental Security Income) created inevitable conflicts between providers' profit motives and client requirements for more or less restrictive settings (Emerson et al., 1981; Edgerton, 1975; Scull, 1981). Inner-city planners faced political pressure to take advantage of a restructuring urban context that held potential for private-sector gentrification plus state-supported urban renewal and economic development. These events forced planners to make difficult trade-offs between clients' well-being and fiscal gains for hard-pressed municipal budgets. With the advent of dramatic reductions in social spending and increasing demands for services due to recession and deindustrialization, we are, in effect, witnessing unprepared human agents practicing deinstitutionalization in a structural setting that has been dramatically transformed.

So, what is to be done? In this final part of the book, we address the normative implications of our work. In chapter 9, we develop planning policies to assist those responsible for human-service delivery; and in chapter 10, we close by returning to the wider context of community-based care. But before moving to praxis, however, we return to the inner-city ghetto, or zone of dependence, which has become something of an 'icon' in this study. Our view of this icon has undergone significant changes during the analysis. The ghetto began in the core of nineteenth-century cities as a zone of transition, an incipient zone of dependence. As institutional alternatives were introduced and expanded, it became a secondary locale of human-service delivery in a decaying inner city. Finally, it became the unwitting target of the deinstitutionalization juggernaut and was transformed into the service-dependent ghetto.

First recognized as a surprising side-effect of deinstitutionalization, the ghetto soon became appreciated for its positive, supportive characteristics. For the service-dependent, the inner city had, in essence, become a coping network. Now, however, new signs are being read into the iconography of the ghetto. It has taken on a pathological character – a place where social problems are exacerbated and reproduced. For instance, many homeless are reputedly migrating from the dangerous and violent Skid Row area of Los Angeles to the safer environs of Santa Monica and West Hollywood.

We want to use this disturbing picture of pathology as a point of departure in developing planning strategies for human-service delivery. In this chapter, we reexamine the iconography of homelessness and use the landscape of the ghetto as a text for reinterpreting the present and anticipating the future.

HOMELESSNESS RECONSIDERED

Homelessness, at its most elementary level, is caused by a series of adverse events. These include eviction, loss of job, discharge from an institution, personal crises (such as divorce or domestic violence) and withdrawal of financial support (City of Chicago Task Force on Emergency Shelter, 1983). These are experiences that, in the normal course of events, can be absorbed by their victims with tolerable levels of discomfort. However, for the groups of 'potentially homeless', such events are sufficient to propel them into homelessness. It is, of course, difficult to define the potentially homeless person, but the demographic composition of the homeless provides some insight into this question.

About half of the people who are currently homeless are victims of economic circumstances – ordinary people who are simply down on their luck (Robertson, Ropers and Boyer, 1985, p. 20). This group includes many young people, women and families. Another quarter of the homeless population consists of ex-psychiatric patients and substance abusers; and the remainder are victims of personal crisis or natural disaster. It must be remembered that these figures are broad generalizations and the composition of the homeless population in any district will necessarily reflect local conditions. For example, in some cities, at least half the homeless are ex-psychiatric patients or persons exhibiting mental disorders (Alter et al., 1984).

Two of the major preconditions for homelessness can be inferred from such data: economic hardship and deinstitutionalization. During the recent economic downturn, poverty levels and unemployment reached alarming proportions. Deindustrialization and economic restructuring are causing acute hardship and have been associated with a shrinkage of budgets available for social welfare programs. The Welfare State is now being restructured increasingly to 'privatize' welfare provision. Direct state services are being replaced by commercial and nonprofit service sectors, and the general level of service provision is being curtailed. Both the restructuring of the economy and the Welfare State have had fundamental consequences for the fledgling deinstitutionalization movement. The recession placed massive new demands on the welfare safety-net at the same time as that network was being severely cut back and recast. This was surely a recipe for disaster. The deinstitutionalization movement, one might say, never stood a chance.

The supply of shelter to meet the needs of the newly homeless is extremely limited. The construction of low-income and assisted housing programs in the US has effectively halted. Fewer than half the six million housing units recommended in 1968 by then-President Johnson were ever built. Department of Housing and Urban Development-sponsored renovations and construction declined to a total of 203,113 units under Carter (1979), to just over 55,000 units under Reagan in 1983 (Alter et al., 1984, p. 22–3). Such stock as already exists has been severely depleted. This is especially the case in the SRO hotel and cheap lodging-home sectors, where government-sponsored gentrification and urban-renewal schemes have removed much housing suitable for the service-dependent. In Chicago, for example, 300 SRO units were lost to gentrification in 1981–2, and a total of 18,000 units have been demolished or converted since 1973 (Fustero, 1984, p. 59; City of Chicago, 1985, p. 23). In New York, government-sponsored urban-renewal legislation encouraged the demolition of SROs and their replacement by luxury apartments; between 1975 and 1981, over 31,000 units were lost (Kasinitz, 1984). Remaining housing opportunities tend to be confined to the inner city, as we have seen, as a result of vociferous community opposition and the zoning practices of risk-averse land-use planners.

In summary, the inner-city landscape is one in which a rapidly increasing demand for assistance is met by a diminished capacity to supply both shelter and services. The population at risk in this system must be regarded as 'potentially homeless'. The subsequent experience of a single adverse event is sufficient to tip this marginalized population into homelessness.

The descent into homelessness is not, however, the end of our account. A reading of the ghetto landscape suggests the emergence of a pathological condition: 'chronic homelessness'. The experience of life on the streets is actively creating a new set of social problems that are likely to perpetuate the crisis of homelessness.

THE CULTURE OF CHRONICITY

What causes a person, once homeless, to remain homeless? The answer to this question lies somewhere in the pathology of everyday life on the streets. There is sufficient evidence in the literature to suggest that it is the *experience of service-dependency* that primarily determines the fate of the homeless. Five factors appear to determine whether or not an individual will escape from homelessness. These factors are:

- the experience of shelter;
- financial status;
- availability of assistance;
- personal status; and
- street experience.

The experience of shelter services themselves can exacerbate the homeless condition. Some shelters may exclude certain groups of people through eligibility requirements (no mentally disabled, for example). Other shelters have intrusive routines of intake and residence which can often have a degrading and humiliating effect on residents. In addition, living conditions in shelters, including the threat of violence, can often depress the morale of the newly homeless (Baxter and Hopper, 1982).

Without shelter, the daily life of the homeless individual is precarious. Financial resources are minimal. Welfare payments are so low that survival is barely possible. Canadian welfare payments are now set at a level exactly equal to one-half of the official poverty line (*Macleans*, 13 January 1986). The homeless in Los Angeles receive sufficient funds for three weeks' SRO accommodation; the fourth week of rent and the entire food budget are left unaccounted for. The incomes of the homeless are frequently supplemented by day labor (for example leafletting), begging and prostitution (City of Chicago, Task Force on Emergency Shelter, 1983, pp. 33–55). Wage earnings are inadequate to permit the acquisition of stable housing options.

The fate of the homeless person depends not only on income and financial assistance. Other forms of support are necessary, including soup kitchens, job-search services, help with clothing and so on. While agencies providing such support do exist, access to their services is frequently rationed by waiting lists and subject to intrusive bureaucratic rules. (Until recently, Los Angeles County's notorious '60-day rule' allowed welfare officers to suspend claimants' payments for some real or perceived breach of agency rules.) A day in the life of the homeless is often spent standing in line: for food, for shelter vouchers, for welfare interviews (Rousseau, 1981).

How well one stands up to the rigors of life on the street depends very much on personal strength, both emotional and physical. It is difficult to remain optimistic and healthy when cleanliness is an impossible goal, sleep is a luxury and nutritional food a scarcity. To sleep in the open in wintertime can cause death through freezing; in the summer, sunburn and sunstroke. To sleep in public shelters at night often leaves lice infestations by morning and empty pockets to boot (Baxter and Hopper, 1982). Other everyday experiences of life on the streets can accelerate the downturn in morale, physical appearance and health status. Muggings are a common problem; the homeless are constantly harassed by police and other street people. In Chicago, one sample of homeless people reported their major daytime activity as 'moving or walking', largely for self-protection and to remove themselves from continual harassment (City of Chicago Task Force on Emergency Shelter, 1983).

Under these circumstances, it is not surprising that the descent into 'chronic' homelessness can be sickeningly quick. Anecdotal evidence from Long Beach, California, reports of one shelter that refused beds to people who had been homeless for more than two weeks, on the grounds that they were already beyond rehabilitation. Most cities report that the length of the 'homeless episode' is steadily increasing. If our analysis is correct, then the primary impetus for chronic homelessness is the practice of social welfare programs. The social dislocation associated with homelessness is being exacerbated by a caring system stretched beyond its limits. As a consequence, the *experience of homelessness itself perpetuates homelessness.*

Homelessness thus has a 'cumulative' effect on its victims. Once on the street, physical and mental health problems surface rapidly, even among those who were victims of economic dislocation rather than service-dependency. For example, depression appears to be common among homeless people with no previous record of psychiatric disorder. As time passes, the dividing line between those with a history of mental disability and those with street-induced mental health problems becomes increasingly blurred. The culture of chronicity has taken hold; the causes and solutions of the homeless problem become hopelessly entangled.

THE POLICY PRISM

Nothing on the immediate horizon is likely to lessen or solve the problem of homelessness, or the general problems faced by service-dependent groups in the teeth of the crisis of deinstitutionalization. First, demographic trends and medical/psychiatric advances will mean lowered rates of growth in developmentally disabled and retarded populations but also an increase in their survival rates. The elderly population will live longer and grow larger through the first two decades of the twenty-first century as the post-1945 baby-boom generation ages. Improvements in psychotherapeutic techniques are always possible but most likely there will continue to be long-term mentally disabled populations dependent on collective resources for support.

Secondly, new and more intense needs for human services may arise. For example, the rise of female labor-force participation and domestic independence, along with changes in public attitudes about divorce, promise to increase disorganization of the family and expand the need for social guidance counseling, child welfare services and care for battered women (40 per cent of the homeless women who turn up in public havens are battered wives; Ellen Bassuk, quoted in Karlen et al., 1986, p. 20). Services for men have already become more prevalent and are likely to be increasingly necessary as traditional gender roles are redefined. Thirdly, the long-term economic picture for the US and Canada is uncertain but there is little cause for optimism. Huge federal deficits linger; the competitive position of North American industries in the global economy is clearly lagging; world currency conditions are highly unstable; and the debt of the Third World has reached crisis proportions. In light of such conditions, the economic likelihood of expanding surpluses for social programs is small.

The increasing demand for service supports and the long-term economic situation have crucial implications for the service-dependent population, particularly the homeless. Unless more resources are devoted to social spending, continued attacks on existing levels of welfare and human-service support are more likely than increased spending. A cyclical economic recovery could provide employment and income to that portion of the service-dependent population which can successfully compete in the labor force. This could halve the number of homeless as the employable are reabsorbed back into the labor force. It is a highly improbable scenario, however, given industrial restructuring and the disappearance of many job categories (Roderick, 1985). Moreover, the 25–50 per cent of the homeless who are alcoholics, drug abusers, mentally disabled, or ex-offenders are likely to remain so. And there is every expectation that the ranks of this group will be swollen by those economically dislocated homeless who have succumbed to the culture of chronicity and *become* service-dependent, psychiatrically unstable, or criminals as a result of their experiences on the streets

Thus service-dependency and homelessness will remain societal problems for the foreseeable future. The situation of New York City is illustrative. According to recent reports, 'the number of homeless families seeking shelter from New York City will double this year [1986], while the number of single homeless adults will grow at a slower rate, about 22 per cent.' (*New York Times*, 12 January 1986: I:19). The city is currently sheltering more than 4,000 families, more than double the figure of late 1984. The number of single homeless adults housed by the city rose from 6,785 in 1984 to 8,700 in 1985 (*New York Times*, 12 January 1986, p. I:19). The 4,000 families and 8,700 individuals represent a daily shelter population of 23,500 homeless persons. They are housed in 55 hotels and nine family shelters. The city's current shelter budget is $200 million (*Toronto Globe and Mail*. 20 January 1986, p. A6). The rise in homeless population is not confined to New York; in Los Angeles County, the number of people *seeking* emergency housing rose from 1,900 per month in 1984 to 5,000 per month in early 1985 (County of Los Angeles, 1985, p. 27). Across the country, young children reputedly constitute the fastest-growing segment of the homeless population (Karlen et al., 1986, p. 20).

The increasingly vociferous calls for reinstitutionalization (new asylums, new jails) are a tacit recognition of the persistence of service-dependency and homelessness. It is ironic that support for reinstitutionalization seems to derive from some of those same constituencies that hitherto supported deinstitutionalization. Fiscal conservatives have realized that social problems have failed to disappear yet solutions must be found; they have turned toward privatization as a way to minimize costs while avoiding both long-term commitment of public funds and the creation of new welfare bureaucracies.

Many professional groups that once supported deinstitutionalization also appear somewhat disenchanted. The supporters of the 'new asylum' are frequently found in the ranks of the penal and psychiatric professions. They seem, in part, to be concerned with reestablishing their territorial claims over traditional client groups, many of whom were lost to other community-based helping professions and the legal system with the onset of deinstitutionalization. This is despite the fact that the majority of state and local mental health funds still go toward institutions that now house only 37 per cent of the nation's chronically mentally disabled and a fraction of their former inmate populations. This has resulted in staggering staff-to-patient ratios: this rate now exceeds 1.5:1 in public and private mental hospitals nationwide (Morgenthau et al., 1986, p. 15). But battles over turf continue noneless, typically buttressed by demands to make involuntary institutional commitment easier (Morgenthau et al., 1986; Los Angeles County Community and Senior Citizens Services Department, 1985, Attachment B:12).

We categorically reject the reinstitutionalization alternative. In the chapters that follow, we explore the normative implications of our preceding analysis. Two views on the policy 'prism' are offered, although a slight turn in this prism could provide different political and practical emphases. But our perspectives (we believe) constitute a significant point of departure in a long-overdue discourse around *alternatives to reinstitutionalization*. In chapter 9, we consider public policy strategies that seek to assist *human agents* in the tasks of deinstitutionalization. Here, we examine the rights and obligations of local communities in providing for the service-dependent population and define practical options and decision-making tools through which planners might develop community-based service opportunities. In chapter 10, we step back to look again at the *structural context* for welfare solutions. From our vantage point, only a renewed political commitment to close the circle – to complete the process and promise of deinstitutionalization – can ultimately insure a humane and caring system of social welfare in the city.

9

Community politics and the planning of human services

As we have documented in previous chapters, the most troubling and common locational outcomes of deinstitutionalization have been the ghettoization of service-dependent and homeless populations in decaying central-city areas and the subsequent dismantling of these ghettos in the face of gentrification and urban renewal. In ghetto environments, access to treatment resources may be greater (Davidson, 1982) and clients may be able to become part of developing coping networks. But opportunities for social integration within the everyday community are restricted as client interpersonal contacts become confined to service providers and others involved in the coping networks (Hull and Thompson, 1981). In some cases, nonclient residents of these areas have also been affected negatively by disproportionate levels of risk and burden in providing for the needs of dependent populations. But despite such costs of ghettoization, ghetto dismantling has disrupted the only mechanisms available to dependent persons trying to sustain themselves outside institutions. Under either scenario – ghettoization or ghetto dismantling – residents of affluent (nonghetto) localities have avoided their obligation to help, an obligation that is at the heart of community care philosophy as well as societal standards of fairness and justice.

Unless we return to large-scale confinement of service-dependent populations, essential human services will be community-based and the problems facing the community have to be addressed. We must evaluate critically the kinds of policies (and nonpolicies) that foster both ghettoization and ghetto dismantling and formulate purposive policies that more equitably and humanely resolve the locational problems attendant upon community-based service delivery.

In this chapter, we assess the advantages and disadvantages of concentration (or ghettoization) versus dispersal of community-based services and clients and argue that some dispersal of the system is needed. While such a change can infringe on local rights to self-determination, urban communities are nonetheless obliged to support dependent populations. We then provide a normative guide for resolving location-linked problems of community-based support systems for service-dependent populations. This guide is premised on the need to protect both client and community rights, while being cognizant of the inherent conflicts that arise between these groups. In respecting rights and recognizing obligations, our recommendations do not identify a specific normative distribution of facilities or clients, but instead furnish a basis for development of practical policy frameworks for the equitable and democratic resolution of locational conflicts over service-dependent populations.

BENEFITS AND COSTS OF ALTERNATIVE SERVICE CONFIGURATIONS

The development of locational policies should be grounded in an understanding of the benefits and costs engendered by alternative spatial distribution schemes. In the discussion that follows, we systematically detail both the desirable and deleterious aspects of two spatial distributions of human services and clients. Numerous additional configurations could be evaluated, but we consider here only the polar extremes: concentration (or ghettoization) and dispersion of services and clients.

Benefits and costs of concentration

Most of the attention on the ghetto has focused on its problematical consequences rather than on its potential benefits (Aviram and Segal, 1973; Wolpert and Wolpert, 1976; Wolch, 1980). However, as we have argued, a concentrated pattern of service facilities furthers client and community interests in several ways.

To the extent that linkages exist between elements of the service system, facility clustering may be efficient (White, 1979). Such linkages are likely to be found where a service provider represents an element in a continuum of care, a complement or near substitute for another service, or where a service requires the cooperation of varied support functions. These interdependencies frequently take the form of shared staff, information, or resources, as well as coordination of programs, especially when services or referrals are provided to overlapping client groups. In such cases, proximity of location may be desirable from both the client and provider perspectives. Clustering will promote interaction and can thereby encourage multiple-purpose trip-making, may reduce overall costs and by facilitating coordination, may improve the quality of services provided. To the extent that such tendencies increase the 'attractiveness' of elements of the service system, service utilization may increase.

Concentration may also be preferable where economies of scale in service provision exist. High fixed costs, particularly for specialized facilities or staff training, may create unacceptable inefficiencies in a dispersed network. Thus clients may best be served by a concentrated configuration of facilities if threshold populations required for specialized services are high. Such efficiencies also clearly benefit the citizen–taxpayer.

Concentration may promote self-help and development of nurturing systems of mutual support (Smith, 1976; Wolpert, Dear and Crawford, 1975; Dear et al., 1980). Ghettoization may translate into political visibility for clients and thus conceivably aid formation of coalitions dedicated to improvements in the quality of community care. This configuration may also be preferable where the cost of overcoming opposition to more scattered locations is great. And, certainly not the least of benefits from concentration are those enjoyed by nonghetto residents. Their isolation from the ghetto allows them to avoid their obligations to help and to escape its perceived negative consequences while reaping the social benefits that a community-care system provides.

The costs of concentration include those borne directly by clients in the form of greater risks of victimization and reduced opportunities for interaction with nonclient populations. Inappropriate community 'norms' are likely to evolve in areas saturated with service-dependent groups, further militating against chances for personal growth (Estroff, 1981). Such costs may impact subpopulations differentially, with the more dependent enduring relatively greater levels of hardship because of forced interaction with incompatible client groups (Wolch 1981b). And, though ghettoization may create political visibility, the isolated setting may also serve to estrange the larger community from the needs of its more disadvantaged members (Lamb, 1979a).

Nonclient residents of the ghetto also bear the burden of its costs, the magnitudes of which generally decrease (or are perceived to decrease) with increasing distance from community care hubs (Dear, 1974; Dear, Taylor and Hall, 1980). Frequently cited spillovers are monetary, for example declines in property values or barriers to positive land-use succession; or they may be intangible, for example, increased threats to personal safety and probability of exposure to peculiar behaviour. In either case, concentration may pose a disproportionate burden for the residents affected (Segal and Baumohl, 1981; Johnson and Beditz, 1981; Steadman, 1981; Sosowsky, 1978).

Externalities that affect the entire community can also arise. For example, behavioral differences observed among ghetto populations may have divisive social consequences if they serve to polarize community attitudes (Wolch and Gabriel, 1985). Any reduction in a locality's property tax base due to the tax-exempt status of services may reduce the level of urban services provided throughout the entire city. Depending on the nature of funding sources for human services, enclaves of the service-dependent can create disproportionate fiscal stress among jurisdictions in a region. Increased demand for community care can conceivably abet shifts in the mix of public goods, or crowd out other locally funded services (Wolch, 1981a). Analogously, voluntary programs may come to emphasize rehabilitative efforts, thus giving short shrift to integrative activities that in fact can serve to reduce the incidence of dependency (Politser and Pattison, 1980; Reddy and Smith, 1973; Segal and Baumohl, 1981; Kammeyer and Botton, 1968; Volkman and Cressly, 1963; Arnoff, 1975). Lastly, ghettoization imposes inequitable obligations on the host community to support service-dependent clients that other communities have shirked.

It is vital to note that many of the negative spillovers of ghettoization are perceived rather than real (i.e. documented empirically). In most ghetto areas, for example, property value effects are not discernible, nor are crime rates always higher than in other communities (Breslow and Wolpert, 1977; Dear, 1974; Dear and Taylor, 1982). While community fears and claims of impaction are not always well founded, they are nonetheless legitimate concerns to be considered in the design of community care configurations.

Benefits and costs of dispersion

Though location *in* the community does not guarantee support *by* the community, dispersion can facilitate the kind of social integration that ghettoization constrains. Opportunities for growth may be improved where clients' living environments reflect those qualities available to nonclients in the course of their everyday life (Wolfensberger, 1972). And significantly, the spillover costs associated with community care facilities and burdens on local fiscs are equalized across jurisdictions.

Nevertheless, it may be costly to deliver the kinds of services afforded by concentration to a more dispersed client population. Benefits of clustering and economies of scale can be exploited less readily. Clients may be underserved in communities if their numbers do not support needed services, or if access to a limited number of such facilities is inadequate. Although some amount of community opposition has been found to be useful to client progress (Segal, Baumohl and Moyles, 1980), placement in a hostile community typically has deleterious consequences for the reintegration of service-dependents. Suburban communities have been found to be much less accepting of community care facilities and clients than ghetto areas typified by transience, low social cohesion and heterogeniety of land uses and social class (Trute and Segal, 1976; Smith, 1978; Davidson, 1982; Taylor et al., 1984). Also, from the community's perspective, centrally mandated equalization of the distribution of clients and facilities between communities can erode local discretionary power and control.

COMMUNITY RIGHTS AND OBLIGATIONS

Is either concentration or dispersion of community-based services optimal? Our analysis of benefits and disbenefits suggests that arguments in favor of ghettoization are primarily efficiency-based, while those promoting dispersion are more equity-oriented. It is not entirely clear whether dispersion or concentration represents the more desirable spatial outcome for service-dependent groups; but winning and losing communities may be more readily identified under alternative distribution schemes. Both patterns can lead to legitimate conflicts between clients and communities and among communities, over location rights and support obligations. In the absence of public intervention, conflict resolution seldom inures to the benefit of clients or the politically weak. So, we are left with ghettos that, despite their benefits, can have distinct drawbacks and only shallow power to ameliorate them.

In attempting to resolve locational conflict over facility siting it is crucial to identify the nature and extent of community rights and to respect those rights while balancing them along with the rights of clients and other local communities. Communities have distinct obligations as well as rights, however. The national policy of deinstitutionalization has created obligations for local communities to provide support opportunities for clients, despite the possibility that such obligations may reduce the community's ability to control its own internal development and environmental goals. These obligations are to clients who need integrative, nonstigmatized support networks and physical surroundings. Communities also have obligations to a society that purports to value a fair geographical distribution of burdens and resources and which has collectively determined that community-based care is in the best interest of clients and the nation.

In the remainder of the chapter, we explore public policy alternatives that could improve the community-based service system. First, in the next section, we consider a model for *local* community-based service provision and outline the land-use and planning policies available to local jurisdictions attempting siting decisions to create an effective community-based support network. These policies for individual localities are, however, alone insufficient to address the service distribution issues across larger metropolitan jurisdictions, particularly inequities related to a service-dependent ghetto in the central city. Thus in the subsequent section, we examine a model of the *regional* community care planning problem, and propose regional institutions and policies that may serve as a further basis for conflict resolution (the last two sections).

PLANNING STRATEGIES FOR LOCAL COMMUNITIES

The deinstitutionalization movement has presented urban communities with manifold issues that have not previously been on the local policy agenda. Since so much of the human-service delivery system is organized, coordinated and funded by nonlocal government agencies, the primary issues facing local jurisdictions have been related to the physical integration of community-based services into the local environment. The formation of service-dependent population ghettos highlights the problems and experiences of cities in responding to the physical–spatial realities of deinstitutionalization. The problem is how to assign service facilities and client users to subareas of the city in order to improve their placement outcomes and social integration. The experience of ghetto formation indicates that good intentions are frequently sacrificed to the *realpolitik* of neighborhood organizations and business interests, hence concentrating the dependent in restricted urban zones in order to avoid support obligations for residents of more powerfully defended districts.

In this section, we examine a model of the client–service assignment problem facing those local jurisdictions that must make the land-use decisions necessary to accommodate community-based supports. This model suggests several practical planning strategies that could be adopted by local governments seeking to resolve problems associated with the spatial distribution of community-based clients and service facilities.

Intraurban assignment models

Following the lead of Nirje (1976) and Wolfensberger (1972), Dear and Wolch (1979) specify 'client normalization' as the primary treatment objective of the client–service assignment problem. The normalization principle operates on two distinct levels. For human-service clients, normalization entails achieving a degree of individual mastery over internal drives, symptoms, and the immediate environment and achieving a measure of social and vocational integration. In addition, normalization implies client integration within a normal social network and community settings.[1] Care and treatment in the 'least restrictive' setting is most likely to further the goal of normalization. The assignment problem is thus defined as one of matching clients with a specific level of functioning (social, physical, mental) to service settings characterized by a given level of environmental restrictiveness. Level of functioning varies along a continuum, one end of which represents client autonomy, the other client dependence on services. Autonomous clients are able to live on their own and require only nonresidential services (for example periodic counseling), while dependent clients require more extensive service support to accomplish their daily tasks. Restrictiveness refers to the extent of limitations placed on client behavior and activities, with the most restrictive setting being a 'total' institution such as a mental hospital and the least restrictive setting consisting of voluntarily consumed walk-in services. The objective function of the assignment seeks to match clients to the service settings most suitable to their level of functioning. If the match is optimal, clients will experience the least restrictive environment concomitant with their needs, i.e. the minimum possible 'envelopment' or external control over their lives.

Community factors are brought into the model as constraints on the assignment process. They insure cost-effectiveness, minimum tax burden, or a 'fair' geographical distribution of service settings to prevent ghettoization. A further possible constraint concerns clients, providing for their assignment in a more (rather than less) protective or restrictive setting should the optimal setting be unavailable. This constraint is designed to prevent harm to clients arising (for instance) from placement in inappropriately 'open' environments which they may not be equipped to handle effectively.

The model's objective function and constraints underscore the sources of 'slack' in the assignment system, which may create sub-optimal client–setting assignments. The objective function specifies the desirability of client assignment to the least enveloping or restrictive environment, but a hostile and fearful community can lead to demands for more restrictions on client freedoms. Such attitudes can also constrain the types of facilities allowed into the community; if residents are worried about client presence, then service settings on the 'open' end of the environmental continuum may be excluded from the jurisdiction. Available opportunities may be skewed and assignments thus overly restrictive of client behavior.

The goal of cost-effectiveness or minimum tax burden, if pursued overzealously can result in underfunding and paucity of service opportunities available to individual communities. Communities have only moderate control over underfunding problems, given that most service resources derive from nonlocal government programs. In addition, there are barriers to independent local service provision initiatives. Localities are caught by the free-rider problem; they may wish for more service resources, but it is not in their best interests to provide these resources from local revenues, because they could be taken advantage of by other local governments which refuse to shoulder their own community care obligations. The outcome for the dependent population may be access only to limited types of service settings and suboptimal assignment outcomes.

The constraint that the assignment follows some criterion for a fair geographical distribution of clients and facilities is central to our concerns. Violation of this constraint leads to 'dumping' clients in certain subareas of the city and to the creation of ghettos. As we have already discussed, ghettoization may occur because of factors operating outside a given jurisdiction (for example, the exclusionary policies of surrounding cities), as well as forces acting within the city. The latter include locational decisions of clients and facilities – mostly in response to scarce resources and accessibility requirements – but also the attitudes and behaviour of neighborhood groups which can either fight against the siting of a human-service facility, or accept it into their midst. The propensity and ability to mount effective opposition to facility entry is strongly correlated with neighborhood income and social status. Thus the sensitivity of local governments to community mobilizations and power differentials leads to regressive siting patterns and a coalescence of clients and facilities in uncontested parts of the city.

Human-service planning strategies at the local level

In order to avoid slack in the community assignment of clients to support settings, local governments must overcome some basic legal and administrative obstacles. One of the foremost reasons that local planning and zoning boards are susceptible to community opposition to facility siting is that law in this area is frequently vague and is continually being contested. Often, the basic definition and legal treatment of institutional land uses such as group homes and halfway houses are poorly articulated and only through evolving case law are their statuses delineated. A second major obstacle to optimal assignment is the attitudes of local residents toward service-dependent populations. As highlighted by Dear and Taylor (1982), residents are often fearful for their personal safety and worry about the potential external effects of facilities such as increased traffic, noise and declining property value. Frequently, such fears are ungrounded but a lack of understanding of clients and their problems – and their mutual communality as human beings – leads to hostility, rejection and exclusion.

Such obstacles are not insurmountable, however. Legal problems and uncertainties can be rectified and attitudes can be changed by new evidence about service-dependent populations, sensitive approaches to facility integration within a neighborhood and recurrent exposure to clients. Below, we outline a series of local planning strategies designed to resolve the issues blocking improvement of the community-based support system.

Local zoning

As the evidence from both Santa Clara County (cf. chapter 6) and Hamilton (cf. chapter 5) illustrates, local jurisdictions frequently use zoning to regulate the entry and location of human-service facilities, particularly residential care installations. Typically, such zoning has been employed to exclude facilities and clients from single-family residential zones, through one of several means:

1 outright exclusion via the designation of facilities as forbidden uses in residential districts;
2 prohibition of group-care homes by defining 'family' (as in 'single-family residential') to exclude the social unit composed of a group of unrelated individuals – clients and staff;
3 use of special-permit or conditional-use requirements which alert local opposition to block facility entry; and
4 imposition of stringent health and safety requirements applicable to institutional (rather than residential) uses, which makes operation prohibitively expensive or impractical.

Zoning laws can, however, be used to encourage and manage the development of a local community care system (cf. chapter 5; also Dear and Laws, 1986). For example, zoning bylaws pertaining to the entire range of human-service facilities can be developed, which are inclusive but which still protect local residents from overconcentration of facilities. Such ordinances would:

1 explicitly define residential care facilities of a specific size-range as residential uses and extend 'by-right' siting privileges to them in residential zones;
2 define larger residential facilities as multifamily uses and extend 'by-right' siting privileges to them in multifamily residential zones;
3 define walk-in nonresidential facilities as commercial uses most similar to medical and legal offices, so that they are permitted in the same areas;
4 identify for special use-permit procedures those larger-scale residential and nonresidential facilities not covered in the above categories;
5 establish 'density' limits for various classes of facilities, specifying either the minimum distance to separate service establishments or the maximum density of facilities or service users allowed in subareas of the city; or identify the impact level of different facility types and specify combinations of low- and high-impact facilities allowed in subareas of the city; and
6 subject facilities to health and safety regulations applicable to similar structures, for instance, to prevent group homes from having to meet business or hospital standards.

Some of these zoning approaches are similar to several state-level preemptive zoning laws currently in effect (US General Accounting Office, 1983). As Schmedemann (1979) argues, certain provisions have drawbacks; for example, if local communities have residential zoning controls that are exclusionary (large-lot or set-back requirements, heavy service hook-up fees, etc.), the 'by-right' inclusion of small residential facilities may be ineffective in permitting these uses because such requirements make facility establishment too costly. In another vein, density restrictions or ceilings may be legally questionable and moreover can have perverse results: favoring early-comers over late-comers without regard to the comparative qualities of their programs; ignoring differences in community character and need for services that affect the appropriateness of facility location; eliminating benefits derived from geographical proximity of functionally linked services; and creating service shortages if limits are set such that areas which are economically feasible for service providers are 'full' even though need remains unmet (Schmedemann, 1979).

These problems indicate that zoning changes alone are not sufficient to overcome problems in client assignment. However, if used in conjunction with other local planning strategies described below, they can be effective policy tools for integrating service-dependent clients in urban communities.

General plan elements

While zoning can set basic guidelines for facility siting, it does not assist the community in proactive planning of the community-based service system. As the experience in housing, transportation and open space indicates, it may be necessary for the community's General Plan to articulate local goals and objectives, problems and needs explicitly and preferred alternatives for goals achievement in the form of a General Plan Element devoted to the community-based service system.

Such an Element would identify current and projected needs of the service-dependent population and delineate the numbers and types of services necessary for their support. The Element would also consider the physical–spatial context of service delivery and designate areas of the city which could serve as service 'hubs', using such criteria as accessibility to public transportation, generic services useful to clients (parks, libraries, etc.) and related human services. Requirements that the Element consider all other city policies and their implications for community-based service delivery could uncover inconsistencies and problems in carrying out recommendations based on analyses contained in the Element. Lastly, the information developed as part of the Element process could be used in the design of workable facility density limits.

Human-service departments

Cities faced with problems of facility saturation and ghettoization can respond by establishing municipal agencies or boards (or subagencies within larger units), which oversee the siting of services and license installations according to health and safety criteria. Such bodies could play a key role in the coordination and integration of human services. First, the department could deal with facilities spanning the entire range of the service spectrum, instead of only one branch of service (the elderly, mentally ill, etc.). Secondly, all service facilities could be licensed by the department. Thirdly, the bureau could designate subareas of the city, keep an ongoing census of services available in each and use this information either to grant or deny licenses to prospective facility operators, given density limits provided in a General Plan Element or zoning ordinance, or developed by the department itself. The information could also be used to spot gaps in the service delivery system, which could be relayed to agencies charged with service development and provider contracting (i.e. Social Services Departments, Mental Health Departments, etc.). Fourth, the department could be the central *locus* for citizen education and participation and technical assistance in finding suitable facility sites for service providers and prospective providers. Lastly, as we will discuss in the final section of this chapter local departments are a central element in planning the intrametropolitan assignment of community care clients and services to local jurisdictions.

Architectural review

Design elements of service facilities can be important influences on community attitudes toward service-dependent clients. For example, Dear and Taylor (1982) found that many neighborhood residents objected to mental health facilities on the grounds that clients often loitered nearby because the clinic had no waiting area sheltered from external view. This surfeit of clients made neighbors feel threatened and uneasy about their children's safety. A second complaint typically centers on building upkeep (Stickney, 1976). Neighbors object to facilities that are in poor repair or detract from the overall aesthetic quality of properties nearby. Both design and maintenance problems of this nature could be alleviated through additions to facility licensing programs carried out by the city human-services department. Facility evaluators could specify architectural features and maintenance levels necessary for different types of facilities and identify changes required prior to granting license applicants their operating permit.

Community education and siting strategies

An important function of local governments in the area of community care is formulating methods for promoting client integration into neighborhood life. Zoning and design changes, improved regulation and planning may create widespread indifference to, rather than active community support for, client rehabilitation. A jurisdiction might embark on a program of community education to quell unfounded fears and concerns and thus encourage development of more accommodating attitudes.

For example, community outreach efforts can acquaint residents with clients. Personal visits to neighbors and public lectures by local human-services staff and dissemination of printed materials, can make educational information on clients and programs available to local civic groups, school children and parent–teacher associations and neighborhood organizations. Also, neighborhood advisory boards can be established to provide a forum for concerns of both residents and providers of local facilities. Perhaps the most important educational efforts are those which involve local residents as volunteers in helping meet client needs and to integrate the service facility and its users into the community fabric (Stickney, 1976).[2]

It is possible that educative efforts, particularly those that do not involve direct contact with clients, may have less impact on attitudes than long-term experience with clients in the community. Supportive attitudes may develop only when neighbors grow accustomed to the presence of service-dependents and interact with them on a frequent basis (Dear and Taylor, 1982). This implies that the ability of facilities to gain initial entrance into the community is an important hurdle and underscores the need for effective facility siting strategies that minimize community opposition.

Two basic siting approaches have been surveyed in the literature on community care: the 'high-profile' strategy, whereby a community is fully informed and involved in the process of facility location, and the 'low-profile' strategy in which facilities are opened with little or no forewarning to the community. Research on the relative effectiveness of these two approaches to siting has produced conflicting results (Orras, 1983). Some studies have found that the high-profile strategy increases acceptance or at least reduces opposition. In such cases, behavior is proceeding rationally according to a learning–response process; that is, behavior is only determined after individuals pass through successive stages of cognition (awareness of a facility) and affect (formation of attitude towards a facility).

Baker et al. (1977) have shown, however, that in several cases, efforts to inform and educate the community about a proposed residential care facility served to increase neighborhood opposition. Yet, communities in which facilities already exist exhibit relatively high levels of tolerance (Mamula and Newman, 1973). Here, individuals appear to have passed through a behavioral–affective–cognitive sequence rather than the reverse (Ray, 1973). Attitude is not created prior to behavior, but rather in response to some pattern of behavior taken in actual situations. Education may be used effectively, then, not to produce awareness, but to reduce dissonance and promote learning through experience. Consequently, a low-profile approach whereby providers consult with few (if any) members of the community prior to opening a facility, may be the more effective strategy for gaining acceptance. Since evidence is decidedly mixed, further research is required to determine how experience and exposure to information affect attitudes towards community care.

STRATEGIES OF ARBITRATION FOR REGIONS

In theory, planning strategies implemented by local communities could improve citizen attitudes toward service-dependent populations, increase acceptance of support facilities and clients and thus eliminate the driving forces behind ghettoization. In practice, however, such local strategies face major limitations for resolving problems of intraregional disparities in community care burdens or inappropriate client environments. First, local planning tools are essentially elective. Localities *desiring* to integrate clients could do so using such approaches, but these policy instruments are incapable of promoting client dispersal to communities actively avoiding their community care obligations. Secondly, the local approaches (except perhaps education) respond to provider pressures for facility siting, which may well include expected level of community opposition and conflict costs. Thus the spatial distribution of demand for facility sites and client opportunities would likely continue in its historical pattern. These limitations suggest the need for an exploration of regional client-to-service assignment systems designed to produce an efficient and equitable allocation of community care resources *across* metropolitan jurisdictions.

Prior models

Models of the optimal method of client-setting assignment discussed in the context of community planning tend to be deficient for regional assignment problems in several important respects. The models are highly abstract and oversimplified, focusing on client characteristics and immediate attributes of service settings; they fail to specify fully the community role in assignment or in offering any means for resolving value conflicts surrounding the regional allocation of community care resources and obligations. The complex dimensions of distributional equity, the role of community in shaping a setting's restrictiveness and therapeutic value and ways of resolving conflicts between client and community rights in the assignment process are barely touched upon.

A model that focuses much more attention on the goals of both clients and communities in the assignment process is found in Wolpert and Wolpert (1976). This heuristic model suggests that four goals should guide assignment of mentally ill clients to a continuum of facilities:

1 economy of treatment
2 client civil and therapeutic rights;
3 client rights to effective and knowledgeable treatment; and
4 development of an inclusive society.

The assignment model itself reflects these goals, with an objective function that maximizes favorable client treatment outcomes, subject to cost constraints identified by participants in the assignment process. Participants include program administrators and helping professionals, as well as receiving communities; relevant costs are program (and hence tax) prices and tangible and intangible spillover effects such as host–community risks, fear, or property-value change.

The basic premise of the model is that client outcomes must be traded off with real and/or perceived costs for others, given their willingness to bear those costs. The model's construct is silent, however, on questions concerning how to use this insight in evaluating real assignments. The Wolperts suggest that 'the assignment structure would be implemented on the basis of the existing distribution of clients to bring about priority corrective reassignment, and to place new entries into proper facilities in the system, all subject to budget constraints' (p. 43). But the data necessary to actually specify an optimal assignment, or to assess the existing assignment, are typically lacking. Moreoever, other than an implicit central assignment authority empowered to correct assignments, there are no mechanisms for adjustment in order to prevent violation of client rights or to impose community and taxpayer constraints. This deficit in fact reflects the real-world experience of deinstitutionalization (particularly of the mentally ill). This the Wolperts acknowledge fully:

> The massive reassignment process which has been proceeding is functionally equivalent to the model which has been discussed here. The actual transfer of patients has tended to favor the preferred assignment according to economy goals. For patients who have been 'dumped' by hospitals prematurely, both therapeutic and civil rights have been violated, as well as rights of the recipient communities. The failure to evaluate treatment outcomes rigorously means that knowledgeability and treatment effectiveness have been hampered. (p. 48).

To this we might add that the rights of some potential host communities *have* been protected or favored at the expense of other communities, thus creating horizontal inequities epitomized by service-dependent ghetto formation.

Despite the insights provided by the model, key questions remain: how can we better balance the goals–achievement of assignment and prevent the denial of basic rights? How can the rights of communities be fairly balanced against the obligations that communities have to support the service-dependent? And how can we design assignment procedures that in and of themselves assure the basic rights of citizens in a representative democracy?

A goals-programming approach

The model we propose is a goals-programming (GP) model and in this section we outline the basic conceptual elements of the model and its operation. (See Appendix to chapter 9, pp. 261–6 for a more technical description of the model.) The GP framework develops an assignment process that insures both client and community rights, effectively balances outcomes when rights conflict and allows for multiple, conflicting goals and trade-offs among objectives. The GP approach permits any spatial assignment outcome to be evaluated (for example, dispersion or concentration) and provides a guide for the development of operational assignment policies necessary to manage the locational conflicts inherent in community-based care.

Briefly, the formal structure of any GP model has five basic elements, as shown in figure 9.1: goals; decision variables; system constraints; goal constraints; and objective function. Goals are outcomes that the assignment seeks to achieve. Decision variables refer to the actual units to be assigned (for example products, people) while system constraints represent absolute restrictions on the assignment process. Goal constraints of the GP model represent

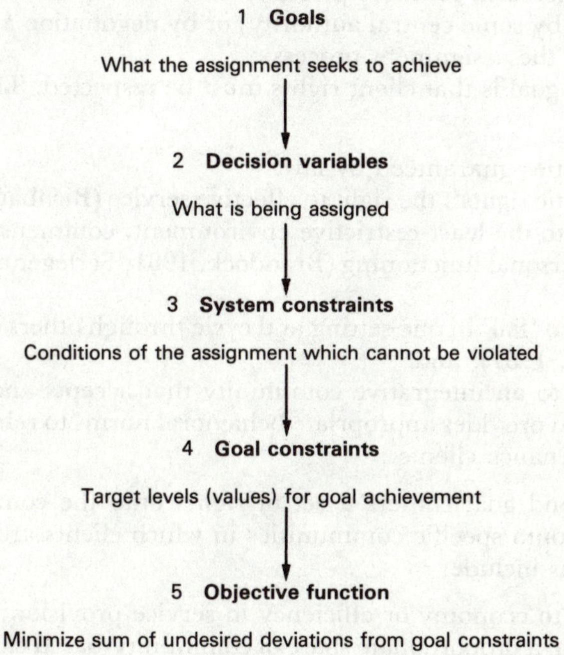

1   Goals

What the assignment seeks to achieve

2   Decision variables

What is being assigned

3   System constraints

Conditions of the assignment which cannot be violated

4   Goal constraints

Target levels (values) for goal achievement

5   Objective function

Minimize sum of undesired deviations from goal constraints

FIGURE 9.1   Elements of a goals-programming model

aspiration or target levels for each goal of the assignment system. For example, a typical objective function might seek to maximize profit by selection of an optimum mix of services, where each service has a given profit margin. Transformed to a goal constraint, however, we would specify the target profit amount and allow for some deviation around that target.

The objective function in GP attempts to minimize the weighted sum of the undesired deviations from targets contained in goal constraints, subject to system constraints. Where more than one goal constraint is desired, goals inherent in the constraints must be ranked according to some priority. Ranking permits deviations of higher-ranked goal constraints to be minimized prior to those of less-important goal constraints.

The goals-programming approach can be applied to the client assignment case (figure 9.2). Two overarching sets of goals guide the specification of the model. These goals encompass and expand on those goals specified in earlier models and serve both to constrain the assignment process and evaluate its outcomes. Goals must typically be rank-ordered in terms of priority, with ranking identified either arbitrarily (by some central authority) or by negotiation among participants in the assignment process.

The first goal is that client rights must be respected. These rights include:

- civil liberties guaranteed by law;
- 'therapeutic rights': the right to effective service (Birnbaum, 1960); the right to the least-restrictive environment, commensurate with level of personal functioning (Braddock, 1981; Ferleger and Boyds, 1979);
- the right to 'fail' in one setting and cycle through others (Segal and Baumohl, 1981); and
- the right to an integrative community that accepts and supports clients and provides appropriate behavioral norms to rehabilitating or maintenance clients.

The second goal confers a set of rights onto the community at large, and onto specific communities in which clients are to reside. These rights include:

- the right to economy or efficiency in service provision;
- the right to a proportionate share of community-based care burden; and

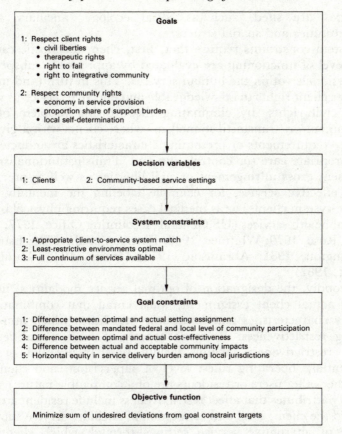

Goals

1: Respect client rights
  - civil liberties
  - therapeutic rights
  - right to fail
  - right to integrative community

2: Respect community rights
  - economy in service provision
  - proportion share of support burden
  - local self-determination

Decision variables

1: Clients   2: Community-based service settings

System constraints

1: Appropriate client-to-service system match
2: Least-restrictive environments optimal
3: Full continuum of services available

Goal constraints

1: Difference between optimal and actual setting assignment
2: Difference between mandated federal and local level of community participation
3: Difference between optimal and actual cost-effectiveness
4: Difference between actual and acceptable community impacts
5: Horizontal equity in service delivery burden among local jurisdictions

Objective function

Minimize sum of undesired deviations from goal constraint targets

FIGURE 9.2 Community care goals-programming assignment model summary

- the right to local self-determination within those boundaries established by the state, which implies that communities are able to evaluate and set limits on the variety of costs imposed by any assignment system.

Decision variables of the model are the clients to be allocated to service settings and the service settings available for client placement. Client groups would be disaggregegated by diagnostic category (i.e. mentally ill, developmentally disabled, probationers, etc.), while service settings would be classified on the basis of two sets of characteristics: facility type (group home, skilled-nursing facility, board-and-care home, etc.) and attributes of communities in which facilities are sited, such as social ecology, ancillary service opportunities and spatial structure.

System constraints require that, first, client diagnostic category and level of functioning are evaluated by appropriate subspeciality professionals within the human services. This in turn (and in part) insures client rights to knowledgeable and effective service as well as their civil rights, by eliminating the growing problem of mis-assignment or 'transinstitutionalism' where clients with a given set of care requirements or presenting characteristics are inducted into inappropriate care (or control) systems. Transinstitutionalism can represent gross infringement of civil liberties as well as preclusion from effective service, for example labeling the mentally ill as justice-system clients, or as medical cases requiring physical but not mental health services (US General Accounting Office, 1977; Scull, 1981; Rose, 1979; Whitmer, 1980; Emerson et al., 1981; Estes and Harrington, 1981; Abramson, 1972; Urmer, 1975; Lamb and Grant, 1982).

Secondly, the designation of optimal service modalities, used to guide actual client assignment, must entail that combination of facility characteristics and community attributes which minimizes setting restrictiveness. Relevant aspects of service facilities that affect restrictiveness include facility type (residential or non-residential); operating rules; level of supervision; and client mix (whether other users or residents are of a compatible nature). Community attributes that affect restrictiveness include resident attitudes toward the client; level and congestion of ancillary service supports; range of alternative service settings through which clients can proceed during their 'careers'; and spatial characteristics that affect ease of client–resident and client–service interactions. Other characteristics necessary to insure client rights to effective service and an integrative community are appropriate technical/program-matic features of facilities and attitudinal and demographic features of communities. The former are beyond our present scope, because they are more appropriately identified by service delivery pro-fessionals. Community attitudes toward clients should be accepting or neutral in order to facilitate client integration, or ancillary community education should be included. Similarly, demographic characteristics, specifically the proportion and mix of service-dependent population, must be selected so that the environment meets criteria for adequate community behavior norms. This condition precludes, for example, the designation of a community already heavily saturated with service-dependents.

The third and final system constraint requires that communities (individually, or collectively within a region) provide a full continuum of service settings, so that clients can have meaningful environmental choices and can move from settings of one level of restrictiveness to another without having to endure unnecessary or harmful changes in personal autonomy (Group for the Advancement of Psychiatry, 1978; Menolascino and Eaton, 1980). This can mean freedom from either excessive control if a client 'fails' (i.e., the level of functioning deteriorates), or inadequate support if level of functioning rises and the client is thrust into an overly autonomous living situation that he/she cannot handle (Felton and Shinn, 1981).

The model's central elements are its five goal constraints. First, the magnitude of the difference between the optimal and actual assignment must not be so great as to violate clients' rights to the least-restrictive environment and integrative community, or the right to effective service. Secondly, the community must be involved in the assignment decision, with involvement structured according to participatory processes that meet nationally accepted norms for democratic governance. Thirdly, the assignment should be the most cost-effective possible, insuring the taxpayer's rights to efficiency in service delivery. This efficiency condition implies that providers offering equivalent services at least cost are selected in the award of contracts and that available economies of scale in service administration and provision will be realized. Fourth, the assignment cannot violate community-set standards for social, fiscal and environmental impacts. Such impacts are externalities of the service system which affect community income, broadly defined. They include changes in land-use compatibility; tax levels and service package level and design; traffic and noise levels; service dependency rates in the population; and property values. This goal constraint maintains the community's right to define its own character and opportunities. Lastly, the client assignment cannot violate the community's right to horizontal equity in service delivery. This constraint prohibits both the 'dumping' of clients onto a small number of specific communities and the avoidance of local obligations to provide support for clients.

The GP objective function can now be stated: the goal of the model is to suggest a client–community assignment that minimizes the undesirable deviations from goal constraint targets related to:

- client rights to least-restrictive environment, integrative community, effective treatment;
- community participation;

- cost-effectiveness;
- community impacts; and
- horizontal equity in service delivery burden.

If the numerical levels and ranges incorporated into the GP model (for example, quantitative targets, deviations, etc.) are too extreme or too narrow, they must be reevaluated and changed. These changes can be made either by lowering (raising) targets, or by expanding the range of acceptable deviation.

Since new clients are continually entering the community framework, either from its own ranks or as a result of deinstitutional-ization, the goals programming is iterative. Each new increment of clients is assigned and reassigned until the cumulative client assign-ment meets goal constraints. Apart from reassignments made necessary by the model, clients are reassigned if and when they experience a change in diagnostic category and/or level of functioning and thus have different service requirements.

IMPLEMENTING THE PLANNING MODEL

The goals programming model becomes operational when parameters of the model are defined: goals are ranked by priority; aspiration or target levels are set for goal constraints; and acceptable deviations and necessary system constraints are specified.

Historically, these parameters have been defined via a political process based on access to power and affluence, within the context of a fragmented system of local governments and a human-service system poorly coordinated both vertically and horizontally. The outcomes of this process have favored some participants over others, often entailing gross violations of rights. As the Wolperts (1976) suggest, efficiency goals have outweighed client rights to a least-restrictive environment, an integrative community and to effective services. Moreover, as the assignment unfolded, host communities that became service-dependent ghettos were heavily burdened relative to other com-munities. Thus one of the most severe infringements of client and community rights arose as a result of highly uneven and eventually inequitable distributions of clients among communities in metropolitan regions.

The root of these distributional problems is an absence of insti-tutional arrangements designed to implement the GP model. In order to fill this fundamental institutional gap, we argue that state or federal legal and administrative mechanisms may be necessary to insure that the system constraints of the model are respected. Moreover, we propose a regional 'fair-share' approach to human-service locational planning which, used in conjunction with arbitration tools, can help to reveal goal rankings, constraint targets and acceptable deviations from these targets.

In the discussion that follows, we identify legal/administrative measures to maintain system constraints. Next we introduce some of the salient features of the regional fair-share concept, compare it with alternatives and then outline how such a policy for the spatial assignment of human-service clients and treatment facilities might work to operationalize the regional planning model.

Insuring system constraints: legal/administrative change

Basic legal and administrative provisions may be necessary to insure that system constraints of the regional planning model are maintained. Such provisions are also basic to the success of local (as opposed to regional) planning for community-based care. These constraints require appropriate matching of clients to human-service subsystems and the use of least-restrictive environmental settings as the optimality criterion. Legal provisions, often guided by court action, have already delineated the basic civil rights of many service-dependent client groups, particularly offenders, the retarded and the mentally ill. Certain therapeutic rights have also been articulated for some client types, such as the right to a least-restrictive environment and the right to service. In addition, professionally designated criteria for matching clients to service subsystems have become integrated into legal practice and administrative regulations. This is exemplified by the use of court-appointed mental health workers to assess the mental instability of offenders and to justify transfer to the mental health care system.

Despite progress in the development of laws and regulatory guidelines, there remain areas in which further legal definition is necessary. First, the process of client–service system matching is often left to professional judgement and results can infringe on civil liberties. An example in the juvenile justice area is the current trend toward diagnosing juveniles as mentally ill and confining them for service *not* on the basis of offense but instead improvement in mental health status. This may, in fact, deprive such juveniles of basic rights (Hylton, 1982). Similarly, peace officers often induct the mentally ill into the criminal justice system, because of lack of training in client assessment; such cases may or may not be brought to the attention of the mental health services (Lamb and Grant, 1982). In order to prevent such mismatches, criteria for referral to service subsystems need to be more clearly articulated, promulgated and in some cases, legislated.

Secondly, the presence of some legislated provisions of service programs themselves impede the matching process. An excellent example is that of Medicare and Medicaid, which reimburse mainly medical services. Mentally ill clients requiring institutional care are routinely obliged to enter nursing homes in order to obtain shelter and physical assistance, but are then left without mental health service supports (Clarke, 1979). This situation could be changed by revision of reimbursement procedures and has been advocated by many (US General Accounting Office, 1977; Seidenberg and Parrish, 1981).

Third, legal changes may be required in order to guarantee clients a full range and continuum of service settings. Since recognition of client rights to a least-restrictive environment and the development by the helping professions of many different classes of service settings, the provision of a continuum of care has assumed central importance (Menolascino and Eaton, 1980; Group for the Advancement of Psychiatry, 1978). Designation of an optimal setting is a hollow exercise if local areas only provide, for example, state hospital beds, skilled-nursing facilities and fully independent living as alternative settings. Legal mandates for a continuum of services may be necessary to encourage cost-conscious or fiscally stressed jurisdictions to fund such services. The issue is already in the courts.

Identifying priorities, targets and deviations:
a regional fair-share approach

The key elements of the regional planning model are its goals and their attendant rankings; targets of the goal constraints; and acceptable deviations from those targets. The specification of these parameters jointly involve local communities, clients, the professions and central government; but as noted earlier, there currently exist no institutional mechanisms designed to bring these participants together. Rather, the reliance on a fragmented political process and *ad hoc* service delivery planning has produced *de facto* parameter specifications that imposed severe burdens on many participants, particularly clients and saturated communities.

In contrast, a fair-share approach to the problem offers many advantages, both in terms of meeting societal standards of fairness, and also on the pragmatic grounds of its flexibility and politically contingent nature. The fair-share concept focuses on one central goal constraint of the model – equitable distribution of community care burdens across local jurisdictions. But a fair-share policy, as envisioned here, also provides a forum for political communication and negotiation, the outcomes of which will represent other GP parameters. As an ongoing process, fair-share planning and client allocation also serve as a fluid and flexible means for continual adjustment of parameters as local conditions change. In the discussion that follows, we offer a rationale for fair-share and detail our own vision of a fair-share approach in practice.

A rationale for fair-share

Fair-share policies involve a change in the distribution of the spatial externalities associated with public facilities and specific populations in order to increase the equity of their incidence pattern. The idea of fair share is most often associated with the equitable allocation of low-income housing among local jurisdictions within a metropolitan area. In addition, fair-share policy has been applied to the case of fiscal resources (regional tax-base sharing), education, business and environmental pollution.

Spatial externalities, for example those arising from a community care facility, may be considered as income (pecuniary or psychic), with negative spillovers diminishing income while positive spillovers augment it. By altering the distribution of externality-linked income, fair-share policies are in effect redistribution schemes that seek to lessen income disparities within the population. However, externalities are distinguished from other forms of income by their horizontal (or spatial) distribution and as such may be viewed as rights in and to location. Moreover, externalities are further distinguished in that their distribution is often determined indirectly by political procedures. To the extent that disadvantaged groups are constrained from influencing the outcomes of public decision-making, negative external impacts will tend to be distributed regressively; and since the disadvantaged are often concentrated spatially, the horizontal distribution of externalities is likely to be highly uneven (Wolpert, 1976).

Herein lies one general rationale for fair share. That the same groups of people should be found at the bottom of both vertical and horizontal (spatial) income distributions, particularly when such distributions are created by public action, is anathema to any society that values justice, fairness and equality. In the case of community-based care, two disadvantaged groups have historically been situated at the bottom of both income scales. Low-income communities unable to mount effective political opposition have been exposed to the preponderance of local impacts arising from the policy switch to community-based care, which has often affected their rights in their neighborhood locations negatively. Secondly, service system clients, almost uniformly lower income, have been relegated to stigmatized and low-quality locations, conferring on them only the least valued rights in and to location.

A second vital rationale for fair share is that unlike other redistribution policies, it is not simply remedial. Rather than attempting to 'fix' the worst effects of inequality once they have occurred, fair-share policies seek to lessen the incidence of inequality itself, by adjusting the base distribution of resources (Baer, 1983). In the community care case, this means not simply compensating clients who have been denied access to appropriate service environments, but instead changing their access to such environments. Similarly, the fair-share process itself may reduce hostility and foster community acceptance of clients by familiarizing neighborhoods with community care and reducing fears and negative perceptions.

In practice fair-share policies have been flexible and politically appealing. As Baer (1983) notes, fair-share policies arbitrarily establish a need for redistribution 'by reference to some percentage of the whole which is politically acceptable (even if there is no reference to data or empirical findings) without regard to estimates of the economic or social costs of enactment. Nor are these costs faced squarely because they are imposed on society at large through the reconfiguration of legal rights' (p. 23). This ambiguity about incidence is complemented in many fair-share programs by 'hold harmless' or grandfathering provisions, which in effect protect vested rights. Holders of such rights – for example, communities that would have to immediately accept their full fair share of clients – might otherwise oppose the fair-share policy. So the policy applies only to the increment or margin, leaving the base of vested rights and hence increasing political feasibility in the process. According to Baer (1983),

These fair-share policies which address the increment but leave the base alone have no ethical or moral rationale . . . Rather, they are politically expedient and perhaps administratively efficacious. They are a political judgement of what can be enacted through reducing the number of people who would be immediately 'taxed' by this new policy, giving them more time to make adjustments to reduce the effects of the tax; and perhaps they are a judgement about the limitations on the size of the change which can be monitored and enforced administratively.

(p. 28)

Alternatives to fair share

A redistribution of location rights effectuated by fair-share policy is not the sole means by which inequities may be remedied. Economists have long advocated compensation schemes by which beneficiaries 'pay off' those bearing the burden of externalities, enabling the achievement of Paretian efficiency (Henderson and Quandt, 1971). Gaps in welfare are lessened even while location rights remain fixed. In practice, compensatory policy is constrained by a number of limitations rising out of the problem of estimating social costs in pecuniary terms and identifying and coordinating beneficiaries who would pay the actual compensation (Downs, 1970).

Even if these limitations could be overcome, it is not clear that pecuniary compensation, when used as the sole redistributive mechanism, would fully address all the problems arising out of a particular assignment of human-service clients. Although compensation for overburdened communities can help them to offset the effects of client concentrations, compensation to *clients* is problematical because of locational intangibles. Clients may be left with little opportunity to experience the benefits of a therapeutic community when money resources rather than location rights are redistributed. Their only solution would be to use financial compensation to move to more desirable and costly neighborhood locations – but that of course implies a different client assignment.

Beyond compensation, density limitations and state-level preemptive zoning offer alternatives to fair share. Density limits restrict the number of service facilities to a specific geographic density, thereby helping to protect communities from facility agglomeration and neighborhood saturation. Preemptive zoning legislation prohibits localities from zoning certain classes of service facilities out of residential and/or nonresidential areas, thereby helping clients to gain access to a broader range of environments (US General Accounting Office, 1983). Although they may be important as a barrier to saturation at the community planning scale (density limits) and useful as a means of limiting local land-use control rights (preemptive zoning),

neither policy presents a solution to the regional locational problems
of the service-dependent population. They are restricted in the scope
of the goals they serve and hence are not able to balance conflicting
goals inherent in the assignment process; they are also essentially
reactive, incapable of guiding participants toward desirable solutions to the assignment problem.

Fair share in practice

Implementation of metropolitan fair-share planning for human-
service delivery involves a significant restructuring of intergovernmental relations, by replacing fragmented lines of service authority
and local community interaction with coordinating institutions and
processes. In what follows, we outline the institutional arrangements
attendant on a fair-share program; the duties and responsibilities of
these institutions; and the planning and arbitration tools available to
develop and adjust the assignment of clients and facilities to local
communities.

Implementation.   The implementation of a regional fair-share policy
entails planning and administrative bodies at both the metro-
regional level and at the local community level. The *two-tiered approach*
is desirable for several reasons. First, the regional organizational
structure is a means of handling what is in fact a regional problem:
regional disparities in community care burdens. In effect, a regional
fair-share planning body provides an arena for negotiation and
arbitration among service providers, client advocates and local communities. Negotiations and arbitration are the means by which the
goals of the client assignment can be articulated and ranked, their
target levels identified and acceptable deviations from targets agreed
upon.

   Secondly, localities are invaluable partners in the development of
a community-based care system. Local jurisdictions can supply the
regional level with detailed information on service-dependent populations, facilities, ancillary urban services and land-use planning.
Such information is essential for the development of workable
regional fair-share plans. Localities must be sensitive to citizen
inputs in order to insure community standards of democratic
governance and a decentralized system for participation typically
proves more effective in this regard than a purely centralized
approach (Ostrom, Tiebout and Warren, 1961). In addition, the
success of a fair-share plan could be threatened if imposed entirely
from above; rather, success depends on successive rounds of negoti-

ations between local and regional levels and among localities. The regional body can serve a broker role for client assignment planning, but localities must be organized effectively to participate in this process, armed with knowledge of community estimates of assignment preferences and spillover costs.

Technical Guidance and Standards. Ideally, the *regional institution* would be overseen by a committee of human-service professionals and local representatives in order to provide technical guidance and to insure that citizen and community standards for democratic process are maintained. The work of the regional organization would include:

1 estimation of the demand for and supply of various service settings along the continuum of care and identification of gaps in service system capacity;
2 development of a fair-share allocation formula to distribute inter-community client population shares;
3 documentation and evaluation of the cumulative client assignment at each time-period, and reassignment if necessary;
4 coordination with state and federal agencies involved in human-service provision in general and deinstitutionalization programming in particular; and
5 provision of technical assistance, information and incentives to private-sector providers and local authorities in order to encourage achievement of the fair-share plan.

These functions are aimed at equity conditions of the assignment, but also at insuring that clients have a full complement of service settings available; that services and planning information are coordinated in an efficient fashion; and that the assignment process is evaluated and reassignments effectuated on the basis of normative criteria such as those suggested in our planning model.

A key aspect of regional institution design is its involvement with almost all types of service-dependent populations. This integrated approach could potentially overcome service duplication, fragmentation and professional boundary-marking behavior that is potentially destructive to effective treatment and rehabilitation. But equally significant is the institution's ability to respond to *aggregate* impacts on the community arising from the many service delivery subsystems that have traditionally operated in isolation, failing to consider the joint effects of siting policies in one locale.

The core charge of the regional body would be development of the fair-share allocation plan. The standard approach to this problem is to estimate regional 'need'. In the case of fair-share housing plans, need is typically defined according to the number of low-income households and the quantity of low-cost housing units available, the discrepancy constituting 'needed' units. Similarly, in the human-services case, regional need could be defined simply as the number of clients requiring community placement. This aggregate need could then be allocated among communities, either by treating each client (regardless of type) as the unit to be allocated, or by allocating each client type separately to local jurisdictions.

Given the various types of clients and facilities to be allocated, however, their differential impacts on local communities and varying needs of clients for normalizing settings, the standard 'needs' approaches are problematical. First, each community may have a separate rank-ordering of relative client acceptability and particular valuations of assignment impacts (Smith and Hanham, 1982: Tringo, 1970; Harasymiw et al., 1976). Ignoring this aspect recognizes community obligations to support clients, but may also infringe on local rights. Secondly, the allocation of each client type separately might easily violate the efficiency conditions of the assignment model. Scale economies in service provision and the agglomeration of advantages resulting from the proximity of interdependent service providers could be lost by adopting this method. The rigidity of such a system could also eliminate the possibility of client/facility trade-offs and the efficient clustering of client groups and increase the likelihood that certain community-based client populations would be below threshold sizes necessary for the provision of special ancillary services.

Given the differential acceptance of client types by communities and the different community resource sets useful to clients, it may be much more effective for the regional body to stipulate a general fair-share allocation expressed in terms of some share of total regional community *burdens*. Such estimates could be developed, for example, utilizing a market-simulation technique (Pushchak and Burton, 1983). The problem is to arrive at compensation levels that would enable communities to accept a public facility in their midst. For the client-assignment problem this approach must overcome problems of estimating social costs. To do so, Pushchak and Burton (1983) suggest the simulation of a market-type situation, in which communities bid for facilities on the basis of their best estimate of the level of compensation required to cancel out their perceived and/or measured social costs. This type of process can serve as an estimating technique to identify regional community care burdens. Using a Delphi process, local community bodies could bid for each specific group of clients according to the pecuniary compensation they would require to accept the group as local residents. The median community bid would be designated as the region's 'social cost' of a client group and a total for service-dependent populations developed from these individual estimates.

The total burden would then be allocated to local jurisdictions, but the precise *content* of the burden would be articulated via a process of negotiation among community bodies and the regional institution. The regional agency would be concerned with achieving community acceptance of needed facilities, while designing an assignment that, within the fair-share framework, protects other client and community rights (effective service, least-restrictive environment, integrative setting and efficiency in service delivery). Localities would strive for the types and numbers of clients that they feel would fit their local environment and minimize spillovers according to their specific valuations.

Bargaining strategies.   Several technical tools could be used as *bargaining strategies* or *arbitration devices* necessary to achieve a mutually acceptable assignment, one that respects all goal constraints set by clients, professionals and communities.

1 *Facilities packaging*. The packaging approach (Austin, Smith and Wolpert, 1970) employs the positive incentive of a side-payment in the form of a desirable facility, as an inducement for community acceptance of a noxious facility. This is often essentially compensation in-kind rather than in cash, although it is possible that the facility package includes not only salutary facilities, but also public policy agreements concerning use of the facility in question, i.e. regulation of parking and traffic around the facility site.

2 *Client/facility trade-offs*. Allowing communities to make trade-offs between clients and facilities with differential acceptability can increase the acceptance of client groups and potentially improve the 'fit' between clients and local settings. A trade-off scheme would define each facility type/size category in terms of some standard in order to develop equivalencies. (The Delphi process outlined above could provide a basis for the development of equivalents.) Communities could then choose between more numerous but lower impact facilities and clients or smaller numbers of higher impact

installations. This approach has already been adopted in some cities (Portland Office of Residential Care Facilities, 1977).

3 *Facility design modifications.* Research has shown that design specifications of facilities including placement on lot, parking provisions, and architectural characteristics, often strongly affect the community acceptance of facilities (Dear and Taylor, 1982). Design features of particular importance to localities and neighborhood groups can be mandated by the regional agency as an incentive to local acceptance.

4 *Program design modifications.* Program design is often a major concern of local area residents who worry about personal safety risks due to inadequate client care and supervision. These fears can be mitigated by changes in program staffing and design. A major avenue for programmatic change is the use of case-managers or support-coordinators (Gonen, 1977; Cohen and Kligler, 1980; Sigelman et al., 1980). Under such a system, each client is assigned a support-coordinator who is responsible for assisting the client to cope and manage daily needs. This labor-intensive strategy may be particularly useful in increasing the acceptability and integration of quasi-independent client groups such as the high-functioning retarded, mentally ill and frail elderly.

5 *Services augmentation.* Ancillary human services can be crucial to client normalization, but the goal of client access to such services often conflicts with goals for equitable community burden, as well as client objectives to live in 'normal' communities unsaturated by service-dependent groups. The spatial dispersion of clients necessary to provide normal settings can limit access to ancillary services and reduce client populations below threshold levels necessary for delivery of special service supports. In order to insure access in a more dispersed assignment situation, local services can be augmented in several ways. First, specialized transportation services can enlarge the spatial range of clients seeking ancillary services. Secondly, local 'generic' or 'universal' services – available to all – can be modified and augmented to enable and encourage their use by clients who otherwise might look to separate facilities for support (Savage et al., 1980; Maluccio, 1980). This can save considerable fixed-facility costs and may also have client-integration benefits. Thirdly, support-coordination systems may be useful to link clients to transportation services, more distant ancillary human services and generic service opportunities. Lastly, informal service networks can be exploited, particularly with the help of support coordinators

(Leutz, 1976; Gonen, 1977). Informal networks of grocers, bankers, landlords and neighbors can be tapped to assist clients in their efforts to cope in the community and to gain independence.

6 *Subcenter client clustering.* The efficiency advantages of client concentration can be replicated in part by allowing client groups of a given type to cluster in regional subcenters whose sizes are acceptable to local communities. As noted earlier, such clustering could produce internal and agglomerative economies of scale in service delivery and bring a community's client population up to thresholds for specialized service supports. Clustering can also permit client self-help groups, some degree of political visibility in the community and reduce client perceptions of helplessness and isolation.[3]

7 *Transfer of facility obligations, fair-share burden pricing, and compensation.* Transfer of facility obligations and fair-share burden pricing are analogous to the transfer of development rights and externality pricing (Hagman and Misczynski, 1978; Kneese and Schultze, 1975; Vickery, 1972; Baumohl and Oates, 1975). Under a transfer of facility obligations scheme, each locality would view its fair-share burden as a 'right to clients' (or to facilities). Communities in a metropolitan area would establish a market for these rights, enabling one locality to offer its rights to other local jurisdictions. In this instance, of course, it is the seller who pays to transfer facility obligations. The price of rights could be established by the market itself, or a minimum could be set at the median burden estimated by the Delphi process (used to arrive at a total cost to be allocated by the fair-share plan).

Fair-share burden pricing would entail the pricing of burdens arising from client/facility types, with a minimum price set at their median cost as estimated again by the Delphi process. This type of pricing scheme would serve three functions. First, communities with higher than median estimates of social cost could pay rather than accept their share or portion thereof, allowing some accommodation of intercommunity differences in valuation. Secondly, the regional body would be able to adjust prices, as an inducement to reluctant communities and as a way to insure client rights to appropriate treatment environments, which could be violated if wealthy communities pay rather than shoulder the locational impacts of clients. Thirdly, the pool of funds arising from a pricing scheme could be used to compensate communities (either in cash or in kind via facility packaging or design modifications) for taking more than their fair-share load. Compensation could be awarded by competitive

bidding, i.e. that locality willing to accept clients for the lowest compensation rate would be allocated the additional assignment.

Community Participation, Information and Planning. As indicated
initially, local human services boards or agencies could provide a
locus for community participation in service provision issues, develop
planning information for their own purposes and for those of the
regional institution and plan the distribution of services. In
particular, local agencies could develop community-burden
valuation assessments and work with the regional body in implementation of the fair-share plan. But in addition, local agencies
could perform vital coordination and information roles, serving to
integrate plans of various care providers and pinpoint service
delivery problems that so often fail to be addressed by individual
service agencies. Here, such planning tools as density limits and
inclusive zoning ordinances could be central, along with sensitive
facility siting strategies and community education programs that
help overcome resistance to and rejection of service clients by neighborhood residents and business interests. Lastly and most importantly, the local agency could work with the city's land-use planners,
aiding in zoning decisions and ordinance development; siting allocated facilities; and resolving inconsistencies between physical and
social planning objectives. Such integration of social and physical
planning, long sought by planning experts, is the key to the success
of a community-based care system in which localities and neighborhoods are crucial components.

FURTHER ISSUES IN FAIR-SHARE PROGRAM DESIGN AND IMPLEMENTATION

The discussion thus far has outlined a general framework for client/
facility assignment which seeks to optimize both client and community well-being. A fair-share plan that includes a panoply of compensatory mechanisms has been offered as a vehicle for defining
acceptable deviations from these often conflicting goals. The process
described clearly requires significant reform in the design and
administration of community-based care and raises a number of difficult issues, the more salient of which are discussed below.

Determining fair share

An appropriate method for determining a fair-share allocation must
be formulated by the regional body. This exercise initially requires
that the size and client mix of the service-dependent population be

estimated – a formidable task given the fragmentation of the service system and the real likelihood that many clients have detached themselves from any type of health or welfare agency. Once total population is figured and the associated community burden estimated, a number of criteria may be employed to allocate a 'fair' quantity of community care clients and facilities to jurisdictions. Most of the same mechanisms offered to redistribute low-income housing are applicable here, including criteria based on a community's proportion of regional population, its existing share of clients and facilities, need, capacity, or availability of employment and services (Bourne, 1981).

A scheme that distributes clients in shares proportional to population initially appears not only simple but intuitively just, perhaps best in keeping within the spirit of fair share. Nevertheless, local capacity constraints, particularly with respect to dwellings for residential care, could conceivably limit the use of this method. However, if allocated shares tend to be small, consequent community adjustment would be minimal. For the most part, existing structures could be readily adapted to accommodate clients. And, because many of these individuals are outside the labor force, a preexisting distribution of job opportunities operates as less of a constraint in a scheme of proportional allocation than in the housing case. The most limiting parameter would appear to be general levels of community acceptance and accessibility to support services, particularly specialized functions for subpopulations. Thus, what is initially defined as 'fair' according to a criterion of proportional share, may, in the manner outlined previously, be modified to compensate for differential costs to communities and clients.

In determining fair share it is also necessary to consider the extent to which clients are to be relocated from their existing places of residence. Though many service-dependent currently live in debilitating environments, relocation may create unacceptable hardship. Perhaps fair share should only apply to future populations of service-dependents, with ghetto areas 'grandfathered' in to exempt them from any further facility burden. Expected growth in client population could be estimated and this figure allocated among nonghetto communities.

Facility and service supply

The discussion thus far has assumed that facility providers will quickly supply appropriate services in response to demand. Yet, given the current system of community care which relies heavily on private operators for the provision of services, we cannot be sure that currently available or privately planned facilities will meet the demand of a given level and mix of service-dependents. It may be that in order to obtain an adequate supply, public-sector incentives may be required. A fair-share program could be compromised unless we develop better models of the market processes of community care, prepare viable forecasts of facility supply and use the information thus obtained to structure provider incentives and coordinate public facility spending programs.

A second consideration concerns the suitability of supply locations. Even communities willing to accept clients may be ill-suited for their support. For example, low-density, affluent suburbs may lack affordable housing or facility sites and may have insufficient urban and commercial services for clients. This possibility is recognized in the GP framework, which defines placement in such communities as a violation of client rights. Nevertheless, such communities have the obligation to help. Strategies for *creating* suitable settings in these areas – either through low-cost housing projects, or government subsidies to facility locators – may be important in expanding the set of appropriate communities (for an example of such a project, see Zanditon and Hellman, 1981). Secondly, careful client matching can partly solve this problem. Service-dependent groups with limited ability to use or benefit from everyday community resources and interaction may, for instance, find suitable niches in outlying suburbs.

Trade-offs and pricing

Formulating trade-off mechanisms such as burden pricing or facilities packaging is no doubt a complex task. Typically, much of the difficulty in solving problems of externalities arises from a general dearth of information available on the magnitude of social costs so imposed. It is apparent that many spillovers, such as increased threats to personal safety, are highly intangible and difficult if not impossible to quantify precisely. Presently, we know little about the magnitude of either potential linkages between elements of the service system or possible scale economies in service provision. Further, information on threshold populations required to support various functions, particularly specialized services for subpopulations, is scant or nonexistent. Thus, currently we have an inadequate database from which to calculate the opportunity costs of alternative plans for facility allocation.

Nevertheless, if acceptable deviations from targeted goals are to be established on the basis of the outcomes of compensatory trade-offs, some estimation of costs is required. Moreover, impacts must be evaluated with some modicum of precision if distorting biases are to be minimized. In the case of burden pricing, inadequate knowledge of the costs associated with a particular allocation plan would lead to inappropriate pricing of the rights to facilities. The existing distribution of facilities would change little if the price is set too low, since communities would find it cheaper to pay the charge rather than accept clients. Conversely, if the price is too high, jurisdictions will accept facilities, but the fine-tuning of the fair-share system would be hindered. In this instance, clients could conceivably find themselves exposed to unduly hostile neighborhoods if communities perceive they are carrying a particularly odious share of the regional burden with no avenues for marginal adjustment.

This problem could be obviated to some extent if the Delphi technique described earlier was employed. Here the median price of community bids for clients and facilities would establish social costs. If this method is to be effective, cost information must be evenly distributed among communities. Because much of the negative impact associated with client assignment is defined subjectively however, relative access to information is less problematic than it might be if, for example, the externality concerned the impact of air pollution on morbidity rates. The Delphi technique might also be ineffective if communities felt they could influence the position of the median. Jurisdictions might purposefully underbid to reduce the median price and therefore the amount they would be required to pay to rid themselves of their facility burden. A number of distorting biases may be introduced whenever the price of public goods is estimated by surveys or bidding techniques of this type. Certainly such tendencies should be considered when designing a burden-charge scheme. Creating a market for rights, as described earlier, is often advocated as a superior method for redistributing the costs of externalities (Eslami, 1983). Where the market sets the price, many of the complexities inherent to a direct pricing policy are avoided.

Several other questions related to compensation mechanisms also merit discussion. Particularly critical are issues related to the secondary incentives inherent in pricing and other compensatory policy instruments such as salutary facilities packaging. Some communities may respond by accepting more than their fair share of clients, in exchange for revenues or in-kind benefits, possibly encouraging new ghetto formation or reinforcing existing concentrated patterns. This incentive can be expected to introduce greater distortion where disparities in fiscal health among communities are pronounced. Such problems might be mitigated if the use of revenues received as part of the assignment negotiation was restricted to community improvements that reduce negative spillover effects of facilities. Revenues might also be used to narrow the range of future deviations from targeted goals, hence lessening the need for compensation in years to come. For example, money could be spent on community education to increase local acceptance of clients and facilities.

The appropriateness of client/facility trade-offs among communities within the context of fair share must also be examined. Fair share effectively gives clients a property right in a community. Clients however, do not retain these rights when communities may use various compensation mechanisms to shift their burden to another locality. Though the outcome of negotiations may be efficient and equitable for cities and certainly superior with respect to these goals than is the current distribution of facilities, clients may be left without a normalizing environment. Nevertheless, compensation provides an important tool for insuring rights to local self-governance and for protecting communities from disproportionate risk. Where negotiation is possible, clients may find communities more accepting of their presence. Within the context of fair share, however, the regional body may find it desirable to establish a range of allocations within which negotiations may take place. The extent to which changes in relative assignment would create nonintegrative settings, reduce access to specialized services or curtail opportunities for agglomerative efficiencies, would of course guide the placement of these limits. The use of such standards as facility density controls (to put an upper limit on concentration) and lower-bound client thresholds (to protect efficiency and service-access goals) may be appropriate in this regard.

A final issue related to compensation concerns the incidence of burden. With respect to location-rights pricing, the determining 'who should pay' is unequivocally established. Should a jurisdiction desire to alter the magnitude of its assigned burden, it can only do so by paying off other localities – whether in cash or with in-kind benefits. For other policy tools, determining who should pay is more difficult. The costs of reducing externalities associated with community care have not been discussed. Especially problematic are compensatory mechanisms related to facility/site design and programmatic specifications (such as requirements for supervising case-managers). There is a certain tradition that would place the property right with the victim, such that the entity creating the spillover is liable for compensation. The victim in the case of community care might be the neighborhood upon which negative impacts are imposed; or it may be the client who has suffered the ill-effects of a deviant environment created by restrictive land-use controls in suburban areas. As Coase (1960) demonstrated, however, the assignment of property rights is superfluous; the outcome will be the same regardless of where the rights are placed since in either case the social costs represented by the externality will be internalized.

Nevertheless, we might very well be concerned about who is required to pay – client, facility provider, or community – if it can be demonstrated that a particular assignment of rights is more equitable or more practical to implement. Again, as the price of 'buying into' an integrative community, facility locators could be required to provide modifications deemed appropriate by the community, thus placing the property right with the community. Alternatively, placing the property right with the provider is consistent with the concept of fair share. Doing so, however, would not necessarily preclude a city from 'reasonable' exercise of its police powers. Facility locators could be expected to pay if requirements are modest; where more stringent demands are made, the community may appropriately be required to carry part of the burden. If extraordinary modifications are determined as part of the overall regional allocation process, then conceivably other cities could be asked to pay. In such cases the regional body could establish guidelines for determining what is and is not reasonable.

SUMMARY

Our developing system of community-based support services has yet to attain its ostensible goal of client integration into local social life. Inadequate funding and coordination of services, coupled with no attention to the spatial implications of the client/facility assignment process, have been cited as principal factors contributing to unsatisfactory community support provisions. In particular, service-dependent population ghettos developed in many inner cities.

Despite its potential benefits, including agglomeration efficiencies, scale economies in service delivery, client networking and political visibility, the ghetto has typically failed to provide the kind of support environment conducive to social reintegration. Moreover, ghettos have implied an inequitable distribution of community support obligations among localities within regions.

Building on earlier research, we have proposed models for the assignment of clients to service settings and for communities that attempt to redress these deficiencies. We distinguish between the community and regional client-assignment problem; the former places clients in neighborhoods within a given city, while the latter concerns the distribution of clients and services between cities located in a region. As our analysis makes clear, the two problems are conceptually distinct and call for policy solutions that differ in both form and content.

The community assignment process has been characterized as a programming problem. System 'slack' or suboptimality arises when constraints calling for efficiency in service provision, client protection from excessive autonomy, or a 'fair' geographic distribution of facilities and clients are violated. Our exploration of the reasons for constraint violation suggested several policies which, if implemented by local governments, could overcome problems of inappropriate client assignment within municipal jurisidictions. These policies include changes in zoning for various types of human-service facilities; limitations on facility density; use of architectural criteria in licensing decisions; addition of a Human Services Element in community General Plans; creation of Human Services agencies charged with the task of licensing new facilities according to health and safety, geographic and other service-delivery system-design criteria, as well as the provision of technical assistance to service providers entering the city; and lastly, provision of citizen education programs designed to reduce fears and increase community acceptance and integration of service-dependent populations.

Because local adoption of these policy options is voluntary, problems of ghettoization and inequitable distribution of community burdens among metro-area jurisdictions may remain and require higher-level policy responses. The regional client-assignment problem is a complex one, involving the rights of both individual clients and communities. We have cast this problem as a goals-programming model, which elucidates the nature of the dilemma posed by often-conflicting objectives of protecting client therapeutic and civil rights, as well as rights of host communities to an equitable share of regional support burdens and to protection from what they consider to be excessive spillover effects of client placements. These rights are goals that are not absolute but which can be scaled upward or downward depending on client and community preferences and tolerance limits and which can change if preferences change or if new conditions create a revised calculus for goals definition. When rights conflict, the optimal solution is one that minimizes the sum of deviations from levels of goals attainment desired by clients and communities. Implementation of the model in a real-world context requires that mechanisms be established for rank-ordering objectives of clients and communities and for identifying appropriate levels for desired goals and acceptable deviations from those goals.

We have argued that in the absence of appropriate institutions or explicit mechanisms for bringing together the multiple groups holding a stake in the assignment process, the client–service setting assignment evolves out of an informal negotiation process. Typically, benefits and costs of the assignment are distributed according to the relative bargaining power of clients, service providers, governments and local community groups, a power that in turn is largely a function of relative affluence and political clout. One result of this process has been the service-dependent ghetto. Instead of this informal and inequitable process, we offer a regional fair-share approach to the assignment problem and suggest that this is a viable method for determining an efficient and equitable metropolitan distribution of community support resources and obligations. Such a program would lessen the inequities conferred by current practice onto clients and ghetto residents, but would also constitute a politically flexible mechanism that considers the rights of participating groups.

We have advocated a two-tiered approach to the implementation of such a fair-share plan and have described the respective roles of a regional body and local service agencies or boards in the assignment process. The regional body, assuming a coordinative and technical role, would estimate supply and demand for community-based facilities and would allocate to each local jurisdiction a fair share of the region's total burden of support for service-dependent populations residing there. The regional body would also act as a broker, negotiating between communities to determine the exact configuration of client assignments. Local service boards would provide not only a *locus* for community participation in service decisions, but would function as sources for planning information and citizen evaluations of facility impacts.

Numerous compensatory instruments for achieving acceptable client assignments have been described, including facilities packaging; modifications in program and facility design; service augmentation and subcenter clusters; client/facility trade-off schemes; fair-share burden pricing; and transfers of facility obligations between communities. The limitations of these tools in practice were also explored, as were additional considerations related to the elaboration of workable fair-share plans for community support services.

If local tasks of service delivery planning can be accomplished and if issues in the implementation of fair-share planning and arbitration policies can be resolved, troubling ethical dilemmas still remain with respect to solving the problem of the service-dependent ghetto. A service/client assignment that 'bribes' communities into accepting clients as residents may strike many as loathsome and objectionable. Trade-offs and 'markets' for facility obligations which use service-dependent residents as bargaining chips in intercommunity power struggles can rob them of their human dignity and right to privacy. It is possible, however, that nothing less than community exposure to clients on a recurrent basis facilitates the formation of positive attitudes and client integration and hence an initial allocation becomes indispensible to future community care outcomes. Without a change in spatial distribution, there may be little improvement in the current plight of ghettoized service-dependent populations and saturated communities and less hope for the future. Granted, laws and regulations could be imposed exogenously on local jurisdictions; but such an approach would be ineffective in promoting client growth if it creates hostile community environments. The approach we offer here recognizes the urgent need for change yet is cognizant of the real objections to centrally mandated regulations and policies that go against the local grain. Increasing community acceptance and accommodation of the service-dependent population may be a slow and arduous process, but the policy avenues described here may initiate the client integration process and promote a more inclusive, open society. At the very least, they represent a more equitable alternative to our present system of community-based human-service delivery.

10

The view from the future

SUMMARY

This book began by exploring the central question about the service-dependent ghetto: what set of social forces could have produced this particular urban form? The roots of the ghetto, we have argued, are to be found in the processes of urbanization and the Welfare State. Contemporary North American cities have developed a distinctive spatial structure that includes an inner-city zone of transition, the incipient service-dependent ghetto. This was a deteriorated area of inexpensive accommodation for transients, unemployed, social outcasts and the disabled and it remains a continuing phenomenon of modern cities. Since World War II, the zone of transition has expanded and intensified as a result of rapid suburbanization of population and employment activities. The accelerated decay in urban core areas has in some cases become so severe that residential and nonresidential abandonment is common.

Cities have also been the traditional focus for public welfare and human-service delivery. Initially, private charitable organizations located in the urban core, near client populations. Later, public asylums and other large-scale institutions became the preferred treatment setting for dependent populations and their locational patterns became the dominant spatial expression of human-service policy. Most recently, the policy of deinstitutionalization discharged many service-dependent persons into unprepared and ill-equipped local communities.

Against this backdrop of changing social and spatial structure, individual agents try to satisfy client needs. Everyday practices of helping professionals are designed to match deinstitutionalized populations to existing human services and residential opportunities. Even without professional interventions, service-dependent persons are attracted to areas where support services and housing opportunities are available. Cheap housing, congregate homes and other services tend to be located in the inner city, where facility operators find properties suitable for conversion to group homes, halfway houses, treatment centers and other agencies. The inner city is also where service providers find most of their clientele and the least community opposition to the service-dependent and their facilities. In contrast, affluent city neighborhoods and suburban jurisdictions have typically excluded service-dependent populations and their support services. Land-use planners have also encouraged facility siting in the core of the city, viewing the historical zone of transition as a risk-free, uncontroversial setting for facility locations. Thus because of the everyday activities of helping professions, clients, communities and urban planners, community-based human services and their clientele have become concentrated in the oldest and most deteriorated part of the inner city: the service-dependent ghetto.

The contemporary service-dependent ghetto is the result of a complex of historical forces. The social history of 'dependency' during the nineteenth century reveals a pervasive conception of the service-dependent population as deviant, dangerous and pauperized. As the wage-labor system spread and the problem of dependency grew, the most popular therapeutic response was institutionalization for the dependent classes. Out of this Jacksonian belief in institution-based moral treatment there evolved a reliance, by the late nineteenth century, on the institution for purely custodial functions and for protection of urban communities from the depredations of disease and degeneracy. During this period, state involvement in the support of dependent populations grew, in the forms of fiscal aid to institutions and outdoor (i.e., in-home) relief. The latter was expanded as a result of popular demands despite the concerted attack against it by the increasingly specialized helping professions. By the late nineteenth century, these professions had diversified into branches for children, the poor, sick, insane, retarded and criminal classes; and they had become organized and integrated into a growing state welfare bureaucracy. The dichotomization of service support into institutional and outdoor relief was paralleled by a dualistic spatial organization of dependent populations designed to insure their segregation from others and control their behavior. They either resided in rural or urban-fringe asylums, or were segregated in an incipient service-dependent ghetto: the pauper warrens of the Victorian city core.

The service-dependent population of the early twentieth century expanded markedly because of the needs of returning World War I veterans and the poverty associated with the interwar years. Patterns of service delivery came under severe attack from Progressives who sought to reform institutions, to individualize treatment regimes via detailed casework and to extend community-based services, all by extending the role of the state in everyday life. Progressive efforts failed to alter the scale or custodial character of institution-based treatment and their success at community service delivery was minimal, until the passage of Social Security in the 1930s. However, after the period of active Progressive effort, human-service workers became increasingly professionalized, each field oriented to ever-finer demarcations of client types; and the realm of state involvement in welfare broadened in the form of social insurance and expanded penal, medical, mental health and child care institutions and services.

Divisions between institutional and in-home service provision remained strong in the twentieth century and principles of segregative control of dependents continued to shape spatial patterns of service delivery. Large-scale asylums continued to be sited in rural or urban peripheral areas, but the growth of cities since the nineteenth century left many large institutions squarely within the new, enlarged boundaries of the expanding metropolis. Land uses and populations of these growing industrial cities became increasingly differentiated; suburbanization and growth of the downtown areas during this era led to a clear identity of the Central Business District-fringe as a zone of dependence that housed the noninstitutionalized dependent populations.

General philosophies of treatment and care became manifest as a specifically urban phenomenon across North America. This is well displayed in the realm of psychiatric care in the urban locales of the Province of Ontario. Following the discovery of the asylum in the early 1800s, the Province quickly adopted a policy of opening asylums in most of its major urban centers. This adoption of public responsibility for care was matched by a private, voluntary-sector response in the provision of relief and charity, often initiated by religious orders. The nineteenth-century institutions were typically sited on the urban fringe. But as cities expanded, these sites gradually became quite central, ending up in what had become incipient service-dependent ghettos, as the example of downtown Toronto shows. Therefore, at the beginning of the twentieth century, the essential geographical prerequisites for the development of a service-dependent ghetto were established: namely, large urban-based asylums drawing their clientele from a much wider regional catchment; and an informal community-care sector located in the core area of the city.

When the community mental health 'revolution' took hold in the 1960s and 1970s, a relatively rapid demise of the psychiatric hospital occurred. The deinstitutionalization of hospital-based populations was a response to new treatment philosophies, major advances in chemotherapy, a concern with patients' rights and fiscal pressures. The ex-patients were discharged to a relatively unprepared community. Those who could not return to the support of family and friends – typically the 'chronic' patient – normally found their way rapidly to the inner city. Here, informal and formal support networks already existed and cheap accommodation could be found. This was also the area where a growth industry in providing homes for ex-patients was springing up. A new 'asylum without walls' had been created as ex-patients moved from asylum to ghetto.

Community response to the deinstitutionalization of psychiatric patients have been mixed. Suburban jurisdictions have been very slow to provide facilities and services for ex-patients. Hence, the ghettoization process has been intensified by the exclusionary behavior of the suburbs. The situation has become aggravated still further as planners have adopted siting strategies specifically designed to identify noncontroversial community settings. As a consequence, ex-psychiatric patients are being placed *in* residential communities, but tend not to be part *of* the community.

The service-dependent ghetto in one city – Hamilton, Ontario – is illustrative of the structure and evolution of the ghetto in other North American cities. The emergence of a zone of dependence in Hamilton is rooted in the early history of its inner city, beginning with the founding of the settlement in the early nineteenth century. The first poor and relief populations lived in boarding houses within and adjacent to the core area – a locational pattern that continued essentially uninterrupted into the mid-twentieth century. At that time, deinstitutionalization and a restructuring of the Welfare State caused a chain reaction of events which eventually resulted in a ghetto of service-dependent populations. In Ontario, extensive cutbacks in welfare-oriented budgets, together with the mobilization of the voluntary and private sectors, placed the burden of caring for deinstitutionalized groups on cities. At the same time, an extensive decentralization and suburbanization of economic and population activities in Hamilton opened up the core area for occupation by service-dependent groups. Traditional patterns of urban social structure became overlain with the new welfare population in the service-dependent ghetto.

The contemporary ghetto in Hamilton shows an intense concentration of health and welfare-related institutions in the core area. This institutional pattern is paralleled in the geographical distribution of client populations. Changes in the provision of welfare services have affected the process of ghettoization of the mentally disabled, mentally retarded, physically disabled, elderly and probationers and parolees. The service-dependent ghetto defined by these populations emerges as a tightly defined area around the central city.

The contemporary processes of ghettoization in Hamilton are highlighted by the growth of the 'lodging-home' industry in the city over the past decade. Approximately 90 homes in the city provide shelter and some supervisory care for a population largely consisting of ex-psychiatric patients. Most of the homes have opened since 1975; they are licensed, but their locations are chosen by the operators who run them. Community concerns about this pattern ultimately led to a new zoning law with specific distance-spacing requirements between lodging houses, passed in the hope that the entire city would share in the burden of providing sites for future homes. This has not happened. Most operators of newly licensed homes continue to seek a ghetto location. Community opposition has been appeased (at least temporarily) and the consolidation of the service-dependent ghetto continues.

In Ontario, the future of the ghetto appears to be uncertain. However, in California, steps have already been taken to dismantle it, suggesting the future that may be in store for other urban areas across North America. A service-dependent ghetto arose in Santa Clara County, California, during the late 1960s and the early 1970s, as California evacuated its state mental hospitals and institutions for the retarded, and began community service programs in corrections, retardation, mental health, disability and elderly care. In the absence of policies for, or controls on, the spatial configuration of service supports, a ghetto of service-dependents and facilities grew up in downtown San Jose, where postwar economic development patterns and suburbanization had left core-area land and housing markets susceptible to occupation by marginal uses. This pattern of concentration was reinforced by the exclusionary policies of suburban governments which served to keep services and clients in San Jose and by state policies of facility location which avoided land-use conflict by siting services in the politically feeble core area.

But by the late 1970s, intense conflict over the ghetto itself had erupted, with opposition to the ghetto led by a political coalition of downtown real-estate interests and neighborhood groups. The battle against the ghetto was fueled by rapid housing-price inflation in the region and a growing job–housing imbalance in Santa Clara County, both of which served to create potentials for redevelopment and gentrification of downtown San Jose. The result has been a decline in the service-dependent population of the ghetto and the closure or removal of service supports, a trend exacerbated by fiscal retrench-ment prompted by the California tax limitation (Proposition 13) and by the Reagan program cutbacks. From our vantage-point; we suggest that the dismantling of the ghetto has led to alternative treatment trends, including assignment to inappropriate services, homelessness and a return to institutions, none of which promise to ameliorate the severe problems of the community-based service population.

The problem of misassignment of dependent groups to the criminal justice system and the explosion of homelessness have reached crisis proportions. Evidence for the mentally disabled in California suggests that history is about to come full circle: once again, the call for large-scale shelters for the homeless is being heard, along with arguments for the necessity of 'safe and comfort-able asylums' for the chronically ill. In California, this has led to increases in funding for the moribund state mental hospitals and for homeless shelters. Moreover, the prison population has increasingly drawn in the service-dependent and homeless, prompting (along with other factors) a massive expansion in prison capacity to handle the burgeoning caseload.

Reinstitutionalization will be, we predict, the most likely direction of human-services policy – unless vigorous attempts are made to avert it by fulfilling the promise of deinstitutionalization. Many of the failures of deinstitutionalization policy resulted from a lack of preparedness on the part of human agents involved in the process, in the face of dramatically altered structural constraints and urban forces. In today's North American cities, the advent of chronic homelessness symbolizes a transformation in the landscape of the service-dependent ghetto. Once a coping mechanism for clients, the ghetto has become an icon of pathology in current social welfare practice. Chronic homelessness is best understood as a result not only of life on the streets, but also of the experience of service-dependency itself. In order to resolve the problems of service-dependent groups (including the homeless), policy frameworks designed to assist human agents in their organization and delivery of community-based services are required, along with reforms to relax the political–economic constraints of the 1980s.

The gross inadequacies of social service coordination, interjurisdictional cooperation and physical/social planning integration suggest a vital need to explore the political and technical dimensions of the planning problem facing the human-service system and to design planning and arbitration mechanisms for community-based programs. Careful consideration must be given to the benefits and costs of both service concentration and dispersion, in order to design better systems and to better understand the conflict between client and community rights which emerges from specific locational patterns of service supports. We conclude that the historical conflict over rights has a legitimate basis that must be reconciled by the planning process, but that in addition, there exist strong legal precedents to suggest that local communities also have an obligation to share responsibilities for dependent groups.

Both the protection of rights and the assignment of obligations can be insured via two strategies for action. Planning approaches, involving service coordination, integration of physical and social aspects of community planning, citizen education concerning the dependent and sensible facility siting strategies, have the potential to decrease ghettoization, improve service delivery and further the integration of clients into the community. In metropolitan areas where strong interjurisdictional disparities in class, power and spatial organization create horizontal conflicts, arbitration strategies may prove more effective. A fair-share framework designed to provide interjurisdictional arbitration mechanisms is necessary to insure client and community rights and to distribute support responsibility fairly, thus leading to the development of equitable and efficient human-service systems.

ARCHEOLOGIES OF THE FUTURE

The deinstitutionalization movement can be regarded as the cumulative impact of a broad range of social changes that began in the 1950s. Its effect has been to create the most radical departure in human-services delivery since the first workhouses, prisons and asylums were built over 200 years ago. Under such circumstances, it seems somewhat churlish to criticize the advocates of deinstitutionalization for not planning the new welfare system properly. The many unanticipated and sometimes undesirable side-effects of deinstitutionalization could not have been foreseen without knowledge of later transformations in the social, political and economic climates. Moreover, despite the dilemmas facing community-based services, those early advocates took the first step in delivering what many had called for but which institution-based services had historically failed to provide: humane, caring support for the dependent. Thus deinstitutionalization was – and is – a necessary stage in the evolution of modern human services.

On the other hand, reinstitutionalization is a step backward in our commitment to progressive service-support systems. We do not doubt that a small number of the service-dependent will always require a secluded, protected living situation; but there is no need –either economic or therapeutic – for such quarters to be provided in large-scale institutions. The onus should be on the advocates of reinstitutionalization to demonstrate the requirement for 'new asylums' and we are frankly pessimistic that such demonstrations can be made.

We believe that the earlier arguments in favor of deinstitutionalization retain their validity. So where do we go from here? What will the future look like?

The future archeologist of human services is likely to discover one of two landscapes at the end of the twentieth century. The first is a *landscape of despair*. The perfect metaphor for this terrain is provided by the homeless who nightly populate the beaches of Santa Monica and Venice, California. They sleep next to the ocean at the continent's edge, a little distance from a tide that could sweep them away. This portrait of the landscape of despair presages the collapse of the human-service system and an abandonment of those in need. The lucky and resourceful who manage to survive hang on by their fingernails at the edge of society.

An alternative archeology is invoked by the many engravings of nineteenth-century asylums. These massive, isolated structures epitomized their creators' search for order, control and 'cure'. As Foucault indicated, the asylum was only one episode in the history of haunted places. The future archeologist might discover a new *landscape of haunted places*, reflecting the rebirth of the institution in the 1980s. The trend toward reinstitutionalization will again take the service-dependent out of sight and out of mind. Only the ghosts of the incarcerated will be left to haunt the community. And deinstitutionalization will be recognized as but a brief respite in the history of the enduring institution.

Instead of these alternative archeologies, we call for a *landscape of caring*. This is a landscape in which the potential and promise of deinstitutionalization will be realized. In it, community-based care is the norm: clients would have the right to service provision in their own community and communities would have the obligation to look after their own.

We recognize that political priorities of the restructured Welfare State may stand in the way of the landscape of caring. First, there is an acute *lack of political will* to deal with the problems associated with the unfolding saga of deinstitutionalization. The various levels of federal, state/provincial and municipal governments desperately blame each other for every crisis. Such vertical conflict of interest is further complicated by horizontal disputes among the various sectors responsible for health, welfare and other key human services. When emergency or crisis situations cause a reallocation of tax dollars, the funds often seem to be directed unimaginatively toward buttressing the old institution-based solutions.

Secondly, the absence of political consensus derives partly from the great *inertia in the health and welfare systems*. As we have argued, deinstitutionalization has created a new apparatus of the Welfare State. This has had two consequences. One is that competition over professional dominance and control has intensified as the existing professional elites seek to protect their 'turf' from the incursion of community-based counterparts. (The best example is perhaps the many union-based campaigns by psychiatric hospital workers to persuade the public of the continuing need for asylums and hence, for their jobs.) Another consequence is that the diffusion of authority implied by community care has the paradoxical effect of simultaneously extending and weakening the traditional channels of social control. Doctors, psychiatrists and social workers have penetrated as never before into the everyday lives of individuals; yet the consequent stretching of the ties of authority between professional and client has also meant that a client group's traditional allegiance to one professional elite can no longer be guaranteed. The rediscovery of the institution, in this light, appears as a retrenchment which will once again clarify and consolidate professional control over the various client populations.

Finally, the political reality of *community opposition* must be addressed. The recent history of deinstitutionalization has brought more and more communities into direct contact with service-dependent groups which they had hitherto rarely encountered. Such communities are likely to be more resistant than previous opponents. Attacks by vigilante groups on the homeless even in traditionally accepting neighborhoods are further testimony to a groundswell of intolerance. The problem of opposition is unlikely to diminish. It may yet prove to be the tangential issue on which continued progress toward deinstitutionalization is blocked.

If these hurdles are to be overcome, how can we set about creating the landscape of caring? The general long-term objective must be to realize the community-based alternative promised by *deinstitutionalization*. This includes a full range of transitional living arrangements for the diverse service-dependent populations, as well as specific programs of care, social integration and employment.

In the short term, the immediate need is for *shelter and services*. For some clients, shelter alone will suffice; for others, ancillary support services will be necessary. Each new program effort should be accompanied by *community outreach*. Neighborhood support for deinstitutionalization must be mobilized; it is vital that neighbors feel willing, able, and – above all – legitimate in supporting community-based care. This can be achieved through tapping the deep roots of tolerance and humanity evidenced in most communities and by increasing neighborhood awareness of the problems of the service-dependent.

The simultaneous existence of tolerant and intolerant dimensions in a community psyche should not be regarded as an inexplicable contradiction. Our experience suggests that communities have generally favorable views of the *problem* of providing community care, but that they often reject the proposed *solution* for service delivery. Specifically, residents share a common concern for problems of the service-dependent, but have no wish to solve those problems in their neighborhood or on their block. A vital part of outreach is therefore a community education program to improve residents' understanding, familiarity and awareness of the problems of service delivery – and to suggest ways in which community participation can assist in overcoming these problems.

One very practical way of proceeding on all these fronts is to develop 'service hubs' throughout our communities. This recommendation stems from our observation that the service-dependent ghetto acts as a coping mechanism for the deinstitutionalized. Why, then, should we not replicate the positive features of the ghetto elsewhere in the city? This would involve identifying those neighborhood centers that already possess a reasonable standard of community and public transportation services; such centers could then be reinforced by the addition of necessary housing, services and employment opportunities. These decentralized hubs would have the effect of opening up a wide range of usable residential alternatives for the service-dependent. The amount of new support infrastructure would be minimal, since the hubs would already operate as independent centers of social interaction. Community opposition would be reduced if only small numbers of people and services were grafted onto an already diverse social fabric and pattern of land use and if all communities were perceived as sharing the 'burden' of caring. Perhaps the best example of a potential service hub is the suburban shopping mall, with its extensive range of services and often good transportation links. The introduction of a few extra housing units and a store-front community service center would transform the mall into another opportunity to build an effective community-based support system.

The concept of the service hub returns us to our point of departure in this book. There, we emphasized the impact of a social process (deinstitutionalization) on a particular geographic location (the inner city). We have concluded by recommending a new urban-based solution to the social problems associated with the evolving deinstitutionalization program. If this or some equivalent solution is not adopted, we run the imminent risk of recreating the landscape of haunted places or a descent into the landscape of despair. In either case, the future archeologist will conclude that the lessons of history and the warnings of this book were overlooked.

Appendix to chapter 5

Mentally disabled

Estimates of the number of mentally disabled in Hamilton were derived using *utilization* figures for the eight major psychiatric facilities in Hamilton (including one provincial psychiatric hospital, three inpatient units, and four outpatient units). For 1976 – the latest date for which complete statistics are available – the number of patients 'on the books' at year's end was taken as a measure of the service-dependent mentally disabled. The total population numbered 2,317.

Mentally retarded

In both Canada and the US it has been estimated that 3 per cent of the population will at some time function in the mentally retarded range of IQ (Effective Advocacy, 1974, p. 8). However, only 1 per cent of the population will probably be classified as being mentally retarded at any given time (Taryon, 1973, p. 327). Based on this 1 per cent estimate approximately 9,196 retarded people are presently living in Hamilton, yet only 3,065 have actually been identified as being retarded. In an attempt to find out the extent of the current service network for the mentally retarded, all Hamilton organizations that provide services for the mentally retarded were contacted. These organizations served a mere 522 people or about 5.6 per cent of the estimated retarded population, or 17.6 per cent of the identified retarded population.

Since 1951, Hamilton and District Association for the Mentally Retarded (HDAMR) has been the primary provider of services in the Hamilton area to people of all ages who have intellectual impairments. The HDAMR is the primary provider of employment for the mentally retarded in the area and approximately 200 adults participate in the vocational programs that it offers. The lack of suitable employment for the mentally retarded is equalled by the lack of suitable residential accommodation. There are only 198 beds available for mentally retarded people in specialized residential facilities in Hamilton. Most of these facilities only provide custodial care. The facilities available only provide for 2.15 per cent of the estimated population of mentally retarded people in Hamilton (or 6.46 per cent of those who are identified as mentally retarded).

Although only 522 mentally retarded people could be investigated through the caseloads of these agencies, this small segment of the total retarded population may be regarded as constituting most of the 'service-dependent' mentally retarded population in Hamilton. This population tends to locate close to the city center but there are important concentrations in other areas (figure 5.4). This reflects the fact that many of the 522 people live in custodial and pseudo-custodial institutions in various parts of the city, or still live in their parents' homes.

Probationers and Parolees

The Probation and Parole Service currently refers clients to over 40 social service agencies in Hamilton. These tend to be primarily located in the core area of the city. The service has specific contracts with such agencies as the Elizabeth Fry Society, which supervises people carrying out community-service orders (i.e. doing community work); the John Howard Society, which provides both supervision and investigation services; and the 'Alternatives for Youth' group, which contracts to provide counseling for people involved in drug and alcohol abuse. The addresses of the total active case-load (13,238 clients) of the Probation and Parole Service in early 1979 were obtained and used to compile figure 5.5.

Physically handicapped

In this study, 'handicapped' is defined in terms of mobility. The actual population of handicapped persons in Ontario has never been documented accurately; various estimates that have been presented range from 8 per cent to 14 per cent of the total population (see Ontario Federation for the Physically Handicapped, 1976). The Department of Housing and Urban Development (HUD) in the US uses the figure of 10 per cent in its estimates of the handicapped population. The Canadian Sickness Survey (1951) estimated that 3.1 per cent of all Canadians were severely or totally handicapped. An American survey for the handicapped found that 1.5 per cent of the American population had trouble getting around and 0.7 per cent of the population were confined to their homes; thus in total, 2.2 per cent of the American population had mobility problems. On the basis of these figures, approximately 3 per cent of the Ontario population (or 200,000 persons) may be physically disabled.

Studies of the handicapped in Hamilton have estimated that 3 per cent of the population (about 15,000 people) were handicapped with respect to mobility. Goodwill Industries in Hamilton suggests that 1.5 per cent of the area's population is physically disabled to the extent that they need workshop services. This represents approximately 7,500 physically disabled individuals, but this figure does not include those handicapped individuals who are homebound. In light of these estimates, 10,000 people in Hamilton may be severely physically handicapped. In order to ascertain the location of the service-dependent physically disabled population in Hamilton, the addresses of all the active cases were secured from the social service agencies that deal with the physically disabled. The 1,473 people thus identified constitute the currently service-dependent physically disabled population in Hamilton (figure 5.6).

Elderly

The number of people over 65 years of age in Hamilton was 40,338 in 1981 (9.3 per cent of the total population); between 1974 and 1979, the over-54 age-group was the fastest-growing cohort in Hamilton. We might therefore expect to see a rapid expansion in institutional accommodation for the service-dependent elderly. In fact, the capacity to provide care for the service-dependent elderly has marginally declined. In 1973, there were six homes for the aged with a total capacity of 1,128 persons. No new homes have been built since and the capacity in this sector has not changed. In 1975, there was a capacity of 1,268 beds in the nursing homes of the Hamilton–Wentworth region, but since then two small homes in the suburban area of the city have closed, resulting in a net loss of 78 beds.

Most of the nursing homes in Hamilton are centrally located, whereas the Homes for the Aged are more scattered across the city. The most probable explanation for this distribution is that nursing homes are private for-profit institutions so they locate mainly in the older central areas of the city where large old buildings can be bought quite cheaply and converted for use. Homes for the Aged are publicly owned or run by large charities and usually provide services from newly constructed facilities. They are therefore not subject to the same locational criteria as for-profit agencies.

Most people aged 70 or over live below the poverty line and are dependent on government transfer payments for survival. They are also dependent on subsidized housing or some form of institutional care, both of which are being supplied in diminishing amounts in Hamilton. Many elderly people await appropriate placements. The ill-defined, dispersed nature of the elderly makes it difficult to provide an accurate picture of the distribution of the service-dependent component of this population. A reasonable approximation of the service-dependent elderly in Hamilton was prepared from data on the population over 70 years of age supplied by the City of Hamilton Planning Department (figure 5.7).

Appendix to chapter 9

DESCRIPTION OF GOALS-PROGRAMMING MODEL

This appendix describes in greater detail the goals-programming model for the regional assignment of clients and community-based care facilities.

The goals-programming model is an extension of linear programming. Unlike linear programming, however, which seeks to maximize (minimize) a goal subject to constraints, the GP framework balances multiple conflicting objectives by permitting trade-offs to occur between these objectives (Turban and Meredith, 1984).

In the area of human-services planning, service objectives can rarely be articulated as some unitary goal. Accordingly, the GP model provides a far more flexible and pragmatic approach to client assignment than does the tradition linear programming framework. Nevertheless, the GP concept has been applied only recently to health and human-service planning (see Franz, Rakes and Wynne (1984), for an example of a probabilistic goals-programming model for guiding the allocation of mental health service resources).

In the case of community residential care, the GP framework may be used to develop an assignment process that effectively balances outcomes where equity and efficiency objectives conflict and where conflicts over client and community location rights arise. Given the many intangibles that the client-location allocation problem must address, the GP approach is a largely heuristic tool which nevertheless offers a useful paradigm for structuring the facility assignment problem. Moreover, this approach permits the evaluation of any spatial assignment (for example, dispersion or concentration) and provides a guide for developing practical assignment strategies to manage the conflicts inherent in community-based residential care.

ELEMENTS OF THE GOALS-PROGRAMMING MODEL

Briefly, the formal structure of any GP model has four basic elements: goals, decision variables, system constraints, goal constraints as well as objective function. Like their linear programming (LP) counterparts, decision variables refer to the actual units to be assigned (for example products, people) while system constraints represent absolute restrictions on the assignment process, with no flexibility allowed (or possible). Goal constraints of the GP model are similar to objective functions in LP; they represent aspiration or target levels for each goal of the assignment system. For example, an LP objective function (or goal) might seek to maximize profit by selection of an optimum mix of outputs, where each product has a given profit margin. Transformed to a goal constraint, however, we would specify the target profit amount and allow for some deviation around that target.

In LP, the objective function is to maximize (or minimize) the value of a single goal subject to constraints. In GP, the objective function is to minimize the weighted sum of the undesired deviations

$$(d_i + / -)$$

from multiple goal constraints, subject to system constraints. For a model with one goal constraint, this objective function could be:

$$\text{Min. } Z = d$$

where the undesirable deviations (d) may be either positive or negative according to whether underachievement or overachievement of the goal constraint target is preferred.

Where more than one goal constraint is desired, they must be ranked according to some priority unless constraints are sufficiently loose to allow achievement of all goals with no deviations from targets. Ranking permits deviations of higher-ranked goal constraints to be minimized prior to those of less important goal constraints.

A GP MODEL FOR COMMUNITY-BASED CARE

In the case of client/facility assignment, two overarching sets of goals guide the specification of the GP model. The first goal is that client rights be respected; the second goal is that rights of the community at large and of the specific communities in which clients are to reside, are upheld. The elements of the GP model, guided by these two broad goals, are described below as they apply in the case of client and residential care facility assignment.

Decision variables

Decision variables of the model are the clients and residential service settings to be allocated among communities:

$$X_{ij}$$

= number of clients of diagnostic category i (mentally ill, developmentally disabled, elderly, etc.), of level of personal functioning j.

$$S(F_q, C_{mk})$$

= residential service setting S, characterized by facility of type q (halfway houses, group homes, etc.) located in community m with k local characteristics (ecology, service systems, spatial structure).

System constraints

As discussed previously, system constraints represent absolute restrictions on the assignment outcome, with no allowance for deviation. In this case system constraints require first, that the client diagnostic category and level of functioning are evaluated by appropriate subspeciality professionals within the human services, to avoid 'transinstitutionalism'. The second system constraint requires that the designated optimal service modality,

$$S^*(F_q^*, C_k^*)$$

used to guide actual client assignment to

$$S(F_q, C_{mk})$$

encompasses that combination of facility characteristics (q) and community attributes (k), which minimizes setting restrictiveness. In effect, this system constraint requires that the optimal (least restrictive) residential service setting, S^*, for a client X_{ij}, be *identified*. The actual assignment of the client to that setting is expressed as a goal constraint in the next section. Relevant elements of (q) affecting restrictiveness include facility type (residential or nonresidential), rules, level of supervision, client mix (whether other users or residents are of compatible nature) and enabling services available there. Attributes (k) of community (m) which affect restrictiveness include attitudes toward the client expressed by other residents of the facility, level and congestion of ancillary service supports, range of alternative residential service settings through which clients can proceed during their 'careers' and spatial characteristics which affect ease of client–resident and client– service interactions. Other characteristics of F_q^* and C_k^* that are necessary to insure client rights to effective service and an integrative community are appropriate technical/programmatic features of facilities and attitudinal and demographic features of communities.

The third and final system constraint requires that communities provide a full continuum of residential service settings.

Goal constraints

The model's central elements are its five goal constraints. First, for each X_{ij}, the magnitude of the difference between S^* and S, or $F_q^* C_k^*$ and

F_qC_{mk}, must not be sufficient to violate clients' rights to the least-restrictive environment and an integrative community, or right to effective service. These attributes could be measured and values assigned to facility types according to some index of restrictiveness, where independent living and institutionalization in a locked facility are at opposite ends of a continuum:

$$S + d_1 = S^* \qquad 1$$

where d_1 = acceptable deviation from optimal assignment, defined jointly by clients and human-service professionals. The sum of the deviations can be either positive or negative, since settings can be either overly restrictive or too unrestrictive.

Secondly, community (m) must be involved in the assignment decision, with involvement structured according to and evaluated against criteria for citizen participation in federal human-service programs (such as those specified for community mental health centers):

$$CP_m + d_2 = CP_n \qquad 2$$

where CP_m = level of citizen participation in community (m) as measured by criteria specified in federal human-service programs; CP_n = federal norm for citizen participation in human-service programs; d_2 = acceptable deviation of CP_m from CP_n which will be positive (assuming that the concept of excessive participation is not applicable).

Thirdly, the assignment

$$X_{ij}, S(F_qC_{mk})$$

should be the most cost-effective one possible, respecting taxpayer demands for efficiency in service delivery. This efficiency condition implies that providers offering equivalent services at least cost are selected in the award of contracts and that available economies of scale in service administration and provision will be realized. Here, levels of efficiency and acceptable deviations can be expressed in monetary units:

$$E + d_3 = E^* \qquad 3$$

where E = efficiency of the assignment; E^* = maximum efficiency; d_3 = acceptable inefficiency (positive since by definition actual efficiency of the assignment can never exceed maximum efficiency).

Fourth, the assignment cannot violate community-set standards for undesirable social, fiscal and environmental impacts. Such impacts are externalities of the service system which affect community income, broadly defined. They include changes in land-use compatibility, tax levels, service package level and design, traffic and noise levels, service dependency rates in the population and property values. This goal constraint maintains the community's right to define its own character and opportunities. In this case, the level of impact and acceptable deviations can often be quantified, for example property-value change, change in vehicles per hour along a neighborhood street, etc. Other impacts (risk of exposure to peculiar behavior, for instance, or simply attitudes about client populations or facilities) are less tangible, but have been measured according to various indices (Smith and Hanham, 1981; Dear and Taylor, 1982) which could be employed here:

$$I_m + d_4 = I^*_m \qquad\qquad 4$$

where I_m = negative impacts of assignment on community (m); I^*_m = negative impact thresholds set by community (m); d_4 = acceptable deviation from impact threshold, either positive or negative.

Lastly, the client assignment cannot violate community (m)'s right to horizontal equity in service delivery. This constraint prohibits both the 'dumping' of clients onto a small number of specific communities and the avoidance of local obligations to provide support for clients. Levels of impact burden and deviation are defined in the same manner as in goal constraint 4:

$$I_m + d_5 = I_m \qquad\qquad 5$$

where I_m = average community impact burden; d_5 = acceptable deviation from mean impact burden.

Objective function

The GP objective function can now be stated:

$$\text{Min. } Z = \sum P_i\, d_i \qquad\qquad 6$$

where P = priority ranking of ith goal constraint; d = the undesirable deviation from ith goal constraint.

The objective function implies that unwanted deviations from goal constraint targets are minimized, in the order of their importance to the assignment. If existing parameter values of the GP model (for example targets, deviations, etc.) preclude a solution, they must be reevaluated and changed, either by lowering (raising) targets, or by expanding the range of acceptable deviation.

Since new clients are continually entering the community framework, either from its own ranks or as a result of deinstitutionalization, the goal-programming model is iterative. Each new increment of clients is assigned and reassigned until the model converges to an equilibrium solution (the cumulative client assignment meets goal constraints). Clients are reassigned if and when they experience a change in diagnostic category and/or level of functioning and thus have different service requirements.

The goals-programming model becomes operational when its parameters are defined: decision variables are identified, system constraints are specified, goals constraints are ranked, their aspiration or target levels are set and acceptable deviations from these targets are identified.

Notes

1 Policies embracing deinstitutionalization have been implemented in several countries, particularly in regard to the mentally disabled (see, for example, the special issue on 'International Perspectives on Deinstitutionalization' in the *International Journal of Mental Health*, 1982/3; Lerman, 1982). The most radical approach has been adopted by Italy, where institutionalization was prohibited by legislative fiat in 1978. Other Western European countries have been slower to deinstitutionalize or have experienced great internal variety in the rate of deinstitutionalization (for example Switzerland). Overall, the United States and England and Wales have been at the forefront of the deinstitutionalization movement (Golman, Morrissey and Bachrach, 1982/3).

2 Note that in the context of urban-based service-dependent populations, our use of the term 'ghetto' differs in certain respects from its more common usage by social scientists in reference to racial or ethnic minorities (i.e. black ghetto; Jewish ghetto). In these latter cases, the term implies spatial concentration; the use of majority force or coercion (physical; legal; social practice) in maintaining the ghetto pattern; and a sense of community and self-identification as ghetto-dwellers. In the case of the service-dependent population ghetto, spatial concentration may be lower in absolute degree; the use of force or coercion is minimal; and a sense of community may or may not be experienced by residents. However, social, economic and political practices, including service delivery policy, planning regulations and land-use zoning, poverty and discrimination, act to eliminate non-ghetto alternatives for the service-dependent. Thus like other ghettos, the service-dependent population ghetto is a coercively constructed element in urban space, not simply a result of preferences for self-segregation (like an ethnic enclave) or the result of purely economic factors.

3 Alternately termed 'transinstitutionalization' in the human services literature.

CHAPTER 2

1 Examples of the extensive literature on the public city include Dear (1977); Dear et al. (1980); Lamb (1979b; 1984); Massey (1980); White (1979); Wolch (1979; 1980; 1981b); Wolpert and Wolpert (1976).

2 Perhaps the best way to enter these debates (at least as they pertain to our analysis) is via the following sources: the early essays by Gregory, Pred and Scott, in Gould and Olsson (1982); the fundamental exposition of structuration theory by Giddens (1984); the geographical interpretation of structuration by Thrift (1983); and the problems of empirical application as discussed in Dear and Moos (1986) and Moos and Dear (1986). Sayer (1984) provides a valuable overview of the methodological and philosophical issues underlying these debates. The recent collection of essays by Gregory and Urry (1985) provides the best overview of the substantive themes found within a single volume, while much of the debate surrounding current developments in the field appears in the journal *Society and Space* (Environment and Planning D).

3 The term 'terrain' is deliberately chosen to convey a sense of place as well as the notion of an arena of conflict, which is the sense in which Foucault uses the term *terrain* (cf. Driver, 1985, p. 443).

4 The evolution of the contemporary Welfare State in the United States, Canada, and Britain are reviewed respectively in Gilbert (1983); Guest (1980) and Mishra (1984). See also Gough (1979) and Offe (1984).

5 See, *inter alia*, Castel et al. (1982); Donzelot (1979); and Jones and Williamson (1979).

6 The logic of capitalist urbanization is summarized in Dear and Scott (1981). The detailed studies by David Harvey provide the best single source on the historical and contemporary processes of urbanization (see especially Harvey, 1982; 1985a, 1985b).

7 This report has been criticized in a special article in *Hospital and Community Psychiatry* (Anon., 1984).

8 This section draws heavily on Dear (1984). See also Baron (1981) and Weber (1978).

CHAPTER 3

1 It is perhaps worth pointing out that the social history of service-dependency is a source of lively controversy. The dimensions of the debate are well encompassed by Ingleby (1985), and in the two edited volumes by Bynum et al. (1985a, 1985b). It is not our intention, in this chapter, to resolve these tensions but to provide a historical geography that transcends their differences.

CHAPTER 4

1 In Upper Canada (later the Province of Ontario), population increased from 70,000 to 1,525,000 between 1806 and 1867 (Splane, 1965, p. 5).
2 Between 1860 and 1890, the City of Toronto's share of funding for the House of Industry grew from 36.7 per cent to 59 per cent of the House's operation budget. During the same period, the provincial share dropped from 25.7 per cent to 9.8 per cent (Pitsula, 1979).
3 Splane (1965), table XVI, details the nature of Ontario's expenditures (in dollars) for social welfare between 1868 and 1893:

TABLE XVI   *Ontario's social welfare expenditures, 1868–93 ($)*

Item	1868	1878	1888	1893
Office of the inspector	1,181	8,068	10,739	15,641
Mental institutions	177,585	457,045	679,940	743,020
Gaols, prisons and reformatories	66,992	174,499	224,793	218,109
Grants to private institutions	39,000	70,673	113,686	164,896
Deaf and blind institutions	—	103,073	86,130	99,901
Assistance to indigents	—	8,791	660	190
Grant to industrial school	—	—	1,000	6,500
Grant to Prisoner's Aid Association	—	—	1,000	1,000
Measures for public health	—	—	7,252	10,700
Inspection of factories	—	—	4,245	4,275
Protection of children	—	—	—	960
Total	284,758	822,149	1,129,445	1,265,192

4 The 1874 Charity Aid Act was the basis of payments of grants to hospitals. Between 1874 and 1893, the number of Ontario hospitals receiving provincial grants increased from 10 to 32. Funds granted rose from $32,684 to $107,312; and the number of patients treated per year increased from 3,466 to 12,392 (Splane, 1965, ch. 5).
5 The same effect was obtained in the US, although it was largely a result of the late nineteenth-century distinction between state and county care. The burden of welfare, which fell largely on the cities, ultimately led to the creation of urban-based institutions for the insane in parallel to the usually isolated, centrally located state institutions. See Deutsch, 1949, pp. 236–61; Fox, 1978, pp. 60–72; Grob, 1973, pp. 118–30; and Grob, 1983, pp. 26, 94.
6 A parallel tendency for urban jails to act as incipient zones of dependence is observed by Splane (1965, p. 135) who noted: 'discharged prisoners

tended to remain in the immediate locality [of jail] where, meeting with associates from the penitentiary, they fell once more into intemperate and criminal habits.'

7 Canada as a whole, and Ontario in particular, experienced a number of population explosions during the past two centuries, mainly associated with immigration. For instance, the period 1850–75 in Ontario was one of extensive economic growth associated with the railway boom. Between 1851 and 1861, the population of British North America grew from 2.3 million to 3.2 million, one half of this growth occurring in Ontario alone. Ontario also shared in the major immigration boom in the early part of the twentieth century (between 1900 and 1913, 2.5 million new immigrants entered Canada), and in the period following World War II.

8 The chief objectives of the US National Committee for Mental Hygiene – founded in 1908 by Clifford Beers – were:

To work for the protection of the mental health of the public; to help raise the standard of care for those in danger of developing mental disorder or actually insane; to provide the study of mental disorders in all their forms and relations and to disseminate knowledge concerning their causes, treatment and prevention; to obtain from every source reliable data regarding conditions and methods of dealing with mental disorders; to enlist the aid of the Federal Government so far as may seem desirable; to coordinate existing agencies and help organize in each State in the Union an allied, but independent, Society for Mental Hygiene.

(quoted in Deutsch, 1949, pp. 314–5)

9 It should be noted that mentally disabled persons had already begun to take up social welfare funds available under legislation that preceded the CAP. For example, between 1955 and 1965, the number of people with psychiatric disability receiving a disabled person's allowance doubled to 1,021 recipients. Many more received help under the General Welfare Assistance and the Rehabilitation Services Acts of 1955 (Allodi and Kedward, 1973, pp. 287–8).

10 The maps in Figures 4.5 and 4.6 were redrawn from data published in Joseph and Hall (1985).

CHAPTER 5

1 No full accounting of the dollar costs and savings of the deinstitutionalization movement has yet been provided. The residential-care alternative is undoubtedly a cheaper form of accommodation than a hospital bed. But hospital costs are generally expressed as an overall operating cost per patient per day (including food, services, administrative and other costs); on the other hand, a lodging-home cost typically refers only to board. Direct comparison of costs is therefore

uniformative, since the full costs of lodging-home care should also take account of providing welfare or disability payments, plus other ancillary services (such as medical care). In addition, many discharges have occurred without substantial reductions in institutional staffing. In the case of psychiatric hospitals, for example, the loss of patients has tended not to be accompanied by parallel reductions in psychiatric and social workers. In the case of prisons, the probation and parolee version of deinstitutionalization has been implemented with no reduction in prison staff or inmate levels; in fact, these levels have both increased. When a full accounting is possible, we suspect that deinstitutionalization and restructuring (at least up to 1986) will be seen to have vastly increased budgets, staffing levels in all sectors and numbers of population served. This will likely seem a paradoxical result in a political climate apparently dedicated to restraint in spending and government intervention.

2 It is by now well established that the availability of specialized social services is a significant factor in stimulating client movement to urban areas. Sizeable portions of the new migrants remain in the local area after discharge from care (see Dear, 1977, for more detailed evidence on the Hamilton case).

3 The 'service-dependent index' (SDI) in figures 5.3–5.8 is reported as follows:

1 Proportion of service-dependent population i (x_i) greater than one standard deviation (σ);
2 Proportion of population x_i greater than the population mean (μ), but less than σ; and
3 Proportion of population x_i less than the population mean μ.

4 Unless otherwise indicated, all references and quotations in this section are from Dear et al. (1980). This study reports on a follow-up of 169 people either preparing for discharge from Hamilton Psychiatric Hospital or in various stages of community living.

CHAPTER 7

1 Note that our use of the term 'reinstitutionalization' in the remainder of this book is intended to include the potential institutionalization of those who have never been institutionalized previously (for example the young chronic adult patient; cf. Lamb et al., 1985).

2 This trend toward erection of shelters is mirrored across the country. For example, the City of New York opened a shelter on an isolated and uninhabited island, which now houses an average of 500 to 600 persons daily (Baxter and Hopper, 1982, p. 30); the city also began a $64 million shelter-building program (Boodman, 1985). In Boston, the State Department of Mental Health converted a gymnasium into a shelter exclusively

for the homeless mentally disabled (Nickerson, 1985a, p. 22). Bergen County opened a shelter in 1984 (Parisi, 1985, p. I36:4); and Massachusetts in 1984/5 allocated $5.3 million for a total of 1,500 shelter beds in 17 public and 60 private shelters for the homeless (*New York Times*, 6 January 1985, p. I36:4).

3 Certain rights have already been withdrawn in some cities. For example, Mayor Koch of New York succeeded in altering city policy regarding incarceration of the homeless. Currently, when the temperature drops to a given level, police are authorized to pick up the homeless and place them, either voluntarily or involuntarily, in shelters, hospitals, or jails.

4 These efforts are related to those of other states to overhaul involuntary commitment procedures. For example, the State of Virginia has doubled funding for commitment systems, providing for greater ease of committal. The state has also introduced a 'provisional discharge' program (similar to parole), which would compel the discharged individual to agree to outpatient treatment and medication, with noncompliance resulting in reinstitutionalization without hearing or ability to appeal (Boodman and Moore, 1985, p. D4).

5 The call for an outdoor home in Saugus is ironic. The site is the same one proposed as a new state prison by Los Angeles Mayor Tom Bradley. His selection of the Saugus location came after an earlier proposal to site the prison close to downtown was defeated by neighboring community groups, which claimed that their area was already saturated with criminal justice facilities. The residents of Saugus, however, have launched a vociferous attack on the Mayor's new site selection, thus jeopardizing the proposal's success.

CHAPTER 8

1 The following sources are indicative of the extensive literature on this topic: Chu and Trotter, 1984; Levine, 1981; Lewis, 1982; Smith, 1983; Kirk and Therrien, 1975; Rose, 1979; Talbott, 1979; Klerman, 1977; Pepper and Ryglewicz, 1982; Braun et al., 1981; Bassuk and Gerson, 1978; Scull, 1981; Coates, 1976; Warren, 1981; Bachrach, 1981; California State Commission on Organization and Government, 1983.

CHAPTER 9

1 Although widely accepted, the normalization principle is clearly controversial, as it assumes that the fundamental definition of normalcy and a range of 'normal' behaviors can be specified by experts. Inherent in the concept of normalization is the assumption of abnormality or deviance. This classification in effect 'labels' the client. Although there is no simple predictable consequence of attaching a specific label to an individual, the

potential for damage is ever present, whether or not the individual accepts the label (Hobbs, 1975). This process of creating categories of 'difference' is important in setting social limits on what is tolerated as normal or deviant behavior (Fincher, 1977). Large numbers of people may be stigmatized or excluded from the normal category on the basis of the absence of one or more desirable characteristics. Such stigmatization also has the convenient outcome of 'blaming the victim' for deviation from sociocultural norms.

2 One recent initiative of interest is that undertaken by the Ontario Division of the Canadian Mental Health Association (CMHA) in conjunction with Ministry of Health funding. Over an 18-month period, diverse methods of public education were utilized to increase province-wide awareness of the problems facing the mentally disabled. The program was based on three premises:

1 underlying general community attitudes show a relative high degree of tolerance for disabled people;
2 specific opposition groups are confined to a vocal minority in very close proximity to a potential facility site; and
3 awareness and familiarity with the disabled tends to diminish opposition.

The CMHA's volunteer-based program was successful in sustaining the general level of community tolerance during a volatile period of facility expansion and in improving community awareness of the needs and problems of the mentally disabled.

3 The development of decentralized 'service hubs' is currently being developed as part of the Canadian Mental Health Association's national policy priorities (CMHA, 1984). Some Ontario cities have also incorporated such a strategy in their formal process of land-use planning.

References

Abramson, M., 'The Criminalization of Mentally Disordered Behavior: Possible Side-effects of a New Mental Health Law', *Hospital and Community Psychiatry*, 23: 13–16 (1972).

Ackerman, T., 'Hired Guns for an East Side Patrol', *Downtown News*, III (17 July 1985).

Ahr, P., and Holcomb, W., 'State Mental Health Directors' Priorities for Mental Health Care', *Hospital and Community Psychiatry*, 36: 39–45 (1985).

Allderidge, P., 'Hospitals, Madhouses and Asylums: Cycles in the Care of the Insane', *British Journal of Psychiatry*, 134: 321–34 (1979).

Allodi, F. A., and Kedward, H. B., 'The Vanishing Chronic', *Canadian Journal of Public Health*, 64: 279–89 (1973).

—— ——, 'The Evolution of the Mental Hospital in Canada', *Canadian Journal of Public Health*, 68: 219–24 (1977).

Alter, J., et al., 'Homeless in America', *Newsweek*, CIII: 20–9 (2 January 1984).

Anderson, M., *The Federal Bulldozer* (Cambridge, MA, MIT Press, 1964).

Anderson, T., 'Thousands Released; Few Treatment Facilities', *California Journal*, 15: 215–18 (1984).

Appelbaum, P. S., 'The Zoning Out of the Mentally Disabled', *Hospital and Community Psychiatry*, 34: 399–400 (1984).

Arce, A., et al., 'A Psychiatric Profile of Street People Admitted to an Emergency Shelter', *Hospital and Community Psychiatry*, 34: 812–17 (1983).

Arnoff, F. N., 'Social Consequences of Policy Toward Mental Illness', *Science*, 188: 1277–81 (1975).

Association of Bay Area Governments, *Development Fees in the San Francisco Bay Area: A Survey* (Berkeley, CA, ABAG, 1980).

Austin, M., Smith, T. E., and Wolpert, J., 'The Implementation of Controversial Facility-Complex Programs', *Geographical Analysis*, 2: 15–29 (1970).

Aviram, U., and Segal, S., 'Exclusion of the Mentally Ill', *Archives of General Psychiatry*, 29, 126–31 (1973).

Axinn, J., and Levin, H., *Social Welfare: A History of the American Response to Need* (New York, Harper and Row, 1975).

Bachrach, L. L., 'Research on Service for the Homeless Mentally Ill', *Hospital and Community Psychiatry*, 35: 910–13 (1984a).

——, 'Interpreting Research on the Homeless Mentally Ill', *Hospital and Community Psychiatry*, 35: 914–16 (1984b).

——, *Deinstitutionalization: An Analytic Review and Sociological Perspective* (Rockville, MD, National Institute of Mental Health, 1982).

——, 'A Conceptual Approach to Deinstitutionalization of the Mentally Retarded: A Perspective from the Experience of the Mentally Ill', in R. H. Beuininks et al. (eds), *Deinstitutionalization and Community Adjustment of Mentally Retarded People* (Washington DC, American Association of Mental Deficiency, 1981), 51–67.

Baer, W., *Towards a Theory of Fair Share* (Los Angeles, CA, School of Urban and Regional Planning, mimeo, 1983).

Baker, B. L., Seltzer, G. B., and Seltzer, M., *As Close as Possible* (Boston, MA, Little, Brown and Company, 1977).

Baron, R. C., 'Changing Public Attitudes about the Mentally Ill in the Community', *Hospital and Community Psychiatry*, 32: 173–8 (1981).

Bassuk, E. 'The Homeless Problem', *Scientific American*, 251: 40–5 (1984).

——, and Gerson, S., 'Deinstitutionalization and Mental Health Services', *Scientific American*, 238: 46–53 (1978).

Baumohl, W. J., and Oates, W. E., *The Theory of Environmental Policy* (Englewood Cliffs, NJ, Prentice-Hall, 1975).

Baxter, E., and Hopper, K., 'The New Mendicancy: Homeless in New York City', *American Journal of Orthopsychiatry*, 52: 393–408 (1982).

Beamish, C., *Space, State and Crisis: Toward a Theory of the Public City* (Unpublished MA Thesis, Department of Geography, McMaster University, Hamilton, Ontario, 1981).

Beigel, A., and Levinson, A. I. (eds), *The Community Mental Health Center: Strategies and Programs* (New York, Basic Books, 1972).

Bell, Leland V., *Treating the Mentally Ill* (New York, Praeger Publishers, 1980).

Birnbaum, M., 'The Right to Treatment', *American Bar Association Journal*, 46: 499 (1960).

Black, T., 'Private Market Housing Renovation in Central Cities: a U.L.I. Survey', *Urban Land*, 3–9 (1975).

Bloom, B. L., *Community Mental Health: A General Introduction* (Monterey, CA, Brooks/Cole Publishing Co., 1977).

Bluestone, B., and Harrison, B., *The Deindustrialization of America* (New York, Basic Books, 1982).

Boffey, P., 'Community Care for the Mentally Ill Termed a Failure', *New York Times*, I1:2 (13 September 1984).

Boodman, S., 'Ex-patients Struggle to Adjust on Outside', *Washington Post*, A16 (12 May 1985).

—— and Moore, M., 'Virginia Panel Approves Involuntary Commitment Change', *Washington Post*, D4 (18 January 1985).

Bourne, L., *The Geography of Housing* (New York, V. H. Winston, 1981).

Boyer, P., *Urban Masses and Moral Order in America, 1820–1920* (Cambridge, MA, Harvard University Press, 1978).

Braddock, D., 'Deinstitutionalization of the Retarded: Trends in Public Policy', *Hospital and Community Psychiatry*, 32: 607–15 (1981).

Braun, P. et al., 'Overview: Deinstitutionalization of Psychiatric Patients: A Critical Review of Outcome Studies', *American Journal of Psychiatry*, 138: 736–49 (1981).

Breslow, S., and Wolpert, J., *The Effect of Siting Group Homes on the Surrounding Environs* (Princeton, NJ, Princeton University School of Architecture and Urban Planning, mimeo, 1977).

Bronzan, B., 'State Leaders Fad the Treatment Problem', *California Journal*, 35: 22 (1984).

Brown, P., 'The Transfer of Care: U.S. Mental Health Policy Since World War II', *International Journal of Health Services*, 9: 645–62 (1979).

——, 'The Mental Patients Rights Movement and Mental Health Institutional Change', *International Journal of Health Services*, 11: 523–40 (1981).

Brown, T., 'Architecture as Therapy', *Archivaria*, 10: 99–123 (1980).

Burgess, E. W., 'The Growth of the City', in R. E. Park and E. W. Burgess, *The City* (Chicago, University of Chicago Press, 1967a).

——, 'Can Neighborhood Work Have a Scientific Basis?', in R. E. Park and E. W. Burgess, *The City* (Chicago, University of Chicago Press, 1967b).

Burgess, T. J. W., 'A Historical Address on Our Canadian Institutions for the Insane', *Transactions of the Royal Society of Canada* (Section iv), 3–116 (1898).

Bynum, W. F., Porter, R., and Shepherd, M., *The Anatomy of Madness* (New York, Tavistock Publications, 1985a), vol. 1: *People and Ideas*.

—— —— ——, *The Anatomy of Madness* (New York, Tavistock Publications, 1985b), vol. 2: *Institutions and Society*.

California Legislative Analyst, *Analysis of the 1985–86 Budget Bill* (Sacramento, CA, CLA, 1985).

California State Commission on California State Government Organization and Economy, N. Shapell, Chair, *Community Residential Care in California* (Sacramento, CA, CSCCSGOE, 1983).

California State Department of Health, *Special Study on Community Care in Santa Clara County* (Sacramento, CA, CSDH, 1973).

——, Facilities Licensing Division, *Directory of Community Care Facilities, 1975* (Sacramento, CA, CSDH, 1975).

——, *Facilities Licensed by the Department of Health Services, Licensing and Certification Division* (Sacramento, CA, CSDH, 1978, 1979).

California State Department of Social Services, Community Care Licensing Division, *Directory of Community Care Facilities, 1979* (Sacramento, CA, CSDSS, 1979).

—— ——, *Information System Directory Report* (Sacramento, CA, CSDSS, 1982).

California State Legislature, Senate Select Committee on Proposed Phase-out of State Hospital Services, Senator Alfred Alquist, Chair, *Final Report* (Sacramento, CA, CSL, 1974).

Caplan, R. B., *Psychiatry and the Community in Nineteenth-Century America* (New York, Basic Books, 1969).

Castel, R., Castel, F., and Lovell, A., *The Psychiatric Society* (New York, Columbia University Press, 1982).

Castells, M., 'The Wild City', *Kapitalistate,* 4–5: 2–30 (1976).

Central Mortgage and Housing Corporation, *Housing for the Handicapped* (Ottawa, CMHC, 1973).

Chu, F. D., and Trotter, S., *The Madness Establishment* (New York, Grossman, 1974).

City Council of Hamilton, *Hamilton: Canada. Its History, Commerce, Industries and Resources* (Hamilton, Ontario, Herbert Lister, 1913).

——, *Report on Existing Conditions* (Hamilton, Ontario, CPCH, 1945).

City of Chicago, Department of Planning, *Housing Needs of Chicago's Single, Low-Income Renters* (Chicago, CCDP, 1985).

——, Task Force on Emergency Shelter, *Homelessness in Chicago* (Chicago, CC, 1983).

Clare, A., *Psychiatry in Dissent* (London, Tavistock Publications, 1976).

Clark, G., and Dear, M., *State Apparatus: Structures and Language of Legitimacy* (London, George Allen and Unwin, 1984).

Clarke, G. J., 'In Defense of Deinstitutionalization', *Milbank Memorial Fund Quarterly/Health and Society*, 57: 461–79 (1979).

Clay, P., *Neighborhood Revitalization: The Recent Experience* (Cambridge, MA, MIT Press, 1978).

Clayton, J., 'City's Skid Row Shelter Will Set Up on New Site', *Los Angeles Times*, I2 (7 July 1985).

Coase, R. H., 'The Problem of Social Cost', *Journal of Law & Economics*, 3: 1–44 (1960).

Coates, R. B., 'Community-based Corrections: Concept, Impact, Dangers', in L. E. Ohlin, Miller, A. D., and Coates, R. B. (eds), *Juvenile Correctional Reform in Massachusetts* (Washington DC, National Institute for Juvenile Justice and Delinquency Prevention, US Department of Justice, 1976), 23–34.

——, and Miller, A. D., 'Neutralization of Community Resistance to Group Homes', in Y. Bakal (ed.), *Closing Correctional Institutions* (Lexington, MA, Lexington Books, 1973), 67–84.

Cohen, S., 'The Punitive City: Notes on the Dispersal of Social Control', *Contemporary Crises*, 3: 339–63 (1979).

Cohen, H. J., and Kligler, D. (eds), *Urban Community Care for the Developmentally Disabled* (Springfield, Ill, Charles E. Thomas, 1980).

Coll, B. D., *Perspectives in Public Welfare* (Washington DC, US Government Printing Office, 1969).

Collins, K., *Women and Pensions* (Ottawa, Canadian Council on Social Development, 1978).

Comptroller General of the US, General Accounting Offices, *Returning the Mentally Disabled to the Community: Government Needs to Do More* (Washington DC, Government Printing Office, 1977).

Community Resources Consultants of Toronto and Social and Community Psychiatry Section, Clarke Institute of Psychiatry, *Psychiatric Aftercare in Metropolitan Toronto* (Toronto, CRCT, mimeo, 1981).

Congressional Quarterly, Inc., *Budgeting for America: The Politics and Process of Federal Spending* (Washington DC, Congressional Quarterly, Inc., 1982).

Connell, R., 'State Accused of Shirking Its Duty on the Homeless', *Los Angeles Times*, II1 (18 June 1985a).

——, 'L.A., Firms on Skid Row OK 1-year Plan on Shelter for the Homeless', *Los Angeles Times*, II3 (2 November 1985b).

Cousineau, D. F., and Veevers, J. E., 'Incarceration as a Response to Crime', *Canadian Journal of Criminology and Corrections*, 15 (1973).

Cupaivulo, A. A., 'Community Residences and Zoning Ordinances', *Hospital and Community Psychiatry*, 28: 206–10 (1977).

Dain, N., *Concepts of Insanity in the U.S., 1789–1865* (New Brunswick, NJ, Rutgers University Press, 1965).

Davey, I., and Doucet, M., 'The Social Geography of a Commercial City, *ca.* 1985', in M. B. Katz (ed.), *The People of Hamilton, Canada West* (Cambridge, MA, Harvard University Press, 1975).

Davidson, J. L., 'Location of Community-based Treatment Centers', *Social Service Review*, 55: 221–41 (1981).

——, 'Balancing Required Resources and Neighborhood Opposition in Community-based Treatment Neighborhoods', *Social Service Review*, 56: 55–71 (1982).

Dear, M. J., *Locational Analysis for Public Mental Health Facilities* (Unpublished Ph.D. Dissertation, Philadelphia, PA, University of Pennsylvania, 1974).

——, 'Psychiatric Patients and the Inner City', *Annals of the Association of American Geographers*, 67: 588–94 (1977).

——, *Community Outreach for Group Home Planning: A Communications Strategy for Gaining Community Acceptance of Group Homes* (Toronto, Ontario Secretariat for Social Development, 1984).

——, Clark, G., and Clark, S., 'Economic Cycles and Mental Health Care Policy', *Social Science and Medicine*, 13c, 43–53 (1979).

——, et al., *Coping in the Community: The Needs of Ex-Psychiatric Patients* (Hamilton, Ontario, Canadian Mental Health Association, 1980).

——, and Laws, G., 'Anatomy of a Decision: Recent Land Use Zoning Appeals and Their Effect on Group Home Location in Ontario', *Canadian Journal of Community Mental Health*, 5:1, 5–17 (1986).

——, and Moos, A., 'Structuration Theory in Urban Analysis: 2. Empirical Application', *Environment and Planning A*, *18*: 351–73 (1986).

——, and Scott, A. J., *Urbanization and Urban Planning in Capitalist Society* (New York, Methuen, 1981).

——, Taylor, S. M., and Hall, G. B., 'External Effects of Mental Health Facilities', *Annals of the Association of American Geographers*, 70: 342–52 (1980).

—— ——, *Not on Our Street* (London, Pion Ltd., 1982).

——, and Wolch, J. R., 'The Optimal Assignment of Human Service Clients to Treatment Settings', in Stephen M. Golant (ed.), *Location and Environment of Elderly Population* (Washington DC, V. H. Winston, 1979), 197–210.

Deutsch, A., *The Mentally Ill in America*, 2nd edn (New York, Columbia University Press, 1949).

Donzelot, J., *The Policing of Families* (New York, Pantheon, 1979).

Dowall, D. E., 'The Effects of Land-use and Environmental Regulations on Housing Costs', in R. Montgomery and D. R. Marshall (eds), *Housing Policy for the 1980s* (Lexington, MA, Lexington Books, 1980).

——, *The Suburban Squeeze* (Berkeley, CA, University of California Press, 1985).

Downey, J. P., 'How Ontario Cares for Its Feeble-Minded', *Social Welfare*, 5: 179–81 (1923).

Downs, A., 'Uncompensated Costs of Urban Renewal', in J. Margolis (ed.), *The Analysis of Public Output* (New York, Columbia University Press, 1970).

Driver, F., 'Power, Space and the Body: A Critical Assessment of Foucault's *Discipline and Punish*', *Society and Space: Environment and Planning D*, 3: 425–46 (1985).

Economic Research Associates, *Memorandum to RTKL and the City of San Jose* (San Francisco, CA, ERA, 1980).

Edgerton, R. B., 'Issues Relating to the Quality of Life Among Mentally Retarded Persons', in M. J. Begab and S. A. Richardson (eds), *The Mentally Retarded and Society: A Social Science Perspective* (Baltimore, MD, University Park Press, 1975).

Emerson, R. M., Rochford, E. B., Jr., and Shaw, L. L., 'Economics and Enterprise in Board and Care Homes for the Mentally Ill', *American Behavioral Scientist*, 24: 771–85 (1981).

Eslami, K., *Transferable Development Rights, Zoning Auction, and Zoning by Eminent Domain* (Los Angeles, University of Southern California, School of Urban and Regional Planning, mimeo, 1983).

Estes, C. L., and Harrington, C. A., 'Fiscal Crisis, Deinstitutionalization and the Elderly', *American Behavioral Scientist*, 24: 811–26 (1981).

Estroff, S. E., 'Psychiatric Deinstitutionalization', *Journal of Social Issues*, 37: 116–31 (1981).

Fainstein, N. I. and Fainstein, S. S., 'Restructuring the American City: A Comparative Perspective', in N. I. Fainstein and S. S. Fainstein (eds) *Urban Policy Under Capitalism* (Beverly Hills, CA, Sage Publications, 1982).

Fainstein, S. S., et al., *Restructuring the City* (New York, Longman, 1983).

Felton, B. J., and Shinn, M., 'Ideology and Practice of Deinstitutionalization', *Journal of Social Issues*, 37: 158–72 (1981).

Ferleger, D., and Boyds, P. A., 'Anti-institutionalization: The Promise of the *Pennhurst* Case', *Stanford Law Review*, 31: 717–52 (1979).

'50,000 in State Prisons', *Los Angeles Times*, I:2 (24 December 1985).

Fincher, R., *An Examination of the Notion of Difference and its Implications for Community Survival Courses for the Deinstitutionalized Mentally Ill and Mentally Retarded* (Princeton, NJ, Princeton University School of Architecture and Urban Planning, mimeo, 1977).

Fingard, J., 'The Winter's Tale: The Seasonal Context of Pre-industrial Poverty in British North America, 1815–1860', *Canadian Historical Association Historical Papers*, 65–94 (1974).

Finkel, A., 'Origins of the Welfare State in Canada', in L. Panitch (ed.), *The Canadian State: Political Economy and Political Power* (Toronto, University of Toronto Press, 1977), 344–70.

Foucault, M., *Madness and Civilization* (New York, Vintage Books, 1973).

——, *Discipline and Punish: the Birth of the Prison* (New York, Pantheon, 1977).

——, *Power/Knowledge: Selected Interviews and Other Writings, 1972–1977*, ed. C. Gordon (Brighton, Sussex, Harvester Press, 1980).

Fox, R. W., *So Far Disordered in Mind: Insanity in California, 1970–1930* Berkeley, CA, University of California Press, 1978).

Franz, L. S., Rakes, T. R., and Wynne, A. J., 'A Choice-constrained Multiobjective Model for Mental Health Services Planning', *Socio-Economic Planning Sciences*, 18: 89–95 (1984).

Freedman, A. M. 'Historical and Political Roots of the Community Mental Health Centers Act', *American Journal of Orthopsychiatry*, 37:487–94 (1967)

Fried, M., 'Grieving for a Lost Home: Psychological Cost of Relocation', in L. J. Duhl (ed.) *The Urban Condition* (New York, Simon and Schuster, 1963).

Frieden, B., *The Environmental Protection Hustle* (Cambridge, MA, MIT Press, 1979).

Fustero, S., 'Home on the Street', *Psychology Today*, 56–63 (February 1984).

Gabriel, S. A., and Wolch, J. R., 'Spillover Effects of Human Service Facilities in a Racially Segmented Housing Market', *Journal of Urban Economics* (1984).

——, Katz, L., and Wolch, J. R., 'Local Land-use Regulation and Proposition 13: Findings from a Recent Survey', *Taxing and Spending*, 2: 73–81 (1980).

Gans, H. J., *The Urban Villagers* (New York, Free Press, 1962).

Gailey, J. B., 'Group Homes and Single-family Zoning', *Zoning and Planning Law Report*, 4: 97–102 (1981).

Giddens, A., *The Constitution of Society* (Berkeley, CA, University of California Press, 1984).

Gilbert, A., *Capitalism and the Welfare State* (New Haven, Yale University Press, 1983).

Golant, S. M., and McCaslin, R., A Social Indicator Model of the Elderly Population's Social Welfare Environment', in S. M. Golant (ed.), *Location and Environment of Elderly Population* (Washington DC, V. H. Winston, 1979), 181–96.

Goleman, D., 'Lawsuits Try to Force Care for the Mentally Ill', *New York Times*, III1:4 (24 April 1984).

Gonen, A., *An Innovative Community Support System for Mentally Handicapped Adults*, Working Paper (Princeton, NJ, Princeton University School of Architecture and Urban Planning, mimeo, 1977).

Gough, I., *Political Economy of the Welfare State* (London, Macmillan, 1979).

Gould, P. and Olsson, G. (eds), *The Search for Common Ground* (London, Pion, 1982).

Grebler, L., and Mittlebach, F., *The Inflation of Housing Prices* (Lexington, MA, Lexington Books, 1982).

Gregory, D., and Urry, J., *Social Relations and Spatial Structures* (London, Macmillan, 1985).

Griffen, J. D., and C. Greenland. 'Institutional Care of the Mentally Disordered in Canada – A 17th Century Record', *Canadian Journal of Psychiatry*, 26:274–7 (1981).

Griggs, B. S., and McCune, G. R., 'Community-based Correctional Programs: A Survey and Analysis', *Federal Probation*, 36, 1972.

Grob, G. N., *Mental Institutions in America* (New York, The Free Press, 1973).

——, *Mental Illness and American Society 1875–1940* (Princeton, NJ, Princeton University Press, 1983).

Group for the Advancement of Psychiatry, *The Chronic Mental Patient in the Community* (New York, Group for the Advancement of Psychiatry, 1978).

Guest, D., *The Emergence of Social Security in Canada* (Vancouver, University of British Columbia Press, 1980).

Hagman, D., and Misczynski, D., (eds), *Windfalls for Wipeouts: Land Value Capture and Compensation* (Chicago, American Society of Planning Officials, 1978).

Hanly, C., *Mental Health in Ontario* (Toronto, Queen's Printer, 1970).

Harasymiw, S. J., Horne, M. D., and Lewis, S. C., 'A Longitudinal Study of Disability Group Acceptance', *Rehabilitation Literature*, 37: 98–102 (1976).

Harvey, D., *Limits to Capital* (Oxford, Basil Blackwell, 1982).

——, *The Urbanization of Capital* (Baltimore, MD, Johns Hopkins University Press, 1985a).

——, *Consciousness and the Urban Experience* (Baltimore, MD, Johns Hopkins University Press, 1985b).

Heal, L. W., Sigelman, C. K., and Switzky, H. N., 'Research on Community Residential Alternatives for the Mentally Retarded', in R. J. Flynn and K. E. Nitsch (eds), *Normalization, Social Integration, and Community Services* (Balitmore, MD, University Park Press, 1980), 215–58.

'Help for the Homeless', *Toronto Globe and Mail*, A:6 (10 January 1986).

Henderson, J. M., and Quandt, R. E., *Microeconomic Theory* (New York, McGraw-Hill, 1971).

Henshaw, C., 'Communities Caring for Their Mentally Ill', *New York Times*, I26:4 (31 May 1984).

Herbert, D. T., 'Social Deviance in the City: A Spatial Perspective', in D. T. Herbert and R. J. Johnson (eds), *Social Areas in Cities: Processes, Patterns and Problems* (Chichester, John Wiley and Sons, 1978).

Hernandez, M., 'Workers at 11 State Mental Hospitals Sue Over Safety', *Los Angeles Times*, I24:3 (6 June 1985).

Heseltine, G. F., *Toward a Blueprint for Change: A Mental Health Policy Program Perspective* (Toronto, Ontario Ministry of Health, 1983).

Hinkley, B., *Report of Lodging Homes, Halfway Houses and Nursing Homes* (Hamilton, City of Hamilton, 1977).

Hobbs, N., *The Future of Children* (San Francisco, Jossey-Bass, 1975).

Holcomb, H. B., and Beauregard, R. S., *Revitalizing Cities* (Washington DC, Association of American Geographers, 1981).

Hospital and Community Psychiatry 34: Special Section on Deinstitutionalization (1983).

Hornblower, M., 'Epidemic of Homelessness Blamed on Federal Cuts in Social Spending', *Washington Post*, A6 (21 November 1984).

Huguenin, E., ' "Homeless": A New Name for the Mentally Ill', *Washington Post*, C8 (18 November 1984).

Hull, J. T., and Thompson, J. C., 'Factors Which Contribute to Normalization in Residential Facilities for the Mentally Ill', *Community Mental Health Journal*, 17: 107–13 (1981).

Humber, J. M., 'The Involuntary Commitment and Treatment of Mentally Ill Persons', *Social Science and Medicine*, 15: 129–33 (1981).

Hurd, H. M., *The Institutional Care of the Insane in the United States and Canada*, 4 vols. (Baltimore, MD, Johns Hopkins University Press, 1916–17).

Hylton, J. H., 'Rhetoric and Reality: A Critical Appraisal of Community Correctional Programs', *Crime and Delinquency*, 28: 341–73 (1982).

Ingleby, D., 'Mental Health and Social Order', in S. Cohen and A. Scull (eds), *Social Control and the State* (Oxford, Basil Blackwell, 1985).

International Journal of Mental Health 11: 'International Perspectives on Deinstitutionalization' (1982–3).

Jacobs, P., 'Mental Case Law: Matter of Rights', *Los Angeles Times*, I1 (18 March 1985a).

——, 'Model Mental Health Plan Seeks to Double Spending', *Los Angeles Times*, I3 (20 March 1985b).

——, 'Panel OKs Major Reforms in Aid for State's Mentally Ill', *Los Angeles Times*, I3 (18 May 1985c).

——, 'Parents' Groups Decry Inequities in State Aid for the Mentally Ill and the Retarded', *Los Angeles Times*, I3 (19 May 1985d).

James, F. J., *Back to the City: An Appraisal of Housing Reinvestment and Population Change in Urban America* (Washington DC, The Urban Institute, 1977).

Jarvis, E., *Insanity and Idiocy in Massachusetts: Report of the Commission on Lunacy, 1855* (Cambridge, MA, Harvard University Press, 1971).

Jobson, K. B., 'Dismantling the System', *Canadian Journal of Criminology and Corrections*, 19 (1980).

Johnson, P. J., and Beditz, J., 'Community Support Systems: Scaling Community Acceptance', *Community Mental Health Journal*, 17: 153–60 (1981).

Jones, K., *A History of the Mental Health Services* (London, Routledge and Kegan Paul, 1972).

——, and Williamson, K., 'Birth of the Schoolroom', *Ideology and Consciousness*, 6: 59–110 (1979).

Jones, R. E., 'Street People and Psychiatry: An Introduction', *Hospital and Community Psychiatry*, 34: 807–11 (1983).

Joseph, A., and Hall, G. B., 'The Locational Concentration of Group Home Networks in Toronto, Canada', *The Professional Geographer*, 37: 143–55 (1985).

Kammeyer, I. C. W., and Botton, C. D., 'Community and Family Factors Related to the Use of a Family Service Agency', *Journal of Marriage*, 30: 488–98 (1968).

Karlen, N., et al., 'Homeless Kids: "Forgotten Faces"', *Newsweek*, 20 (6 January 1986).

Kasinitz, P. 'Gentrification and Homelessness', *Urban Social Change Review*, 17: 9–14 (1984).

Katz, M. B., *In the Shadow of the Poorhouse: A Social History of Welfare in America* (New York, Basic Books, 1986).

——, *Poverty and Policy in American History* (New York, Academic Press, 1983).

——, *The People of Hamilton, Canada West* (Cambridge, MA, Harvard University Press, 1975).

——, Doucet, M. J., and Stern, M. J., *The Social Organization of Early Industrial Capitalism* (Cambridge, MA, Harvard University Press, 1982).

Kirk, S. A., and Therrien, M. E., 'Community Mental Health Myths and the Fate of Former Hospital Patients', *Psychiatry*, 38: 209–17 (1975).

Kirkbride, T. S., 'Propositions Relative to the Construction of Hospitals for the Insane', *American Journal of Insanity*, 11: 160–2 (1854).

——, *On the Construction, Organization and General Arrangements of Hospitals for the Insane* (New York, Arno Press, 1973; reprint of 2nd edn, Philadelphia, 1880).

Klerman, G. L., 'Better But Not Well: Social and Ethical Issues in the Deinstitutionalization of the Mentally Ill', *Schizophrenia Bulletin*, 3: 617–31 (1977).

Kneese, A. V., and Schultze, C. L., *Pollution, Prices and Public Policy* (Washington DC, The Brookings Institution, 1975).

Krasnick, C. L., 'In Charge of the Loons: A Portrait of the London, Ontario Asylum for the Insane in the Nineteenth Century', *Ontario History*, 19: 138–84 (1984).

Krauthammer, C., 'For the Homeless: Asylum', *Washington Post*, A15 (4 January 1985).

Lamb, H. R., 'Roots of Neglect of the Long-term Mentally Ill', *Psychiatry*, 42: 201–7 (1979a).

——, 'The New Asylums in the Community', *Archives of General Psychiatry*, 36: 129–34 (1979b).

——, 'What Did We Really Expect from Deinstitutionalization?', *Hospital and Community Psychiatry*, 32: 105–9 (1981).

——, 'Young Adult Chronic Patients: The New Drifters', *Hospital and Community Psychiatry*, 33: 465–8 (1982).

——, 'Deinstitutionalization and the Homeless Mentally Ill', *Hospital and Community Psychiatry*, 35: 899–907 (1984).

——, and Edelson, Majorie, B., 'The Carrot and the Stick: Inducing Local Programs to Serve Long-term Patients', *Community Mental Health Journal*, 12: 137–44 (1976).

——, and Grant, R. W., 'The Mentally Ill in an Urban County Jail', *Archives of General Psychiatry*, 39: 17–22 (1982).

——, and Lamb, D., 'A Nonhospital Alternative to Acute Hospitalization', *Hospital and Community Psychiatry*, 35: 728–30 (1984).

——, and Peele, R., 'The Need for Continuing Asylum and Sanctuary', *Hospital and Community Psychiatry*, 35: 798–801 (1984).

Lambert, C., *Retarded Adults, Their Adjustment and Community Milieu* (Toronto, Ministry of Community and Social Service, 1976).

Lane, D., 'The Politics of Growth in San Jose', *California Journal*, 9: 324 (1978).

Lang, V., *The Service Emerges in Ontario 1945–1973.* (Toronto, Ontario Economic Council, 1974).

Lauber, D., and Bangs, F., Jr., *Zoning for Families and Group Care Facilities* (Chicago, American Society of Planning Officials, 1974).

Lavell, A. E., 'The Beginning of Ontario Mental Hospitals', *Queen's Quarterly*, 49: 59–67 (1942).

Laws, G., and Dear, M., 'Coping in the Community', in C. Smith and J. Giggs, *Location and Stigma* (London, George Allen and Unwin, forthcoming 1987).

'Lawsuits Try to Force Care for the Mentally Ill', *New York Times*, III1:4 (24 April 1984).

League of California Cities, *Resolution 24: Relating to Mental Health Treatment and Facilities* (San Francisco, CA, General Assembly, League of California Cities, 1985).

Leighton, A. H., *Caring for Mentally Ill People* (Cambridge, Cambridge University Press, 1982).

Lerman, P. *Deinstitutionalization and the Welfare State* (New Brunswick, NJ, Rutgers University Press, 1982).

Leutz, W. N., 'The Informal Community Care-giver: A Link Between the Health Care System and Local Residents', *American Journal of Orthopsychiatry*, 46; 678–88 (1976).

Levine, M., *The History and Politics of Community Mental Health* (New York, Oxford University Press, 1981).

Lewis, D. K., 'Female Ex-offenders and Community Programs: Barriers to Service', *Crime and Delinquency*, 28: 40–51 (1982).

Lipton, F. R., Sabatini, A., and Katz, S. E., 'Down and Out in the City: The Homeless Mentally Ill', *Hospital and Community Psychiatry*, 34: 817–21 (1983).

Lipton, G., 'Evidence of Central City Revival', *American Institute of Planners*, 43: 136–47 (1977).

Los Angeles County, Community and Senior Citizens Services Department, *Report of the Countywide Task Force on the Homeless*, (Los Angeles, CA, LACCSCSD, 1985).

——, Department of Mental Health, *Memo to Board of Supervisors on Allocation of 1985–86 State Augmentation Dollars* (Los Angeles, CA, LACDMH 2, July 1985).

Lubove, R., *The Professional Altruist: The Emergence of Social Work as a Career, 1880–1930* (Cambridge, MA, Harvard University Press, 1965).

Lyons, R., 'How Release of Mental Patients Began', *New York Times*, III1:2 (20 October 1984).

MacDougall, K., 'Rich–Poor Gap in U.S. Widens During Decade', *Los Angeles Times*, I1 (25 October 1984).

Maluccio, A. N., *Alternatives to Institutionalization – A Selective Review of the Literature* (Saratoga, CA, Century Twenty-one Publishing, 1980).

Mamula, R. A., and Newman, N., *Community Placement of the Mentally Retarded: A Handbook for Community Agencies and Social Work Practitioners* (Springfield, ILL, Charles C. Thomas, 1973).

Manderscheid, R., et al., 'A Review of Trends in Mental Health Services', *Hospital and Community Psychiatry*, 35: 673–4 (1984).

Marshall, J., *Madness: An Indictment of the Mental Health Care System in Ontario* (Toronto, Ontario Public Service Employees Union, 1982).

Martyn, L. B., *The Face of Early Toronto: An Archival Record 1797–1936* (Sutton West, Paget Press, 1982).

Marxist–Leninist Organization of Canada. *They Say Cutback, We Say Fightback!' An Analysis of the Economic Strategy of the Ontario Government and the Development of the Anti-Cutbacks Movement* (Montreal, Marxist–Leninist Organization of Canada, 1980).

'Massachusetts Expanding Aid for Homeless', *New York Times*, I36:4 (6 January 1985).

Massey, D. S., 'Residential Segregation and Spatial Distribution of a Non-labor Force Population: The Needy, Elderly, and Disabled', *Economic Geography*, 56: 190–200 (1980).

McFarlane, C. G., 'Ontario's Temporary Absence Program', *Canadian Journal of Criminology*, 21 (1979).

McKnight, J. 'Professionalized Service and Disabling Help' in I. Illich et al. (eds.) *Disabling Professions* (London, Marion Boyars, 1977).

Mechanic, D., *Mental Health and Social Policy* (Englewood Cliffs, NJ, Prentice-Hall, 1969).

Menolascino, F. J., and Eaton, L. F., 'Future Trends in Mental Retardation', *Child Psychiatry and Human Development*, 10: 156–68 (1980).

'Mental Care Home Hit with Stiffest Fine', *Los Angeles Times*, I:33 (20 June 1985).

Mishra, R., *The Welfare State in Crisis* (Brighton, Sussex, Harvester Press, 1984).

Moos, A. and Dear, M., 'Structuration Theory in Urban Analysis: 1. Theoretical Exegesis', *Environment and Planning A*, *18*: 231–52 (1986).

Morgantheau, T., et al., 'Abandoned', *Newsweek*, 14–19 (6 January 1986).

Morse, G., et al., *Homeless People in St Louis: A Mental Health Program Evaluation, Field Study, and Follow-up Evaluation* (St Louis, Missouri Department of Mental Health, 1985).

Moscovitch, A., *The Welfare State in Canada: A Selected Bibliography, 1840–1978* (Waterloo, Wilfrid Laurier University Press, 1983).

Mounsey, S. C., 'Contracting Out a Government Service', *Canadian Journal of Criminology*, 19 (1977).

Moyles, R. C., *The Blood and Fire in Canada: A History of the Salvation Army in the Dominion, 1882–1970* (Toronto, P. Matrins Association Ltd., 1977).

Mundy, J., 'On the Various Modes of Public Provisions for the Insane', *American Journal of Insanity*, 21: 533–54 (1864–5).

Murphy, J. G., and Datel, W. E., 'A Cost-benefit Analysis of Community Versus Institutional Living', *Hospital and Community Psychiatry*, 25: 165–70 (1976).

Mylea, J. F., 'The Aged, the State and the Structure of Inequality', in J. Harp and J. R. Hofley (eds), *Structured Inequality in Canada* (Englewood Cliffs, NJ, Prentice-Hall, 1980).

Nickerson, C., 'Reformers' Dream that Went Astray', *Boston Globe*, I1 (10 March 1985a).

——, 'Young and Mentally Ill. They Drift to the Fringes of Society', *Boston Globe*, I1 (2 March 1985b).

Nirje, B., 'The Normalization Principle and its Human Management Implications', in R. Kugel and A. Shearer (eds), *Changing Patterns of Residential Services for the Mentally Retarded*, (Washington DC, Presidents Committee on Mental Retardation, 1976), 179–96.

Noyelle, T. 'The Rise of Advanced Services', *APA Journal* 49: 280–90 (1983).

Offe, C., *Contradictions of the Welfare State* (Cambridge, MA, MIT Press, 1984).

Ontario Ministry of Health, *Health Statistics* (Toronto, Province of Ontario, 1979).

Ontario Provincial Secretariat for Social Development, *Community Living for the Mentally Retarded in Ontario* (Toronto, OPSSD, 1973).

Ontario Public Service Employees Union (OPSEU), *Ontario's Mental Health Breakdown* (Toronto, OPSEU, 1980).

Ontario Welfare Council, *And the Poor Get Poorer . . .* (Toronto, Ontario Welfare Council, 1981).

Orras, G. L., *Community Diagnosis and Entry Strategies Used in Establishing Neighborhood Facilities for the Developmentally Disabled* (Unpublished Ph.D. Dissertation, Los Angeles, University of Southern California, 1983).

Ostrom, V., Tiebout, C. M., and Warren, R., 'The Organization of Government in Metropolitan Areas: A Theoretical Inquiry', *American Political Science Review*, 55: 831–42 (1961).

Ouimet Report, *Report of the Canadian Committee on Corrections* (Ottawa, Queen's Printer, 1969).

Paddock, R., 'Governor Tours Prison, Denies that Trip is Campaign Related', *Los Angeles Times*, I16 (23 July 1985).

Palmer, J. L. and Sawhill, I. V., *The Reagan Experiment* (Washington DC, The Urban Institute, 1982).

Parisi, A., 'Bergen County Dedicates Home for Homeless', *New York Times*, I36:4 (24 April 1985).

Park, R. E., 'Community Organization and Juvenile Delinquency', in R. E. Park and E. W. Burgess, *The City* (Chicago, University of Chicago Press, 1967).

Pepper, B., and Ryglewicz, H., 'Testimony for the Neglected: The Mentally Ill in the Post-deinstitutionalized Age', *American Journal of Orthopsychiatry*, 52: 388–92 (1982).

Perlman, R., and Gurin, A., *Community Organization and Social Planning* (New York, John Wiley and Sons, 1972).

Petersen, D. (ed.), *A Mad People's History of Madness* (Pittsburgh, University of Pittsburgh Press, 1982).

Pierce, L. H., and Hauck, V. B., 'A Model for Establishing a Community-based Foster Group Home', *Child Welfare*, LX: 475–82 (1981).

Pitsula, J. M., *The Relief of Poverty in Toronto, 1880–1930* (Ph.D. Dissertation, York University, 1979).

Politser, P. E., and Pattison, E. M., 'Social Climates in Community Groups: Toward a Taxonomy', *Community Mental Health Journal*, 16: 187–200 (1980).

Portland Office of Residential Care Facilities, *Density Guidelines for the Siting of Residential Care Facilities* (Portland, OR, PORCF, 1977).

'Prisons: Making Room', *Los Angeles Times*, II:4 (2 September 1985).

Pushchak, R., and Burton, I., 'Risk and Prior Compensation in Siting Low-level Nuclear Waste Facilities: Dealing with the NIMBY Syndrome', *Plan Canada*, 23: 68–80 (1983).

Ray, M. L., *Marketing Communication and the Hierarchy-of-Effects* (Cambridge, MA, Marketing Science Institute, 1973).

Reddy, R. D., and Smith, D. H., 'Who Participates in Voluntary Action?', *Journal of Extension*, 11: 17 (1973).

Reich, R., 'Care of the Chronically Mentally Ill – A National Disgrace', *American Journal of Psychiatry*, 130: 911–12 (1973).

——, and Siegal, L., 'Psychiatry Under Siege: The Chronically Mentally Ill Shuffle to Oblivion', *Psychiatric Annals*, 3: 33–55 (1973).

Richman, A., *Psychiatric Care in Canada: Extent and Results* (Ottawa, Queen's Printer, 1964).

——, and Harris, P., 'Mental Hospital Deinstitutionalization in Canada', *International Journal of Mental Health*, 11: 64–83 (1983).

'Rise in Homeless is Forecast', *New York Times*, I:19 (12 January 1986).

Robertson, M., Ropers, R., and Boyer, R., *Emergency Shelter for the Homeless in Los Angeles County* (Los Angeles, CA, Basic Shelter Research Project, School of Public Health, University of California, Los Angeles, 1984), Document 2.

—— —— ——, *The Homeless of Los Angeles County: An Empirical Evaluation* (Los Angeles, CA, Basic Shelter Research Project, School of Public Health University of California, Los Angeles, 1985), Document 4, (reproduced pp. 984–1108) in US House of Representatives, Committee on Government Operations, Intergovernmental Relations and Human Resources Committee, Hearings on *The Federal Response to the Homelessness Crisis* (Washington DC, Government Printing Office, 1985).

Roderick, K., 'Homeless – Left Behind by Recovery', *Los Angeles Times*, I:1 (2 February 1985).

Rose, S. M. 'Deciphering Deinstitutionalization: Complexities in Policy and Program Analysis', *Milbank Memorial Fund Quarterly*, 57: 429–60 (1979).

Rosen, G., *Madness in Society*, (Chicago, University of Chicago Press, 1975).

Rosenblatt, A., 'Concepts of the Asylum in the Care of the Mentally Ill', *Hospital and Community Psychiatry*, 35: 244–50 (1984).

Rosenzweig, N., *Community Mental Health Programs in England: An American View* (Detroit, Wayne State University Press, 1975).

Rothman, D. J., *The Discovery of the Asylum* (Boston, MA, Little, Brown and Company, 1971).

——, 'The State as Parent', in W. Gaylin, et al., (eds), *Doing Good: The Limits of Benevolence* (New York, Pantheon Books, 1978).

Rothman, D. J. *Conscience and Convenience: The Asylum and its Alternatives in Progressive America* (Boston, MA, Little, Brown, 1980).

Rousseau, A. M., *Shopping Bag Ladies* (New York, Pilgrim Press, 1981).

Rubin, J., 'The National Plan for the Chronically Mentally Ill: A Review of Financing Proposals', *Hospital and Community Psychiatry*, 32: 704–13 (1981).

Salamon, L. M., and Abramson, A. J., *The Federal Budget and the Nonprofit Sector* (Washington DC, The Urban Institute, 1982).

San Jose Department of City Planning, 'University Area Task Force Draft Report', (San Jose, CA, SJDCP, 1979).

San Jose Department of City Planning, 'Building Permit Survey', 1975–1979 (San Jose, CA, SJDCP, 1980).

San Jose Department of City Planning, 'Building Permit Survey', 1977–1981 (San Jose, CA, SJDCP, 1982).

Santa Clara County, *Annual Budget* (San Jose, CA, SCC, 1978–9; 1979–80; 1980–1; 1981–2; 1982–3).

Santa Clara County Board of Supervisors, Meeting Minutes (San Jose, CA, SCCBS, 1976–9).

Santa Clara County Department of Social Services, Unpublished Data on Public Assistance Caseloads (San Jose, CA, SCCDSS, 1970, 1975, 1980).

Santa Clara County Department of Social Services, News Releases (San Jose, CA, SCCDSS, 25 August 1981; 18 November 1981; 30 March 1982; 14 May 1982).

Santa Clara County Housing Task Force, '*Housing in Santa Clara County*' (San Jose, CA, SCCHTF, 1977).

Santa Clara County Manufacturing Group, *Vacant Land in Santa Clara County: Implications for Job Growth and Housing in the 1980s* (San Jose, CA, SCCMG, 1980).

Santa Clara County Planning Department, *Special Census* (San Jose, CA, SCCPD, 1975).

Santa Clara County Planning Department, *A Report on Zoning and Non-medical Community Care Facilities in Santa Clara County* (San Jose, CA, SCCPD, 1976).

Santa Clara County Planning Department, Housing Task Force, *Housing: A Call for Action* (San Jose, CA, SCCPD, 1977).

Savage, V. T., Novak, A. R., and Heal, L. W., 'Generic Services for Developmentally Disabled Citizens', in A. R. Novak and L. W. Heal (eds), *Integration of Developmentally Disabled Individuals into the Community* (Baltimore, MD, Paul H. Brookes, 1980), 75–90.

Sawers, L., and Tabb, W., (eds), *Snowbelt/Sunbelt: Urban Development and Regional Restructuring* (New York, Oxford University Press, 1984).

Saxenian, A., *Silicon Chips and Spatial Structure: The Industrial Basis of Urbanization in Santa Clara County* (Berkeley, CA, University of California Institute of Urban and Regional Development, 1981), Working Paper 345.

Sayer, A., *Method in Social Science* (London, Hutchinson, 1984).

Scheerenberger, R. C., *A History of Mental Retardation* (Baltimore, MD, Paul H. Brookes, 1983).

Schmedemann, D. A., 'Zoning for the Mentally Ill: A Legislative Mandate', *Harvard Journal of Legislation*, 16: 853–99 (1979).

Schmidt, P., 'Democracy's Scrap Heap: Rehabilitation of Long-stay Mental Hospital Patients', *Canada's Mental Health*, Supplement 46 (1965).

Scull, A., *Decarceration: Community Treatment of the Deviant – A Radical View*, (Englewood Cliffs, NJ, Prentice-Hall, 1978).

——, 'Madness and Segregation Control: The Rise of the Insane Asylum', in Robert Perlman and Arnold Gurin (eds), *Community Organization and Social Planning* (New York, John Wiley and Sons, 1972).

——, 'A New Trade in Lunacy', *American Behavioral Scientist*, 24: 741–54 (1981).

——, 'Deinstitutionalization and the Rights of the Deviant', *Journal of Social Issues*, 37: 6–20 (1981a).

Segal, S. P., 'Attitudes Toward the Mentally Ill: A Review', *Social Work*, 23: 211–17 (1978).

——, 'Community Care and Deinstitutionalization: A Review', *Social Work*, 24: 521–7 (1979).

——, and Aviram, U., *The Mentally Ill in Community-based Sheltered Care*, (New York, John Wiley and Sons, 1978).

——, and Baumohl, W. J., 'Social Work Practice in Community Mental Health', *Social Work*, 26: 16–24 (1981).

—— ——, and Moyles, E. W., 'Neighborhood Types and Community Reaction to the Mentally Ill: A Paradox of Intensity', *Journal of Health and Social Behavior*, 21: 345–59 (1980).

Seidenberg, G. R., and Parrish, J., 'Medicare Provider Status for Community Mental Health Centers: An Overdue Reform', *Administration in Mental Health*, 8: 202–13 (1981).

'Shortchanging Mental Health', *Los Angeles Times*, II:4 (28 June 1985).

Sigelman, C. K., et al., 'Factors that Affect the Success of Community Placement', in A. Novak and L. Heal (eds), *Integration of Developmentally Disabled Individuals into the Community* (Baltimore, MD, Paul H. Brookes 1980), 57–74.

Siggins, M., 'Madness in South Parkdale', *Today Magazine*, 6: 6–10 (1982).

Simmons, H. G., *From Asylum to Welfare* (Downsview, National Institute on Mental Retardation, 1982).

Simon, B., *Mind and Madness in Ancient Greece* (Ithaca, NY, Cornell University Press, 1978).

Siren, A., 'An Analysis of Correctional Services for Adults in Ontario', *Canadian Journal of Criminology*, 14 (1979).

Smith, C. J., 'Innovation in Mental Health Policy: The Political Economy of the Community Mental Health Movement, 1965–1980', *Society and Space, Environment and Planning D*, 1: 447–68 (1983).

——, 'Residential Neighborhoods as Humane Environments', *Environment and Planning A*, 9: 585–97 (1976).

——, 'Urban Structure and the Development of Natural Support Systems for Service-dependent Populations', *The Professional Geographer*, 33: 457–65 (1981).

——, and Hanham, R. Q., 'Any Place But Here! Mental Health Facilities as Noxious Neighbors', *The Professional Geographer*, 33: 326–34 (1981).

—— ——, 'Deinstitutionalization of the Mentally Ill: A Time-path Analysis of the American States', *Social Science and Medicine*, 15D: 361–78 (1981).

Social Planning Council of Hamilton, *Lodging Homes in Hamilton* (Hamilton, Ontario, Social Planning and Research Council, 1980).

Social Planning Council of Metropolitan Toronto. *Caring for Profit: the Commercialization of Human Services in Ontario* (Toronto, Social Planning Council of Metropolitan Toronto, 1984).

Sosowsky, L., 'Crime and Violence Among Mental Patients', *American Journal of Psychiatry*, 135: 33–42 (1978).

Splane, R. B., *Social Welfare in Ontario, 1791–1893* (Toronto, University of Toronto Press, 1965).

Steadman, H. J., 'Critically Reassessing the Accuracy of Public Perceptions of the Dangerousness of the Mentally Ill', *Journal of Health and Social Behavior*, 22: 310–16 (1981).

Stedman-Jones, G., *Outcast London* (London, Oxford University Press, 1971).

Sternlieb, J., et al., *America's Housing* (New Brunswick, NJ, Center for Urban Policy Research, 1980).

Stickney, P., *Gaining Community Acceptance: A Handbook for Community Residence Planners* (White Plains, NY, Westchester Community Service Council, 1976).

Stoesz, D., 'A Wake for the Welfare State: Social Welfare and the Neo-conservative Challenge', *Social Service Review*, 55: 398–410 (1981).

Stoner, M. R. 'The Plight of Homeless Women', *Social Service Review*, 57: 565–81 (1983).

Stumpf, J., and Terrell, P., *Proposition 13 and California Human Services*. (Millbrae, CA, National Association of Social Workers, Inc., 1979).

'Suffering in the Street', *New York Times*, IV22:1 (16 September 1984).

Sumka, H., 'Neighborhood Revitalization and Displacement', *APA Journal*, 45: 480–7 (1979).

'Summary of the Major Items Vetoed', *Los Angeles Times*, I 18:2 (29 June 1984).

Sundeen, R. A., and Fisk, S., 'Local Resistance to Community-based Care Facilities', *Journal of Offender Counseling Services and Rehabilitation*, 6: 29–42 (1982).

Sylph, J. A., Eastwood, M. R., and Kedward, H. B., 'Long-term Psychiatric Care in Ontario', *Canadian Medical Association Journal*, 114: 233–7 (1976).

Talbott, J., 'The Need for Asylum, not Asylums', *Hospital and Community Psychiatry*, 35: 209 (1984).

Taylor, S. M., et al., 'Predicting Community Reaction to Mental Health Facilities', *Journal of the American Planning Association*, 50: 36–47 (1984).

Test, M. A., 'Effective Community Treatment of the Chronically Mentally Ill: What is Necessary?', *Journal of Social Issues*, 37: 71–86 (1981).

Thrift, N., 'On the Determination of Social Action in Space and Time', *Society and Space*, 1: 23–57 (1983).

Trattner, W. I., *From Poor Law to Welfare State* (New York, The Free Press, 1974).

'The Growing Ranks of the Homeless', *Macleans*, 28–9 (13 January 1986).

Tringo, J. L., 'The Hierarchy of Preference Toward Disability Groups', *Journal of Special Education*, 4: 295–306 (1970).

Trotter, S., and Kuttner, B., 'The Mentally Ill: From Back Wards to Back Alleys', *Washington Post*, (24 February 1974).

Trute, B., and Segal, S., 'Census Tract Predictors and the Social Integration of Sheltered Care Residents', *Social Psychiatry*, 11: 153–61 (1976).

Tuke, D. H., *The Insane of the United States and Canada* (New York, Arno Press 1973; reprint of 1885 edn, London, H. K. Lewis).

Turban, E., and Meredith, J., *Fundamentals of Management Science*, 3rd edn (Plano, TX, Business Publications, Inc., 1984).

US Department of Commerce, Bureau of the Census, *Census of Population and Housing* (Washington DC, Government Printing Office, 1970).

US Department of Health and Human Services, Social Security Administration, *Social Security Beneficiaries by Zip Code: San Francisco Region in 1979* (Washington DC: Government Printing Office, 1980).

US Department of Health and Human Services, *Toward a National Plan for the Chronically Mentally Ill* (Washington DC, Government Printing Office, 1980).

US Department of Health, Education and Welfare, Social Security Administration, *Social Security Beneficiaries by Zip Code: San Francisco Region in 1975* (Washington DC, Government Printing Office, 1976).

US Department of Housing and Urban Development, *A Report to the Secretary on the Homeless and Emergency Shelters* (Washington DC, Government Printing Office, 1984).

US General Accounting Office, *Returning the Mentally Disabled to the Community: Government Needs to Do More* (Washington DC, Government Printing Office, 1977).

US General Accounting Office, *An Analysis of Zoning and Other Problems Affecting the Establishment of Group Homes for the Mentally Disabled* (Washington DC, Government Printing Office, 1983).

US National Institute of Mental Health, *Deinstitutionalization: A Sociological Perspective* (Washington DC, US National Institute of Mental Health, 1970).

United Way of Santa Clara County, *Retrenchment and Transition: An Analysis* of the Impacts of Public Sector Funding Reduction on Human Services, Education and the Arts in Santa Clara County (Santa Clara, CA, UWSCC, 1982).

Urmer, A. H., 'Implications of California New Mental Health Law', *American Journal of Psychiatry*, 132: 251–4 (1975).

Vickery, W. S., 'Economic Efficiency and Pricing', in S. Muskin (ed.), *Public Prices for Public Products* (Washington DC, The Urban Institute, 1972), 53–72.

Volkman, R., and Cressly, D., 'Differential Association and the Rehabilitation of Drug Addicts', *American Journal of Sociology*, 69: 129–42 (1963).

Vollmer, T., 'County Hit for Big Bite by Soaring Relief Costs', *Los Angeles Times*, II1 (9 July 1985a).

——, 'County Hopes to Modify Aid for Homeless', *Los Angeles Times*, II1 (17 July 1985b).

Walker, R., 'A Theory of Surburbanization', in M. Dear and A. Scott, *Urbanization and Urban Planning in Capitalist Society* (New York, Methuen, 1981).

Wallace, E., 'The Origin of the Welfare State in Canada, 1867–1900', *Canadian Journal of Economics and Political Science*, 16: 383–93 (1950).

Ward, D. *Cities and Immigrants: A Geography of Change in Nineteenth Century America* (New York, Oxford University Press, 1971).

——, 'The Victorian Slum: An Enduring Myth?', in *Annals, Association of American Geographers*, 66: 323–6 (1976).

Warren, C. A., 'New Forms of Social Control', *American Behavioral Scientist*, 24: 724–40 (1981).

Weaver, J., *Hamilton: An Illustrated History* (Toronto, Lorimer, 1982).

Weber, D. E., 'Neighborhood Entry in Group Home Development', *Child Welfare*, LVII: 627–42 (1978).

Weinberg, J., 'The Chronic Patient: The Stranger in our Midst', *Hospital and Community Psychiatry*, 29: 25–8 (1978).

Weiss, M., 'The Origins and Legacy of Urban Renewal', in P. Clavel, Forester, J., and Goldsmith, W. W., (eds) *Urban and Regional Planning in an Age of Austerity* (New York, Pergamon Press, 1980).

Welch, R., *Community Living for the Mentally Retarded in Ontario: A New Policy Focus* (Toronto, Government of Ontario, 1973).

White, A., 'Accessibility and Public Facility Location', *Economic Geography*, 55: 18–35 (1979).

Whitmer, G. E., 'From Hospitals to Jails: The Fate of California's Deinstitutionalized Mentally Ill', *American Journal of Orthopsychiatry*, 50: 65–75 (1980).

Williams, J. I., and Luterback, E. J., 'The Changing Boundaries of Psychiatry in Canada', *Social Science and Medicine*, 10: 15–22 (1976).

Williston, W., *Present Arrangements for the Care and Supervision of Mentally Retarded Persons in Ontario* (Toronto, Ontario Department of Health, 1977).

Wilson, J. Q., (ed.), *Urban Renewal: The Record and the Controversy* (Cambridge, MA, MIT Press, 1966).

Wolch, J. R., 'The Residential Location of the Service-dependent Poor', *Annals of the Association of American Geographers*, 70, 330–41 (1980).

——, 'The Spatial Impact of Social Policy: The Role of Facility Location in Urban Development', in R. C. Rich, (ed.), *The Politics of Urban Services* (Lexington, MA, Lexington Books, 1981a).

——, 'The Location of Service-dependent Households in Urban Areas', *Economic Geography*, 57: 52–67 (1981b).

Wolch, J. R., and S. A. Gabriel. 'Local Land Development Policies and Urban Housing Prices', *Environment and Planning A,* 13:1203–76 (1981).

—— ——, 'Development and Decline of Service-dependent Ghetto', *Urban Geography*, 5: 111–29 (1984).

—— ——, 'Dismantling the Community-based Human Service System' *Journal of the American Planning Association,* 51:53–64 (1985).

Wolfensberger, W., *The Principle of Normalization in Human Services* (Toronto, National Institute on Mental Retardation, 1972).

Wolpert, J., 'The Dignity of Risk', *Transactions Institute of British Geographers*, 5: 391–410 (1980).

——, 'Regressive Siting of Public Facilities', *Natural Resource Journal*, 16: 103–15 (1976).

——, and Wolpert, E., 'The Relocation of Released Mental Hospital Patients into Residential Communities', *Policy Sciences*, 7: 31–51 (1976).

——, Dear, M. J., and Crawford, R., 'Satellite Mental Health Facilities', *Annals of the Association of American Geographers*, 65: 24–35 (1975).

Woods, R. A. (ed.). *The City Wilderness: A Settlement Study* (New York, Garrett Press, 1970; reprint of edn by Houghton, Mifflin and Company, 1898).

Woogh, C. M., Meier, H. M. R., and Eastwood, M. R., 'Psychiatric Hospitalization in Ontario: The Revolving Door in Perspective'. *Canadian Medical Association Journal*, 116: 876–81 (1977).

Workman, B., 'Asylums for the Chronic Insane in Upper Canada', *American Journal of Insanity*, 24: 42–51 (1867).

Zanditon, M., and Hellman, S., 'The Complicated Business of Setting Up Residential Alternatives', *Hospital and Community Psychiatry*, 32: 335–9 (1981).

'Zoning, Group Homes for the Mentally Disabled, and a GAO Study's Controversial Results', *Hospital and Community Psychiatry*, 35: 177–92 (1984).

Index of subjects

Index of works cited